MW01130635

Following the Formula in *Beowulf*, *Örvar-Odds saga*, and Tolkien

"Fox describes a method of reading and composition that reaches back into the origins of European storytelling, a method that worked for *Beowulf* and for J. R. R. Tolkien. Fox takes his reader from the smallest phrase, through nested motifs, scenes, and plots, to the formulaic patterns of myths themselves. Norse sagas, ancient Germanic languages, early medieval Latin—all play recurring roles in a gripping analysis built on the very formula that underlies *The Hobbit*. Highly recommended to anyone who wants to understand ancient storytelling techniques."
—Stephen Harris, *Professor of English, University of Massachusetts, Amherst, USA*

"This learned and engaging book unlocks the intricate artistry of *Beowulf*, demonstrating subtle and meaningful repetitions and variations at the level of diction, half-line, fitt, digression, and theme. Fox also unearths fascinating new connections with Germanic alliterative verse, biblical tradition, heroic legend, Norse saga, and folktale. This is a book that all *Beowulf* scholars will want to read."
—Francis Leneghan, *Associate Professor of Old English, University of Oxford, UK, and author of* The Dynastic Drama of Beowulf *(2020)*

Michael Fox

Following the Formula in *Beowulf*, *Örvar-Odds saga*, and Tolkien

palgrave
macmillan

Michael Fox
Western University
London, ON, Canada

ISBN 978-3-030-48133-9   ISBN 978-3-030-48134-6   (eBook)
https://doi.org/10.1007/978-3-030-48134-6

© The Editor(s) (if applicable) and The Author(s), under exclusive license to Springer
Nature Switzerland AG 2020
This work is subject to copyright. All rights are solely and exclusively licensed by the
Publisher, whether the whole or part of the material is concerned, specifically the rights
of translation, reprinting, reuse of illustrations, recitation, broadcasting, reproduction
on microfilms or in any other physical way, and transmission or information storage and
retrieval, electronic adaptation, computer software, or by similar or dissimilar methodology
now known or hereafter developed.
The use of general descriptive names, registered names, trademarks, service marks, etc. in this
publication does not imply, even in the absence of a specific statement, that such names are
exempt from the relevant protective laws and regulations and therefore free for general use.
The publisher, the authors and the editors are safe to assume that the advice and
information in this book are believed to be true and accurate at the date of publication.
Neither the publisher nor the authors or the editors give a warranty, expressed or implied,
with respect to the material contained herein or for any errors or omissions that may have
been made. The publisher remains neutral with regard to jurisdictional claims in published
maps and institutional affiliations.

Cover credit: INTERFOTO/Alamy Stock Photo

This Palgrave Macmillan imprint is published by the registered company Springer Nature
Switzerland AG
The registered company address is: Gewerbestrasse 11, 6330 Cham, Switzerland

PREFACE

On May 1, 2015, I was invited to talk at the Old English Colloquium at the University of Toronto. I am grateful for the opportunity because it was the first time I patched several of the ideas in this book's chapters together and attached to them the title "Following the Formula." Roy Liuzza asked immediately afterward about using the word "formula" and how I was planning to define it. Almost five years later, having written the book that was first conceived in that talk, I confess that, as then, I cannot answer the question.

Even though formula has been attached to Old English studies since the first half of the nineteenth century, the mix of descriptive and pejorative uses of the term that were in use then has hardly changed. The term was adopted by oral-formulaic studies in the first half of the twentieth century, and formula was again praised and adopted and vilified and scorned. For a time, the author of *Beowulf* seemed dead. The development of theories of formula that did not rest on clear, visible repetition, the recognition of variation, and thinking about formula at different levels of the compositional process, from the deep structure of the half-line to overarching mythic structures, helped to revive the author, even in the absence of any consensus about what formula might mean. Today, the use of the word in the context of *Beowulf* carries with it still, at the very least, a connotation of orality and, for most readers, drags behind it an unwieldy and almost debilitating train of scholarship. The question of oral versus literate or the identification of a possible transitional stage between the two has not been at the forefront of *Beowulf* studies since the 1990s, and the word formula is used by many critics now to denote simply a repeated phrase, half-line, or line, sometimes without any explanation of how repetition becomes formula. If something repeats, it is a formula.

Without repetition of some kind, of course, formula is impossible to recognize. To attempt to define formula, therefore, I start with repetition. The difficulty with such a definition is similar to attempting to identify etymemes: one person's repetition, be it metrical repetition, syntactic repetition, lexical repetition, or semantic repetition, is another person's brand new passage. At the level of story-pattern, one might think of the comparison of *Beowulf* and *Grettis saga*: one person's clear genetic relationship is another person's coincidence. Still, when repetitions of a similar type and quality begin to cluster, as we have seen from the earliest arguments for common authorship of Old English poems, those clusters must mean something. The argument of this book, therefore, is that *Beowulf* can be considered the result of a formula. That formula is in fact very complicated, for it begins with a formula for a story-pattern, and that formula has various smaller levels of formula embedded within it. The story-pattern contains type-scenes or themes and motifs, the themes and motifs are often tied in form and content to digressions and episodes, and themes and motifs and digressions and episodes are almost always expressed in structural formulas of patterned repetition such as envelope patterns and ring structures. The whole, of course, is expressed in Old English verse, that "rhymeless sort of poetry, a kind of bombast or insane prose," as Joseph Ritson apparently called it (D'Israeli 1841, 53; Magennis 2011, 42), the formulaic nature of which is, if not entirely understood, widely accepted. If my argument has merit, then the recognition of formula suggests also a method of reading the poem, and that is largely how the book is structured.

The first chapter of the book, though limited in scope by the constraints of its place in the argument, traces the history of thinking about formula in Old English. The sketch will demonstrate the movement from formula as repetition to formula as method of composition and the way formula has edged in recent years back toward repetition. I make no attempt to arbitrate between theories of how formula works, for I find in every identification and expression of formula a useful way of thinking about the poem (that is, if a pattern seems significant to a reader or group of readers, the pattern is worth considering). The story of formula has mainly been written in the context of oral-formulaic theory, and the chapter reflects that, though the question of *Beowulf's* status within the oral-formulaic tradition is not directly part of my study. Where issues of formula have co-existed with oral-formulaic theory (in studies of structure, theme, and story-pattern), I include those studies in the review. What becomes obvious is that repetition and formula are central, if only implicitly, in every reading of the poem.

The half-line formula is the most commonly recognized formulaic unit in the poem, and I trace *weox under wolcnum* (8a) to demonstrate what can be learned about Old English composition and about the poem from a single half-line. The half-line is significant in its smaller units (in its lexical constituents and its phrase *under wolcnum*), both within the poem and outside it. The half-line is widely considered a formula or at least part of a system, and it has been suggested to participate in a theme that appears also in *Genesis A*. Repetition within the poem links it to several other half-lines ending in *under/to wolcnum*, and one example would seem to link to yet another theme in several Old English poems. The repetition, formulaic or otherwise, clusters around other kinds of repetition that suggest a relationship between poems while also adding depth to the scenes in which it appears. Finally, the half-line connects outside the tradition to Old Saxon half-lines, an interaction that has rarely been explored.

The first numbered fitt of the poem demonstrates a great deal about the poet's method of composition. The fitt expands on the themes of the proem, introduces the poet's method of embedding digressions and episodes, demonstrates how structural features can signal textual divisions and thematic significance, and illustrates the poet's approach to interweaving narrative strands, a method that is tied to the handling of time. In short, the fitt and its concentrated sequence of references to the Old Testament book of Genesis allow us to see much of the poet's method in the space of a few lines. Reading the poem at the level of the fitt connects to the half-line *weox under wolcnum* and looks ahead to the more sustained digressions and episodes, even while hinting at story-patterns related to the poem as a whole.

One of the most celebrated passages in the poem is the Sigemund-Heremod digression. The digression plays a vital role in the poem, binding the two ages of Beowulf's life together, but understanding the nuance of that role requires knowledge of a great deal of background material, for the passage is highly allusive and offers a version of a well-known story that is otherwise unattested. The passage involves itself with many of the themes of the poem—it has been seen as the poem in miniature—and it even offers a suggestion about a significant date in the poem's development.

At the level of whole narratives, *Beowulf* has most often and most productively been compared and contrasted with *Grettis saga*. However, if the broad narrative structures of the two stories are in any way related, that is, if behind the poem and the saga is a kernel of traditional story that develops into the life stories of Beowulf and Grettir, then that kernel, which may be a folktale resembling the basic outline of what is now known as ATU 301, "The Three Kidnapped Princesses," must also lie at the heart of *Örvar-Odds saga*. I would argue that the career of Örvar-Oddr has been overlooked as a *Beowulf* analogue, but perhaps more importantly, the saga has been overlooked as a possible model for the slow metamorphosis and accretion of features that must have happened in the poem and *Grettis saga*. The process has never been articulated for *Beowulf*, but must have been analogous to the shaping of the *Odyssey*, which has recently been persuasively reconstructed by M. L. West (2014).

Finally, the compositional processes that I am calling *Beowulf*'s formula remain productive. One of the poem's best-known readers, J. R. R. Tolkien, intimately familiar with the poem and with hypotheses of a possible folktale behind it, uses his knowledge in two different ways. In his recently published *Sellic Spell*, Tolkien extracts and realizes one element of the formula, the basic story-pattern behind the poem. In *The Hobbit*, Tolkien works through the *Beowulf* formula, selecting and innovating, to come up with a prose narrative that participates in the same tradition as the poem and its Old Norse-Icelandic analogues. Again, the correspondences are notable, but the value of such an analysis lies more in the recognition of what is possible as the formula is deployed.

Larry D. Benson said many years ago that "to prove that an Old English poem is formulaic is only to prove that it is an Old English poem" (1966, 336). With *Beowulf*, however, the notion of formula takes on much more meaning. Formula rests in the half-line as a compositional unit, but those half-lines are the building blocks of every other structure in the poem, reaching out in many different directions, even into the spaces behind the poem, into the history and myth all around it, and into stories not yet told. I hope the following chapters demonstrate the broad applicability of the term formula to the compositional process while at the same time modeling different ways to read the poem, from consideration of a single half-line to the way story-patterns change and can be changed over time.

London, Canada   Michael Fox

REFERENCES

Benson, Larry D. 1966. The Literary Character of Anglo-Saxon Formulaic Poetry. *PMLA* 81: 334–341.

D'Israeli, Isaac. 1841. *Amenities of Literature*, vol. 1. London: Edward Moxon.

Magennis, Hugh. 2011. *Translating Beowulf: Modern Versions in English Verse*. Cambridge: D. S. Brewer.

West, M. L. 2014. *The Making of the Odyssey*. Oxford: Oxford University Press.

ACKNOWLEDGMENTS

This book would not exist without the efforts of many. I would not be in this line of work without Nicholas Watson, Kirsten Wolf, Michael Lapidge, Stephen R. Reimer, Jane Toswell, Brock Eayrs, and Kathleen Fraser. I might not have survived the early years without Marteinn Helgi Sigurðsson and Manish Sharma. This book might never have been completed without the iron will of Tim Freeborn and the patience and kindness of Allie Troyanos and Rachel Jacobe.

I offer this book to the three people who have taught me the most about *Beowulf* and, if inadvertently, also much about other things.

The first warmed winter mornings here in London with *Hrólfs saga kraka* and *Beowulf*—I think of snow seen through windows, people chucking bones, a bottle of Stoli—and looked out for me as long as she could.

The second read the Junius manuscript and *Beowulf* with me over two full years on the eastern edge of the prairie—I think of fall stubble burning in the Red River Valley, the hidden world of devils, what it means to go to war—and sent me on my way.

The third showed me I had come to the right place—I think of restless genius, the only good version of "Hallelujah," respect for those who have gone before—and remained there, in the distance, a comfort and a shield.

This book is for what we have lost, the bones underfoot, the dust in the air.

CONTENTS

CHAPTER 1

Beowulf and Formula

Since serious study of *Beowulf* and Old English poetry began in the nineteenth century, scholars have recognized that the poem repeats itself, repeats and is repeated by other poems, retells and is retold in other traditions, genres, and forms. The scholarship devoted to studies of the poem's repetitions and relationships is almost impossible to control. The word that most often appears in this kind of analysis is "formula," but the term has been applied to such a wide variety of concepts in such a wide variety of fields that what it means for *Beowulf* is, even for most *Beowulf* scholars, uncertain, even while few would disagree with a statement such as "the form of *Beowulf* is generally and basically formulaic" (Haarder 1975, 166). This chapter (and this book) will not offer one definition of formula, either generally or for readers of the poem, but what I hope to demonstrate is that the loose concept of formula is the best way to analyze the poem that we have and to imagine what systems and structures lie hidden beneath and before the words on the page. In other words, formula helps us to understand the compositional processes that generate the poem and, perhaps obviously, also provides an approach to reading the poem, an approach that will be modeled in subsequent chapters. This chapter, therefore, attempts to survey what we know about formula and *Beowulf*, moving from the most widely accepted notion of formulaic composition at the level of the half-line all the way to the poem as a whole, where recognition and discussion of formula becomes rare, all while demonstrating the impossibility of isolating any one level of composition from the others.

© The Author(s) 2020
M. Fox, *Following the Formula in Beowulf, Örvar-Odds saga, and Tolkien*, https://doi.org/10.1007/978-3-030-48134-6_1

1.1   THE FORMULA AND FORMULAIC SYSTEM[1]

The concept of the formula and its extended definitions, everything from the half-line to the full story-pattern, has been part of the discussion of *Beowulf* almost from the beginning.[2] As early as 1840, Jacob Grimm, in suggesting how fitting the "legends" behind *Judith*, *Andreas*, and *Elene* were for conversion into Old English poetry, uses the phrase *hergebrachte epische Formeln* (traditional epic formulas) in his description of how ecclesiastical material is transformed into Old English (1840, vi). Grimm suggests these formulas are so much a part of the tradition that poetry could not be composed without them ("ihre verfasser konnten sich dieser formeln, die damals nach gäng und gäbe waren, nicht überheben"; their authors could not do without these formulas, which were common at the time), and he identifies several formulas across early Germanic literatures (1840, xl–xliv). Grimm is effectively looking at more or less verbatim repetition: for example, he lists *gode pancode* (with slight variation in *Andreas*, *Beowulf*, the *Heliand*, and the *Ludwigslied*) and *ne wæs hit lenge þa gen* (again with slight variation in *Beowulf*, the *Heliand*, the *Ludwigslied*, and *Parzival*). In the same year, just as influentially as it turns out, Ludwig Ettmüller, influenced by contemporary study of the *Nibelungenlied* and basing his conclusion first on the introductory material on Scyld, which he sees as having very little connection with the poem as a whole, concludes that *Beowulf* is the work of more than one poet: "Das Beowulflied nicht von einem Dichter organisch gebildet, sondern aus einzelen Volksliedern zusammengesetzt ward" (the *Beowulf*-poem was not composed organically by one poet, but rather was assembled from individual folk-poems; 1840, 7).

Grimm's recognition of repeated and similar half-lines is explored more fully by Eduard Sievers in his 1878 edition of the *Heliand*. Sievers, under the heading *Formelverzeichnis*, offers over a hundred pages of synonyms (a *synonymischer Teil*, with notes to how they relate to works other than the *Heliand*, most often in Old English) and expressions organized by part of speech and inflection (a *systematischer Teil*, classifications by syntax that anticipate later Old English ideas of formulaic systems based on syntax). Around the same time, building on Ettmüller's sense of the poem's composition, Karl Müllenhoff detects different strands in the composition of *Beowulf*, dividing the poem into an introduction and four parts (fight; fight; homecoming; fight) and then finding two old songs from different sources (the fight with Grendel and the fight with the dragon) and two bridges or continuations (the fight with Grendel's mother and the homecoming) between those old songs, a theory of composite authorship that becomes known as *Liedertheorie.* All told, Müllenhoff identifies the work of six different poets (1869, 193–4).[3] Müllenhoff's theories are the inspiration for the first sustained studies of variation and formulas in *Beowulf.* The synonyms of the poem (including features such as epithets) are first gathered by Karl Schemann in 1882, explicitly to support Müllenhoff's divisions of the poem (1882, 1); in 1886, Adolf Banning, acknowledging Schemann and suggesting that his aims are to do for *Beowulf* what Sievers does for the *Heliand* and to confirm Müllenhoff's findings by looking at how formulas relate across Müllenhoff's divisions of the poem, gathers *Die epischen Formeln im Beowulf;* in 1889, Richard M. Meyer starts to gather and classify different kinds of repetition across Germanic poetry, including sections on *Parallelverse; technische Satzformeln; ceremonielle Satzformeln; andere Satzformeln;* and *wiederholte Verse.* Richard Kistenmacher gathers repetitions of words and word groups in the first part of his study (of *Beowulf* and other poems) and repetitions of half-lines in the second, comparing *Beowulf* to *Elene* in that regard. The identifications of formulas and repetition were almost an industry in the late nineteenth century.

Where Homeric scholarship from the late eighteenth century divides along Analyst and Unitarian lines, with the former seeking the seams of multiple authorship and the latter arguing for one author, for artistic unity, opinions of *Beowulf* develop similarly. Müllenhoff and his followers seek the seams of multiple authorship, and the recognition of the poem's (formulaic) repetition is deployed, as we have seen, to support *Liedertheorie,* but also to advance other theories of authorship. Gregor Sarrazin, most famously, argues on the basis of parallels between *Beowulf* and the signed poems of Cynewulf that Cynewulf brought *Beowulf* into its current form through a process of translation and adaptation, thus agreeing with Müllenhoff while demonstrating a further relevance to repetition across poems.[4] The earlier work of Grimm and Sievers, however, suggests instead a traditional storehouse of words and phrases and, by extension, the possible artistic unity of the poem. Johannes Kail is the most vocal opponent of Sarrazin: Kail argues (later supported by Ellen Clune Buttenweiser [1898]) that the repetition is so ubiquitous as to render arguments for authorship on the basis of shared diction and half-lines ridiculous. Instead, again, the *Parallelstellen* are simply evidence of a storehouse of words and formulas that were in traditional and common use ("Es ist wol das natürlichste, die parallelstellen als einen gemeinsamen poetischen formelschatz zu betrachten, aus welchem alle ags. dichter unabhängig von einander je nach bedarf ihren ausdruck ent- nahmen"; It is no doubt most natural to consider the parallel passages as a common poetic vocabulary from which all Anglo-Saxon poets, inde- pendently of one another, took their phrases as needed; 1899, 32); as Bernhard ten Brink would put it, they were "a common property on which anyone could draw freely," but that common property seems to have been seen in the nineteenth century as a fixed set of "pieces," subject to only slight variation as they are used (Schaefer 1997, 109). By 1905, Friedrich Klaeber, in a collection of textual notes to *Beowulf* (in a section on rhetorical notes with discussion of variation, formulas, epithets, and litotes) could say (with reference to Meyer and Sievers), that "there is no need to remark on Old English (Germanic) poetic formulas in general," for he considered the existence and definition of formula a given (1905, 243). However, John Miles Foley's assessment of Sievers' contribution might do for the nineteenth century as a whole: "The assumptions underlying the editor's arrangement of materials fairly represent the rather inexact concept of 'formula' typical of most of the period" (1980b, 52).

Still, even the earliest scholarship contains hints of the explosion of formulaic studies to come, at almost every level of formula. Jacob Grimm, already in 1823, as has been explored by Eric Stanley, recognizes in a review that *unsere serbischen Lieder*, coming from the warm mouth of the people, exist in an important relationship to Germanic songs of a thousand years ago, thus anticipating the studies of Parry and Lord (1997, 12–15). Henry Munro Chadwick, almost a century later, though without reference to Grimm, begins to approach modern oral theory as he perceives parallels and formulas in modern Slavonic poetry, calling their heroic poetry the "nearest modern analogy" to Germanic heroic verse, noting preservation in an "oral tradition" without a modern sense of authorship. In looking at parallels between Homeric and Germanic formulas, Chadwick attributes them to the oral tradition, thus seeing a continuity from Homeric verse to modern (oral) Slavonic song (1912, 101–2, 320).[5] John S. P. Tatlock's investigation of epic formulas in Layamon is also instructive: Tatlock notes that "the degree of similarity which makes a phrase a formula is impossible to define" and decides that three or more occurrences (in Layamon) make a (similar) phrase a for- mula. He finds little continuity from Old English to Layamon (no shared formulas), and recognizes that instead of borrowing from a common storehouse of "epic formulas," Old English poets "cultivated variety and ingenuity of phrasing," thus anticipating another of the major issues of oral-formulaic theory (1923, 494, 515–16).[6]

Tatlock seems to have been the first to recognize that, though the concept of the formula is clear enough, coming up with a definition poses problems. From the earliest collections of parallel verses, as we have seen, some variation was accepted, but the outer limit of that variation proves difficult to set. Tatlock's list of formulas in Layamon is revealing, for most of the formulas are exact repetitions, yet he groups things like superlative phrases (for example, *aðelest* with different nouns), noun/past participle phrases (for example, noun plus *bidæled*, a "formula" that will be familiar to readers of *Beowulf*, as Tatlock points out), and noun/adverb or adjective phrases (for example, *wunder ane swiðe* with a different adverb or adjective for *swiðe*) under the same headings. Tatlock also realizes that formula varies widely in its context, recurrence, and impact:

> Some are used as epic formulas in the strictest sense, narrating identical events in identical language. But in many cases such a formula or the skeleton of it is thriftily appropriated to an entirely different connection. A few are mere tags which add little. A formula is often used twice or oftener close together; not unnaturally, being freshly in mind. Sometimes the initial occurrence is speedily followed by the second, as if the poet were pleased with his new invention. Some formulas are highly poetic and probably original; others as we shall see may have been traditional in poetry; a few are colorless, commonplaces of daily speech. It is difficult to draw the line between what would stand out to Layamon and his auditors as a distinct formula, and what was a common obvious expression of no individuality, even though often repeated. (1923, 511–12)

Tatlock's conception of formula, in other words, roughly equates the term with repetition, though that repetition is of various degrees and kinds.

Milman Parry's pioneering work on Homer introduces the first definition of formula in 1928, "an expression regularly used, under the same metrical conditions, to express an essential idea" (1971b, 13). These formulas are traditional—"we have found in the *Iliad* and the *Odyssey* systems of epithets and of noun-epithet formulae so extensive as to be explicable only by the conception of a poet faithful in its smallest details to a traditional diction created by bards under the persistent influence of the heroic line" (1971b, 174)—and can result, through repeated use of individual epithets, in a kind of "insensibility" in the reader, where the formulas become "ornamental," a recognition that anticipates differentiation between different kinds of formulas based on their form and frequency (1971b, 127). Parry modifies his definition slightly in later work ("a group of words which is regularly employed under the same metrical conditions to express a given essential idea"), noting also that "usefulness" is a key factor in distinguishing formula from simple repetition. That is, the "essential idea"[7] of a formula must be an idea frequently expressed; if not, the repeated phrase has instead "been brought into the verse for some special effect" (1930, 80–1), a distinction that has important ramifications for thinking about the formulas of *Beowulf*, as we shall see. Parry distinguishes a formula (defined as above) from a formulaic system, which is "a group of phrases which have the same metrical value and which are enough alike in thought and words to leave no doubt that the poet who used them knew them not only as single formulas, but also as formulas of a certain type" (1930, 85). Formulas, in other words, may have no close relatives, and thus not be (demonstrably) part of a system; formulaic systems contain groups of related formulas.[8] Parry's focus moves from tradition (in his earliest work) to orality: "Homeric poetry can be grasped only when one has seen that it is composed in a diction which is oral, and so formulaic, and so traditional" (1932, 6). In such an oral traditional style, "thrift" is a key concept, and Parry makes it clear that "the long efforts of many poets [seeking] the best and easiest way [to tell] the same kinds of stories in the same verse-form" would result in one main formula for any given situation (1930, 73–4). Ultimately, as Foley notes, in the specific realm of Homeric studies, Parry effectively ends the Analyst/Unitarian dispute (1981b, 32).

Parry's student, Albert B. Lord, who had accompanied Parry to Yugoslavia in the 1930s, was left to carry on Parry's work after his death, and the chronology of the study of the formula becomes complicated, for our purposes, by the delay between the completion (1949) and publication (1960) of Lord's thesis, *The Singer of Tales*. Lord's specific contributions pertain more to oral-formulaic theory generally[9] than to formula in Old English, though Lord helpfully supplements Parry's definition of formula by noting that formula ought to be considered "a living phenomenon of metrical language," learned in a process much as language is learned, until the formula becomes "the offspring of the marriage of thought and sung verse" (1960, 30–1, 35–6). Lord begins to note how formulas are related: lines and half-lines are called formulaic "because they follow the same basic patterns of rhythm and syntax and have at least one word in the same position in the line in common with other lines or half-lines" (1960, 47). Lord does not do much to develop the idea of the formulaic system, but he does show how a "substitution system" works, and he looks at some basic syntactic patterns, such as the initial formula "made up of a three-syllable noun in the dative followed by the reflexive" (1960, 35, 47–8). *The Singer of Tales* includes an analysis of *Beowulf* 1473–87 (an analysis that was part of his thesis, and therefore predates the work of Francis P. Magoun, Jr., which is discussed below). On the basis of his analysis of the poem, Lord concludes that *Beowulf* was orally composed, likely not to be "transitional" (that is, in a period between oral and literate composition), and the work of a "single singer" (1995, 105–6; 1960, 198–200). Lord's assessment of later developments in Old English formulaic theory is also quite useful (1995, 117–36).

In 1953, Francis P. Magoun, Jr. took Parry and Lord's work and applied it to *Beowulf* in an article that has been said to have "affected *Beowulf* criticism more than perhaps any other single modern work of scholarship" (O'Brien O'Keeffe 1997, 98). Magoun's restatement of the theories of Parry and Lord stresses how formulas develop over time as "the creation of countless generations of singers" and that the stories told with these formulas are themselves usually "traditional." Oral poetry can therefore be contrasted with "lettered poetry," and for Magoun, poetry is either oral or lettered: "Oral poetry … is composed entirely of formulas, large and small, while lettered poetry is never formulaic, though lettered poets occasionally consciously repeat themselves or quote verbatim from other poets in order to produce a specific rhetorical or literary effect." The talent of the individual singer, however, does matter: "A good singer is one able to make better use of the common fund of formulas than the indifferent or poor singer, though all will be drawing upon essentially the same body of material" (1953, 446–7). Magoun's analysis of the first twenty-five lines of the poem suggests that roughly 70% of the passage's half-lines occur elsewhere, though his more detailed comments differentiate between exact or nearly exact repetition, repetition that looks more like part of a formulaic system (for example, *on geardagum* as part of a *on x-dagum* system), nominal compounds with

second elements that are the core of small formulaic systems, and ken-
nings, where, in Christian expressions, we see "young" formulas. Magoun
returns the notion of "formula" to currency in *Beowulf* studies, kicking
off a period of intense scholarly debate over formulaicity in Old English.

Katherine O'Brien O'Keeffe calls the publication of Magoun's work
a "kill the author of *Beowulf*" moment (1997, 91), and most of the reaction to Magoun's work challenges his conclusions in some way, focusing
on the logic that leads Magoun to claim the poem is oral, on the lack of
consistency and clarity of definitions, and on the apparent lack of originality oral-formulaic composition might suggest. Claes Schaar first points
out the flaw in Magoun's argument: "The proposition 'all formulaic
poetry is oral' does not follow, either logically or psychologically, from
the proposition 'all oral poetry is formulaic'" (1956, 303). Further, that
"lettered poets" should simply ignore the "incomparable advantage" of
the formulas, refined over many years, simply does not make sense (1956,
302). Robert D. Stevick, though generally positive about the new direction for *Beowulf* studies, has concerns about vocabulary (singer/poet;
performance/poem/composition; formulaic; transitional) and recognizes
a persistent problem: "It is not easy to make precise distinctions between
oral poems set down, poems composed 'in the ordinary modern way,'
and poems composed by learned poets using traditional (i.e., oral) formulas" (1962, 383–5).[10] One of the more interesting objections to Magoun
comes from Adrien Bonjour, who, working from Magoun's comments
on the beasts of battle, compares Cynewulf's use of the theme with the
Beowulf-poet's. Bonjour's analysis, while not conclusive, suggests that
the *Beowulf*-poet, because of the timing (late in the poem) and presentation of the theme, is more likely to have been a "lettered author ... of a
greater genius [than Cynewulf]" than to have been an "unlettered singer
... [with] an artistic sense and skill unmatched in all the extant passages
in which the theme is known to occur" (1957, 573).[11] Finally, Larry D.
Benson, building on Schaar's observations about "literary borrowings,"
demonstrates that the *Phoenix* and the *Metres of Boethius* are thoroughly
formulaic, so the fact of formulaicity cannot be used to determine an oral
or literary origin: "Because Old English poetry is formulaic, our study
of it must begin with the exciting and useful techniques developed by
students of oral verse, but because this poetry is also literature, our study
need not end there" (1966, 340).[12]

Although Magoun does not modify the definition of formula offered
by Parry and Lord, those who take up the challenge of oral-formulaic

theory develop that definition in important ways. Robert P. Creed, Magoun's student, completes a thesis that is a formulaic analysis of all of *Beowulf*, a thesis that leads him to conclude that "the diction of *Beowulf* is schematized to an extraordinary degree," with "roughly every fifth verse … repeated intact at least once elsewhere in the poem" (1968, 141).[13] Creed emphasizes that the "essential quality" of the formula is "its usefulness to the singer" as a ready aid to composition. After modifying Parry's definition slightly ("[a formula is] a word or group of words regularly employed under certain strictly determined metrical conditions to express a given essential idea" [1968, 143]), Creed recomposes four lines of *Beowulf* (356–9) to show what the range of the singer's choices might have been. Creed has no new idea of what constitutes a formulaic system, but he follows Magoun (and, therefore, Parry) in recognizing that "in a formulaic or traditional poem, we are frequently able, because of this schematization of the diction, not only to examine the formula which the singer chose, but also to guess at with some measure of assurance, and to examine, the system or entire group of formulas from *among* which he chose at a given point in his poem" (1968, 143). Creed's idea of a system is explored in a separate study of the "*andswarode*-system" (1957, 523–8), an analysis that explores all the formulas in the system, but which does not consider how a formulaic system might work in general (Creed mainly talks about syntactic variation). Where Creed's studies show how formulas may be substituted, Randolph Quirk, though he is not so much talking about formulas as the Old English poetic system generally, takes a different approach, calling a formula "a habitual collocation, metrically defined," noting that the existence of formulas sets up expectations and connections: formulas can be congruous and complementary, can establish variation, or can be incongruous (1963, 150).[14] J. B. Hainsworth, although in the context of a much more sophisticated argument about the Homeric poems exclusively, makes the same point in simpler terms: "The formula is a repetition of content, of words that have between them a bond of mutual expectancy,"[15] and the expectations of the audience can be met, varied, or completely subverted (1964, 155).

Several scholars liken the production of a formula to language,[16] a development that paves the way for a fuller understanding of formulaic systems and a recognition of the fact that any given instance of a formula has a generative "system" or "grammar" behind it, a claim that Lord had made without fully exploring what that grammar might look like (1960,

35–6). Frederic G. Cassidy suggests that "the verbal formula rests upon one or another of a limited number of archetypal syntactic patterns," and that there are twenty-five of these patterns or "frames" in Old English verse (1965, 78).[17] The most complete articulation of such a syntactic frame is W. F. Bolton's "three-word a-verse (X Y Z) in which the first and last words (X, Z) are alliterating content-words and the second word (Y) is a preposition" (1985, 167), a formula we will consider in the next chapter. As Ann C. Watts points out, Cassidy follows Hainsworth in attempting to devise an adequate definition of formula in a tradition with limited data: the repetition that we associate with formulaic composition is not always going to be present to help us identify formulas (1969, 66–8). Although the notion of syntax as the foundation of the formula does not catch on (half-lines would, by necessity, contain a limited range of syntactic structures), the notion of some kind of "deep" structure with "surface" manifestations is important at every level of formulaic composition. Michael N. Nagler, addressing specifically what he sees as an impasse in oral-formulaic studies in Homer, would prefer to ditch the term "formula" and adopt instead the word "family": "Each phrase in the group [the family] would be considered an allomorph, not of any other existing phrase, but of some central Gestalt … which is the real mental template underlying the production of all such phrases" (1967, 281).[18] Nagler specifically invokes Chomsky and, though he does not say so specifically, suggests in his repurposing of the terms "traditional" and "original"—"all is traditional on the generative level, all original on the level of performance"—that the traditional is the deep structure and the original the surface, "not only on the level of the formulaic phrase but also on that of the motif, type-scene, and whole plot" (1967, 273). Nagler's definition is introduced, in a way, to Old English studies by Patrick W. Conner, who defines a formula as "the product—one half-line in length—of a grammar of poetic diction superimposed upon the grammar of the spoken language" (1972, 206), again invoking a Chomskyian understanding of structural levels and grammar (with semantic, syntactic, and phonological components).

The three key figures in the developing understanding of the formula in Old English after Magoun are Donald K. Fry, John Miles Foley, and John D. Niles. Fry, for the first time, prioritizes the formulaic system over the formula, meaning that his definition of formula is simply "a group of words, one half-line in length, which shows evidence of being the direct product of a formulaic system." The formulaic system to which the formula belongs is "a group of half-lines, usually loosely related metrically and semantically, which are related in form by the identical relative placement of two elements, one a variable word or element of a compound usually supplying the alliteration, and the other a constant word or element of a compound, with approximately the same distribution of non-stressed elements" (1967a, 203–4).[19] Fry makes it clear that his notion of system means that identifying formulas is different than it was for Magoun: "[Formulaic] systems remove the necessity for verbatim repetition since we only need find another similar verse from which the system can be abstracted." A formulaic system, in other words, is a "pool of organized diction" (1974, 236). In another study, Fry also makes it clear that Parry's notion of thrift or economy could not apply to Old English verse (1967b, 353–6), and his last comment on the formula explains why, in his view, every meaningful part of Parry's definition is not quite right for Old English:

> An Old English formula may consist of one long compound word rather than a "group of words." The formula may appear only once, not "regularly employed," but be closely related to other formulas from the same system. Since all Old English half-lines are metrically equivalent, "under the same metrical conditions" proves meaningless. And finally, Old English formulas seem to be related only in form, not in content, i.e., they do not "express a given essential idea." (1981, 172–3)

Fry's critique of the applicability of Parry's definition for Old English is taken up by Albert Lord (1995, 120–4), but Fry's focus on a definition specifically for Old English paves the way for John Miles Foley, and his notion of "tradition-dependent" features of oral-formulaic verse.[20]

Foley may be the most important figure in oral-formulaic studies in general; no overview of his contributions to the field will do him justice. His initial treatment of formula in Old English is based on a computer-assisted metrical analysis that demonstrates that "a single rhythmic template ... generates 94% of all lines metrically recoverable from the unique manuscript and the Thorkelin transcriptions" (1976, 207). Instead of focusing on the (visible) syntactic and semantic structures of the formula, Foley looks at deep metrical structure and defines that metrical template as "a rhythmic underlay, one whole poetic line in length with verse (half-line) substitution, which predetermines the structure of its verbal counterpart, the formula" (1976, 219).[21] What we see (or hear) is, therefore, a formula that is the solution to the equation of "metrical idea plus traditional vocabulary" (1976, 212). Foley refines this into one succinct definition of formula in Old English, a definition that incorporates formulaic system, a system that is clearly generative: "A verbal formula in Old English poetry is a recurrent substitutable phrase one half-line in length which results from the intersection of two compositional parameters—a morphemic focus at positions of metrical stress and a limited number of metrical formulas" (1980a, 122; 1981c, 274). What Foley makes clear, in some ways for the first time, is that formulaic patterns are dependent upon tradition, genre, and text; Parry's definition of the formula was for the Homeric formula only, and arguments about the oral-formulaic nature of Old English verse based upon studies that rely on Parry's definition miss the point. Benson's argument, for example, actually demonstrates that "Old English has a certain number of Greek formulas—about the same number in possibly oral and possibly written texts," a problem that disappears with a tradition-dependent definition of formula. Due to the constraints of Old English meter, "we must expect both a lower percentage of classically defined formulas and a higher index of variability among systems in the Anglo-Saxon poetic texts" (Foley 1981c, 271–2).

John D. Niles succinctly describes the problems that comparisons of potentially oral-formulaic texts across traditions have caused, noting, first of all, that because of differences in meter, "the formulaic language of *Beowulf* differs significantly from the formulaic language of Homer" and that the importance of "the stylistic feature of variation" is another tradition-specific feature of Old English narrative poetry (1983, 121). Niles juxtaposes occurrences of Homer's ἔπεα πτερόεντα προσηύδα (he spoke winged words) with b-verses in *Beowulf* ending in *gedryht*, showing that Homer's formula hardly varies, but that *Beowulf* seems to show evidence of a system including verses that are "similar in rhythm and syntax and identical in the relative placement of the word *gedryht*" (1983, 123). This system can be schematized as (x) x x X́ x (x) *gedrýht*, where x indicates an unstressed syllable, X the initial stressed syllable of a noun in the genitive plural, and parentheses an optional element, meaning the system has five iterations in the poem (357b; 431b; 633b; 662b; and 1672b); the sixth occurrence of *gedryht* (*æþelinga gedriht*, 118b), though superficially very similar to the other five (genitive plural noun before *gedryht*), can in fact be shown to belong to a different system *æpelinga(-es)* **X́**, a system with six other occurrences in the poem.[22] In the first system, the genitive noun changes with the demands of alliteration; in the second, which can be an a- or b-verse, the constant element alliterates. The example demonstrates how the surface formula provides an incomplete picture of the formulaicity of Old English verse, a point Niles drives home by illustrating the problems with Fry's putative x́ *mup*-system.[23] A formula in Old English poetry is, therefore, "a rhythmic/ syntactic/semantic complex one half-line in length." Formulas may be identified by their participation in a formulaic system, "a set of verses of a similar metrical type in which one main verbal element is constant" (1983, 126). Having established his definitions, Niles repeats Magoun's 1953 analysis of lines 1–25, showing formulaic systems for each verse but limiting those systems to *Beowulf* alone in order to avoid mixing evidence from different genres, regions, and dates. Niles finds that thirty-three of the fifty verses show evidence of belonging to a formulaic system, a figure that, curiously enough, is roughly comparable with Magoun's findings of reiterated verses. Extending his analysis to the first 500 lines of the poem, Niles finds that 16.9% of the verses are reiterated (Creed's 1955 figure was 16.7%), even though most still are part of a formulaic system, while nearly 63.2% of the verses in the poem are members of an "identifiable formulaic system." Niles concludes that "the diction of *Beowulf* is indeed highly formulaic, but far more important than the repetition of fixed phrases is the substitution of one verbal element for another within flexible formulaic systems filling the half-line" (1983, 128).

   Though Old English definitions of formula and formulaic system have not been substantially reworked since Niles, some innovations and additions to how formula might function have been proposed. Anita Riedinger, first of all, though her findings are more appropriate to the discussion of theme (below), proposes the concept of a formulaic "set" between the formula and the system. Effectively, Riedinger is suggesting that sets participate in a particular theme (a connotation): "One cannot read Old English poetry accurately or with full appreciation of its artistry without an understanding of the connotative meaning of the formulas—an understanding to be gained primarily by an examination of the formulas in context" (1985, 303). Riedinger's observation in a way goes back to Parry, suggesting that a formula recurs when the singer sees a similarity of situation, though the tradition-dependent characteristics of Old English verse mean that the formula will see some variation as it moves from context to context. Riedinger's definition of system—"a group of verses usually sharing the same meter and syntax in which one word, usually stressed, is constant, and the other stressed word or words may be varied to suit the alliterative and/or narrative context"—admits some systems that seem too open to be useful to the singer (such as *x under x*), but does not disagree in any major way with Fry or Niles.[24] A set is defined almost the same way, as "a group of verses usually sharing the same function and system in which one word, usually stressed, is constant, and at least one stressed word may be varied, usually synonymously, to suit the alliterative and/or narrative context," introducing the concept of "function" to the definition of the system. A formula, finally, becomes "the repetition of one general concept + one system + one function" (1985, 305–6). Charles D. Wright points out that Riedinger "is not exactly clear about what constitutes a function" (2012, 162), but the possibilities seem to range from filler (a "tag function," the ornamental or incidental repetition) to communicating theme, "a recurrent image, idea, or event" (a "thematic function" or significant repetition). Riedinger, however, usefully links formula and theme, showing "traditional contexts" are important to understanding formula and formulaic system.

Karl Reichl, in effect, proposes a semantic definition for the formula, suggesting the terms formula and formulaic system be limited "to those repeated expressions which (1) form metrical units and (2) have a recognizably constant lexical nucleus" (1989, 49). For Reichl, the "semantic nucleus" of the formula is the key, not "abstract metrical-rhythmical patterns [or] syntactic structures" (1989, 53). Formulas have types, and those types range from the "rigid formula," with little or no variation, to the "variable formula," which, depending upon the degree of variation, shades into the formulaic system. For example, X *dryhtnes æ* is a variable formula in which the variable part (X), which he calls the "substitution slot," here usually filled with an adverb of time or place, "serves to place the fixed expression into a syntactical context" (1989, 46–7). If, however, the "substitution slot" is filled by nouns, verbs, or adjectives (syntactic items with more semantic weight), then Reichl would call it a formulaic system, as, for example, with *sinces brytta, goldes brytta, beaga brytta*, etc. In the focus on a three-step scale—rigid formula, variable formula, variable formula in a formulaic system—Reichl echoes the earlier classification of Paul Kiparsky, who suggests a classification

system ranging from fixed to free formulas, again without metrical cri-
teria, but there on the basis of a comparison with natural language, with
syntactic structures being key. Kiparsky's complicated attempt to unravel
the grammatical nature of the formula includes the important observation of "three levels of formulaic patterning" (1976, 91): formulas
"crystallize" at deep structure, at surface structure, and in phonological
representation, thus mirroring the three kinds of verbal memory,
"echoic" (auditory trace), "preliminary" (surface structure form), and
"long-term" (deep structure/semantic form).[25]

A further consideration of how formula might impact Old English
poetry has been highlighted by Katherine O'Brien O'Keeffe, who extends
the investigation of formula to the scribe (1990, 191). O'Brien O'Keeffe
"assumes the possibility of one or more transitional states between pure
'orality' and pure 'literacy'" (1990, x). She suggests a "transitional literacy" in the transcription of Old English verse, a model of "participatory
transmission" (1990, 193): in other words, Old English scribes, familiar
with oral traditional verse, could introduce variants as they copied. As she
puts it, the scribe could "read 'formulaically' and … become a participant
in and a determiner of the text" (1990, 191). O'Brien O'Keeffe finds evidence for this participation in the different visual conventions of surviving Latin and Old English verse. A. N. Doane takes the argument a step
further, calling a scribe who copies vernacular poetic texts a "performer":
"The scribe's performance is the product not only of the power of writing, but also of the power of speaking, and the scribe's performance is
therefore considered not as faithful duplication, but as the exercise of
his own 'communicative competence' within the tradition that normally
resides in speaking and traditional memory" (1994, 423). Doane stresses,
again, that this process means that such texts are "emergent" and "subject to ongoing reformulation" (1994, 423–4) as we have seen with traditional oral narratives. Peter Orton reductively writes of the scribe as
"poetaster," altering verse at the level of word and phrase and interpolat-
ing longer passages (2000, 129–61), and Leonard Neidorf dismisses theories of "scribal behavior" in favor of "lexemic theory" (2017, 103–14),
but the observations of Carol Braun Pasternack on the issue have further
interesting implications for the way stories are told and adapted: "This
method of making poetry, in which the roles of poet and scribe-compiler
echo and overlap each other, also blurs the line between poet (or should
I say 'compiler'?) and reader. For if the authority for defining the poem's

dimensions and intent does not clearly rest in the poet, then authority is open to all who would participate in making the poem" (1995, 193).

Recent studies of *Beowulf* and formula, instead of attempting to arbitrate between the developing ideas of formula and formulaic system in Old English, either generalize or pick and choose.[26] Thus, for example, Andy Orchard's *A Critical Companion to Beowulf* offers no definition of formula or formulaic system. Orchard observes that orality is no longer the key question in such investigations (as indeed it is not here). He finds "formulaic repetition in around 40 per cent of the lines of the poem," which is substantially less than Niles' 63.2%, but Orchard is listing "repeated formulas," not verses that seem to be part of formulaic systems (2003a, 86, 274–326). Orchard has something to say about substitution in a system, but rather than define a formulaic system, he directs readers to Fry, Niles, and Riedinger and carefully and clearly demonstrates the interaction of repetition and formula from verbatim repetition at the level of the line and half-line to substitution (synonyms, metrically equivalent expressions, different parts of speech) within "interconnected systems of formulas" (2003a, 87–9).[27] The latest edition of Klaeber's *Beowulf* similarly offers no definition but rather a general overview:

> The fundamental compositional unit employed in the crafting of the poem is thus the flexible formulaic system one half-line in length. The words that, in a given instance, fill the half-line are very likely to be formed on the basis of one or another abstract linguistic pattern useful to poets composing in the alliterative form, regardless of whether or not the resulting verse has the appearance, to our eyes, of a fixed formula. From the perspective of generative composition and its formal procedures, the poet's formulaic language therefore operates as language does in general, only it is more specialized because of the added requirements of meter and alliteration. (Fulk et al. 2008, cxiv)

Though the precise nature of *Beowulf*'s formulaicity does not seem to have been settled, that the poem is formulaic in some fashion is impossible to deny. Still, Lord's last words on the subject of oral-formulaic theory suggest that much remains to be decided, for he insists that there is a significant difference in formulaic usage between *Beowulf* and other poems and argues for evidence of thrift in *Beowulf*, even though most Old English critics would probably not agree (1995, 120, 134–6).

1.2   ACTION-PATTERN, THEME, TYPE-SCENE, MOTIF[28]

The earliest readers of Old English verse notice a kind of repetition that differs from the formula and the formulaic system. Jacob Grimm comments that all the descriptions of battle have something magnificent about them, and he goes on to list occurrences of the wolf, eagle, and raven and to muse on their origin (1840, xxv–xxviii), and Ernst Otto, in 1901, identifies "typical motifs" in Old English secular poetry. However, no systematic study of theme (or type-scene or motif) comes until after Walter Arend, Milman Parry, and Albert Lord: Arend gathers what he calls *die typischen Scenen* (1933) in Homer for the first time—precisely the sorts of themes one would expect, such as feasting, journeys, and assemblies—a book which Parry reviews favorably for how Arend "sees the schematization of Homer's composition," though Arend "fails almost altogether to see the reasons for it" (1936, 358). Parry's review calls Arend's type-scenes "action-patterns" and notes how action-pattern and formula "depend upon one another" (1936, 358). Parry, unfortunately, does not live long enough to explain in detail how theme works or to define it, but he does signal theme as a component of oral song: "The oral song is made up on the one hand of the essential theme, which may in itself be a bare enough thing, and on the other hand of the traditional oral material which furnishes its elaboration" (1971a, 461). Lord, however, revisits the definition and consideration of theme many times over the course of his career. He first defines theme as "a subject unit, a group of ideas, regularly employed by a singer, not merely in any given poem, but in the poetry as a whole," noting how, over time, the more frequently used themes become more fixed in content (1938, 440–1).[29] Lord sees the formula and theme as distinct units, even though they at times coincide, observing that metrical considerations do not apply to theme (1951, 73). Themes are "repeated narrative or descriptive elements" that "function in building songs in much the same way in which the formulas function in building lines"; as with formulas, themes may be simply ornamental (1953, 127). In sequence, therefore, "formulas are … the means of expressing the themes of the poetry," and "the themes lead naturally from one to another to form a song which exists as a whole in the singer's mind" (1960, 49, 94).[30]

The theme, like the formula, explodes into Old English studies as a result of the work of Magoun, this time on the theme of the beasts of battle, though Stanley B. Greenfield, no doubt guided by Magoun's earlier work, writes at the same time on the theme of exile.[31] Magoun's study is based almost completely on Lord's idea of the theme, repeating the idea of ornamental and essential themes (the beasts of battle he considers ornamental) and restating how the theme works in the compositional process: "Anglo-Saxon singers [make] use of themes ... ready made and as ready at hand as the formulas with which [they] will construct or phrase them" (1955, 83). Greenfield's work on exile is a little different, for Greenfield divides the theme into aspects (status; deprivation; state of mind; and movement in or into exile), and the aspects do not necessarily include the same kind of formulaic repetition that Magoun identifies in the beasts of battle theme. Perhaps the most valuable observations of this study, however, are couched in the language of formula rather than theme, even while these statements are true for both and even for levels of composition above the theme:

> The associations with other contexts using a similar formula will inevitably color a particular instance of a formula so that a whole host of overtones springs into action to support the aesthetic response ... Originality in the handling of conventional formulas may be defined as the degree of tension achieved between the inherited body of meanings in which a particular formula participates and the specific meaning of that formula in its individual context. (1955, 205)

Adrien Bonjour, replying specifically to Magoun and Greenfield, suggests that the theme of the beasts of battle in *Beowulf* (3021b–27) "gives us a measure of [the poet's] art in turning a highly conventional theme into a thing of arresting beauty and originality. If ever one can speak of the alchemy of genius it is here" (1957, 571).[32]

As specific examples of themes continue to be identified after Magoun and Greenfield, Donald K. Fry again takes on the problem of a lack of critical vocabulary. Fry usefully surveys the history of the problem of what to call the theme and then chooses to distinguish type-scenes from themes, suggesting that a type-scene occurs within a specific narrative event while a theme does not:

> A type-scene [is] a recurring stereotyped presentation of conventional details used to describe a certain narrative event, requiring neither verbatim repetition nor a specific formula content; and a theme [is] a recurring concatenation of details and ideas, not restricted to a specific event, verbatim repetition, or certain formulas, which forms an underlying structure for an action or description. (1968a, 49–51, 53)

A key feature of these definitions is the flexibility of both type-scene and theme, for "neither themes nor type-scenes are restricted in any way to verbatim repetition, definite metrical patterns, a fixed order of events, details, or ideas, or certain formulas or systems," meaning that some kind of "underlying structure" is what ultimately identifies them (1968a, 53). This underlying structure is basically Greenfield's "aspects"; David K. Crowne's analysis of the "hero on the beach" also focuses on "imagistic details" over verbal correspondence (1960, 371).[33] Lord, for his part, would not agree that "the hero on the beach" is a theme, but he believes it is part of a larger journey theme for which verbal correspondences can be found. Part of the problem is Crowne's expansion of the theme away from its literal elements (from the beach to a doorway or even a general liminal situation), an expansion which limits possibilities for verbal correspondence and which is instructive for formulaic systems and story-patterns as well (1995, 142–56).

John Miles Foley, again, is a key figure in the study of the Old English theme. In his first major attempt to define the theme, he describes it in terms that make the relationship of formula and theme clear. If a formula is the result of the combination of meter which gives form and traditional vocabulary which provides content, then theme is the product of "'episodic impulse' (form) and 'traditional actions' (content)" (1976, 226). Theme, like formula and formulaic system, is tradition-dependent: Old English themes, therefore, exhibit less verbatim repetition, but demonstrate instead "verbal correspondence" through features Foley calls "stave-roots," which he defines as "principally the roots of alliterating words, although non-alliterating words may at times be included" (1976, 221, 231). The other tradition-dependent feature of the Old English theme is its episodic structure, its "initialization" and "termination" through "formal boundary marker[s]" (1976, 227). Foley's 1990 treatment of theme does not differ substantially, but Foley helpfully lists the twenty-four themes reported to date[34] and gives his view of current issues in Old English thematics: Fry's attempt to split the field into type-scenes and themes, the role of verbal correspondence, and the question of theme in general, that is, if the term really works for Old English and, even if a suitable definition were found, how non-thematic units might function (1990, 331–5). Lord had already commented on Fry's distinction, agreeing that type-scene was a useful term for repeated elements of details with little or no verbal correspondence, but suggesting that a theme had to have some verbal correspondence, effectively responding to the first two issues (1974, 205–10). Foley looks at the sea-voyage in *Beowulf*, and he calls the smaller units of the theme both "elements" and "motifs" (like Greenfield's aspects), finding in them "a discernible and dynamic narrative sequence" and verbal correspondence in the form of "single morphs" (his former "stave-root," it would seem), "root words whose systemic content is metrically (and therefore lexically and syntactically) highly variable" (1990, 339–40). Foley also introduces here the concept of "responsion," a "local resonance of morphs," words that "respond to proximate partners, lexical relatives usually no more than about twenty lines away, and often much closer" (1990, 340–41).[35] Finally, though, the theme in the Old English tradition has "a definite, consistent narrative pattern but little or no verbal correspondence" (1990, 357), and that lack of sustained verbal correspondence, of course, has to do with the Old English emphasis on variation.

The most important and most recent reconsideration of type-scene comes from Mark S. Griffith, who again argues for a more strict definition of the term. Griffith begins with G. S. Kirk's definition (from Kirk's commentary on the *Iliad*), "recurrent actions of everyday or heroic life … described again and again in standard language that can be abbreviated or elaborated where necessary" (1993, 179), and makes a cogent argument for the motifs within those actions: "Themes and typescenes must constitute a specific nuclei of motifs which must add up to more than generalized truisms about heroic narrative" (1993, 181). On that basis, Griffith dismisses Crowne's "hero on the beach" type-scene, as it can be reduced to one motif—the presence of a flashing light—that "occurs in a bewildering array of guises" (1993, 181). In other words, Griffith suggests, and I think quite rightly, that a flexibility of definition has led to the admission of so much variation in the study of type-scenes that the type-scene as a category at times collapses. Griffith does show, however, how the "beasts of battle" works as a type-scene, suggesting in terms that will be familiar to us that fixed content is obviously not part of the Old English type-scene yet that the mention of some sub-group of a type-scene's motifs would no doubt bring the others to the audience's mind (1993, 185–6). Griffith, though he denies that the type-scene can be simply ornamental, links the type-scene to the classical rhetorical technique of ekphrasis, that is, a description which is "largely self-contained" with stock subject matter and which delays "narrative movement" (1993, 196). On the basis of his study of the "beasts of battle," Griffith concludes that "formulaic theory still has a place in Old English critical studies as long as it is concerned with the development of a rhetoric that can most economically describe the stylistic features of the texts themselves" (1993, 197).

Fry's attempt to distinguish between type-scene and theme has not really caught on, much like Adrien Bonjour's distinction between episodes and digressions has not been maintained, but it does seem that the term "theme" is more common than type-scene and that motif is now used as Foley used it, for smaller non-narrative units within themes (type-scenes) or, as Stith Thompson would define it in the study of folktale, as "the smallest element in a tale having a power to persist in tradition" (1946, 415). This is how Paul Battles and Charles D. Wright approach the problem of adding a new theme—the scop's repertoire—to Old English studies. The theme has three motifs (copiousness, orality, and antiquity) in different distribution and follows different models (traditional or inspirational). Battles and Wright suggest that this theme—modeling how themes might work overall—is important because it contributes to our understanding of how the Anglo-Saxons conceived of poetry, because we can study its modifications and think about how cultural change is reflected in the theme, and because its identification allows us to muse about intertextual relationships (2018, 4–5). Foley would agree that the effect of the theme is not limited to its place in the text, either, for "echoes from one occurrence of a given theme reverberate not simply through the subsequent linear length of the given poem, but through the collective mythic knowledge of the given culture" (1976, 231). The overall effects of theme cannot, perhaps, be overstated. Paul Beekman Taylor suggests that the repetition of themes "establishes a parallelism of ideas … carries to a particular context the sense of previous contexts in which a theme has appeared … [and functions as] a unifying principle" (1967, 270); Creed, though discussing oral theme, puts it even more succinctly: "The audience—singer included—hears each new performance of a theme counterpointed against all the old performances it has heard" (1961, 101).

Finally, thinking about theme in Old English connects to theme in other fields and looks toward the larger unit of the story-pattern. Joseph Fontenrose, in his study of Delphic myth, defines the theme as "a recurrent feature or episode of traditional stories" (1974, 6). For Fontenrose, the theme is always an integral part of the story (not, it would seem, ever simply ornamental), and subject to variation and obfuscation. As he puts it, "the theme is not identically expressed in every variant or version: it constantly changes its outer dress in accord with the national customs or local features of the places where it is found. It may become obscured or disguised; only a trace of it may be left" (1974, 7). Here, we are clearly entering the realm also of the folktale, as Fontenrose enumerates the themes of his combat myth, but this becomes part of the discussion of story-pattern to follow.

1.3   STRUCTURAL REPETITION

Structural markers such as envelope patterns and ring composition are closely linked with formulas, formulaic systems, and themes, as Foley's identification of initialization and termination of themes through formal boundary markers would suggest, though of course the signaling of narrative threads or units need not revolve around theme. Even though the recognition of ring composition (sometimes known as hysteron proteron or chiasmus, though also known classically as prothysteron or hysterologia) in Homer dates from Aristarchus,[36] Parry and Lord have little to say about it,[37] and Old English scholarship advances at first along separate lines. As in the study of formulas and themes, key related terms have sometimes been used differently. Adeline Bartlett identifies a 1907 observation by Walter Hart as the first mention of what is now commonly known as the "envelope pattern": Hart suggests that "dead is Æschere" (1323b) is repeated in reverse order as *swylc Æschere wæs* (1329b; where *wæs* also stands chiastically for *dead*) and that the pattern is "something like the 'envelope figure' of the Psalms" (1907, 200–1),[38] though the possible biblical origin of the pattern is not fully explored until much later. Bartlett's study, however, introduces several different kinds of patterning and structures to our understanding of Old English poetry. Most prominently, she discusses the envelope pattern, which she defines as "any logically unified group of verses bound together by the repetition at the end of (1) words or (2) ideas or (3) words and ideas which are employed at the beginning" (1935, 9). Bartlett's examples, however, extend immediately into chiastic structures inside her envelope patterns (for example, *The Battle of Maldon*, lines 25–8), and she in fact suggests that the origin of the pattern might be "simple chiasmus," though she later agrees with Hart that the Psalms were the model for the structure in Anglo-Saxon poetry (1935, 25).[39] Bartlett also discusses parallel patterns, "when ... doubling is extended to fully elaborated sentences and to sentence groups" (1935, 30), and classes these into repetition, balance (often more than two; both restatements in different words and repetition via anaphora), and antithesis (only two; parallelism with antithesis). A special category of parallel pattern is the incremental pattern, when the parallelism demonstrates "cumulative force" (1935, 49): her primary example here is the now well-known *com* ... *com* ... *com* sequence of Grendel's approach to Heorot. Finally, Bartlett includes a chapter on what she calls "decorative inset," sections of text that break from the main narrative and range from gnomic expressions to digressions.

Forty years later, Constance Hieatt expands Bartlett's notion of the "envelope pattern" to the level of the fitt—about one-quarter of the fitts in the poem have envelope patterns—and to the digressions and episodes. Indeed, Hieatt offers a summary diagram for the poem as a whole, noting how the envelope patterns lead to an overall chiastic structure (like a ring structure, but without a central, unrepeated element) and interlock fitts and other envelopes in a way that echoes John Leyerle's argument for an interlace structure of the larger poem. Hieatt makes it clear, however, that hers is not a model of "thematic occurrences and narrative events," that is, not the model that will soon be offered by John Niles (1975, 249, 253, 257, and 264–5n29). Niles' work comes in the context of Homeric and oral-formulaic studies, which had progressed through the work of W. A. A. Van Otterlo, who discusses *Ringkomposition* as framing technique either as part of an annular (chiastic) structure or as an instance of single repetition with an anaphoric (a resumption of the main narrative) or inclusive (envelope pattern) function, to the work of J. A. Notopolous, who connects ring composition to oral-formulaic theory.[40] Notopolous classes ring composition as one of three essential "unifying devices," the other two being prolepsis ("foreshadowing") and analepsis ("retrospection"), and suggests that ring composition is specifically connected with digressions (1951, 88). Independently, that is, without apparent knowledge of Bartlett, Hieatt, or Niles (whose work on ring composition first appeared in his thesis of 1972), H. Ward Tonsfeldt rehearses the earlier Homeric study of ring composition and relates it to *Beowulf*: his most detailed example is the Finn episode, and Tonsfeldt shows how the episode's ring structure both unifies the episode and establishes its relationship to the rest of the poem. Overall, Tonsfeldt concludes that "each ring structure is in spirit, if not precisely in form, a microcosm of the whole work" (1977, 452). Further, Tonsfeldt sees a hierarchy that reaches from formula (verbal) to theme (narrative) to ring composition (structural):

themes are made up of formulas, and ring composition can organize either formulas or themes (1977, 443–4). Tonsfeldt, like Hieatt, relates his study to Leyerle's study of interlace, but with added perspectives on the treatment of time and a possible visual aspect of ring structure (the latter a connection made also by Whitman, who connected geometric design in Greek pottery to ring structures). According to Leyerle, the *Beowulf*-poet found "relations between events ... more significant than their temporal sequence," so an interlaced structure (and, by relation, a ring structure) is a device that gives the poet "great freedom to manipulate time," breaking down the linearity of narrative and thus making the poem almost visual, in effect helping us to "see" the poem as a whole while we move through it line by line (1967, 13). In other words, as Tonsfeldt puts it, the structure allows for the "compression of time and the juxtaposition of past and present" (1977, 448).

John Niles finds ring composition at micro- and macro-levels throughout *Beowulf*, concluding that "the poet relies so greatly on this sort of patterning that, for him, balance and symmetry of thought must have been almost second nature" (1983, 153).[41] The overall structure of the poem, determined not by the repetition of words and formulas, as in Hieatt, but instead by narrative events, puts the fight with Grendel's mother at the center:

> If the reader does not become lost in the many byways of the narrative, the large-scale symmetry of its design will be evident: (A) introduction, (B) fight with Grendel, (C) celebrations, (D) fight with Grendel's mother, (C) celebrations, (B) fight with dragon, (A) close. The three great fights that constitute the main body of the poem are separated by two substantial interludes in which the hero's triumphs are celebrated with gifts, feasting, and songs and speeches alluding to legendary heroes. (1983, 157–8)[42]

Niles specifically does not assess orality and ring composition, but, like Tonsfeldt, he develops further structural arguments on the basis of ring structure. He notes that narrative events are regularly linked to one another ("in complex interrelationships"), often as thesis and antithesis, but also in a balance that blends similarities and differences, and the overall structure resembles "a series of major and minor pairs," from the fight with Grendel and the fight with the dragon all the way down to an *uncuð gelad* (1410b) and *cuþe stræte* (1634a). Ring structure and the relationships of events and pairings lead Niles to a conclusion about the thematic center of the poem, that "human success and failure are conceived of as an inseparable pair," and even to some observations on the similarity of story-pattern, as Niles sees in that central fight with Grendel's mother the central journeys and descents of Odysseus, Aeneas, and Christ (1983, 155–9, 162).

Niles' conclusions on how ring structure works are later supplemented by Ward Parks, who puts in different terms the conclusions of Tonsfeldt and Leyerle, noting how "ring structure promotes balance and symmetry," but also that it can function as "a bridge or interface between two plot movements or between a digressive episode and the principal narrative line … ring systems [regularly] interact with or even constitute themselves of other kinds of narrative structures, such as motific or thematic patterns, or narrative sequences" (1988, 241, 251). Because of the physical way in which these structures embed material, too, the technique "conveys an impression of unfolding from within" (1988, 251). Parks, like Notopolous, situates ring patterns as "just one component in a sophisticated narrative weave that makes use of other kinds of narrative organization also, such as themes or type scenes, or Proppian strings of narrative functions, or interlace" (1988, 241). The conclusions of Niles and Parks with respect to the effect of these structures have recently been echoed in useful terms by David Quint in his study of chiasmus in the *Aeneid*: "Virgil deliberately designed the *Aeneid* in order to produce the double effect ['doubling or splitting its meanings'] that divides critics: it is not an either/or but a both/and. The poem performs its own immanent critique" (2018, ix, 1).

The rather obvious connection of ring composition to memory, that is, as a mnemonic device for the oral-traditional singer, has thus in the study of *Beowulf* not been the emphasis. Instead, the envelope patterns, chiastic structures, and ring structures have been associated almost exclusively with aesthetics. Elizabeth Minchin, however, though working exclusively on Homer, suggests that such repetitions might simply be natural, that is, not "self-conscious and artful" (2001, 23). Because ring structures are related to the processes of memory, they become natural features of narratives; in other words, analyses of everyday story-telling demonstrate evidence of repetition and near repetition that resembles ring structure, all the more so if the story contains episodes or digressions (2001, 187–9). Certainly, the notion that every envelope pattern and every ring structure is "self-conscious and artful" and would be recognized by a listening (or even a reading) audience, especially across long sections of the narrative, has been called into question. Niles, however, quotes Whitman on precisely this issue: Whitman surmises that "the human mind is a strange organ, and one which perceives many things without conscious or articulate knowledge of them, and responds to them with emotions necessarily and appropriately vague. An audience hence might feel more symmetry than it could possibly analyze or describe" (1963, 256).[43]

Finally, though, perhaps for obvious reasons—including justified skepticism about the reliability of the poem's fitt divisions and the fact that the line numbers of the poem are a modern invention—there seems to have been no general critical acceptance of such studies, envelope patterns, chiastic structures, and ring structures have been deployed along with fitt divisions in numerical studies of the poem. A series of articles by Thomas E. Hart covers various aspects of repetition, effectively suggesting that it happens according to "tectonic" (numeric) patterns.[44] David R. Howlett considers this a "biblical style," as Walter Hart did in the very beginning, and demonstrates its prevalence in Anglo-Latin and Anglo-Saxon prose and verse. Howlett never presents a full schematic of *Beowulf*; he finds within smaller sections highly complex chiastic and parallel structures, often numerically informed. To give a simple example, he argues that the first three lines of the poem contain a three-part parallelism and that counting words and syllables leads to the discovery that the first part of the parallelism (*Hwæt ... gefrunon*) has eight words and seventeen syllables and the second (*hu ... fremedon*) five words and eleven syllables, both ratios in the golden section of their totals (1997, 506).[45] Eamonn Carrigan finds numerical organization in groups of fitts and the thematic progression of the poem (1967), and Gale Owen-Crocker combines thinking about fitts and chiastic structures in her argument for the significance of the four funerals (2000, 133–57). Yvette Kisor's overview of theories of "numerical composition"—a thorough and engaging read—concludes that whatever we might make of their origins, "the fact remains that the patterns are there" (2009, 76).

1.4   Story-Pattern/Tale-Type

Alexandra Hennessey Olsen's review of oral-formulaic research in Old English studies suggests that scholars who work at the level above the theme have been more interested in myth than in ring structure and envelope patterns. Albert Lord, for example, often discusses myth in an oral-formulaic context, arguing that the themes of traditional narrative song come from myth: "My basic assumption is that in oral tradition there exist narrative patterns that, no matter how much the stories built around them seem to vary, have great vitality and function as organizing elements in the composition and transmission of the oral story texts" (1969, 18; Foley 1981b, 45). That is, as he says later, "on a different level from that of the strictly compositional elements of formulas and themes ... lies a narrative pattern which might be called 'mythic' because in some instances, at least, it seems to have originated in a myth" (1976, 1). In other words, the way oral traditional narrative is composed lends additional meaning to the narrative, meaning which is tied to the fact of oral tradition; one of these "aspects of meaning" is the enrichment that "comes directly from the myth and is *inevitable* in all traditional narrative song" (1959, 1; Olsen 1988, 140). Lord discovers an (1) absence, (2) devastation, (3) return, (4) retribution, and (5) wedding pattern in Homer and Serbo-Croatian oral epics and a (1) father absent or dead, (2) challenge, (3) helper–donor, (4) borrowed equipment, and (5) journey pattern in similarly different traditions (1969; 1976, 4; Foley 1981b, 45, 49). Lord later suggests that the poem is a combination of two widespread patterns with roots ultimately in the Indo-European tradition:

1. A powerful figure is not present or, for various reasons, is powerless in a situation of danger to his people. During the period of his absence, or of his inability or unwillingness to act effectively, things go very badly for those around him, and many of his friends are killed. Finally, the powerful figure returns or his power is restored, whereupon he puts things to right again.
2. The hero and a companion, or companions, encounter first a male monster, which is overcome, and then a female monster, or a divine temptress who wants to keep the hero in the "other" world. The hero's escape from the one and his rejection of the offers of the other involve breaking a taboo and/or insulting a deity, and as a result one or more of his companions is killed. The hero, then, with a question in his mind concerning his own mortality or immortality, goes on a journey in which he learns the answer to that question (1980, 137, 139).[46]

Lord finds the first pattern also in the stories of Achilles and Odysseus, and of course in the figure of Hrothgar at the beginning of the poem, perhaps with a doubled absence of the powerful figure (that is, both

Hrothgar and Beowulf); the pattern is repeated at the arrival of Grendel's mother. The second pattern is somewhat more complex, clearly worked out in the epic of Gilgamesh (Humbaba, Ishtar, death of Enkidu), somewhat changed for Odysseus (Polyphemos, Circe, death of Elpenor, journey to the land of the dead), and "a form in *Beowulf* in which guilt has become a virtue [the adversary is no longer "sacred"] and the pattern is broken, leaving either a gap or at best an enigmatic and unclear vestige" (1980, 141). For Lord, the two patterns offer a "mythic base" which allows both Beowulf's victory over the offspring of Cain and Beowulf's heroic death in old age (1980, 141).

Lord's final comment on the "mythic pattern" is a "generic narrative of the 'monster-slayer'" which he notes he has devised himself instead of relying on Aarne-Thompson (1995, 106). The "sequence of elements" is now quite different from his previous interlocking patterns:

> [The stories begin with] (1) an unusual or special kind of hero, who (2) has a special weapon, or weapons, (3) to encounter a monster, that is, by definition, a special kind of opponent, usually what we would call "supernatural." In the course of that encounter the hero (4) is almost killed but is saved by (5) divine intervention, to (6) kill the monster, thus restoring order and normality to the world of humankind. (1995, 106–7)

Lord's models are Marduk, Gilgamesh, Zeus, Heracles, Achilles, and others: the point is to show that an Indo-European myth is at the "base" of the action in *Beowulf*, providing its "deep structure" (1995, 107). However, Lord reminds us that the mythic story is only one layer or "area" of the poem. The second is Judeo-Christianity, and Lord's comments on the juxtaposition of the mythic and the Christian very much echo J. R. R. Tolkien's notion of the point at which "an imagination, pondering old and new, was kindled" (1983, 26): the mythic tradition "sensed an affinity between its version [of bringing or restoring order] and the biblical story" (1995, 108). The other two areas are "allusions to Germanic history and legend" and other poetic genres such as elegy, boast, and lament. Lord imagines a process of accrual to the ancient theme, all of which "[serve] to strengthen the inherited meaning" (1995, 111). At a general level, Lord concludes, a story-pattern "dramatizes a fundamental anxiety or need of its culture" (1995, 13).

Outside of Lord's work, not much has been done on story-patterns in oral-formulaic studies with respect to Old English,[47] but the study of myth in relation to the poem has been extensive. John D.

Niles' overview of the topic notes problems of definition with the term "myth," and traces mythic interpretations of *Beowulf* from Müllenhoff's idea that a nature myth underpins the poem to what Niles calls the "neo-mythological school," which tries to connect the poem to "an ancient hero pattern, whose ultimate source is a set of archetypes in the unconscious mind" (1997, 222). A particularly relevant example here is Joseph Fontenrose's study of a "combat myth" that in his estimation includes *Beowulf.* Fontenrose is careful to define myth—"a traditional story [and, therefore, at first orally transmitted] that accompanies rituals," with a "plot," "a beginning, a middle, and an end"—and its constituent units, themes, or episodes that can change in their sequences or details (1974, 3–7). His combat myth has ten themes, and each of the ten has several sub-themes; according to Fontenrose, the poem has in its first two fights and its third two important variants of the myth. Fontenrose relates both fights to expeditions to the realm of death (he sees the Breca episode as a doubling of the mere descent) and links the dragon to Chaos and Thanatos (1974, 525–7, 532).

Proponents of oral-formulaic theory, therefore, have engaged somewhat with the idea of an overarching story-pattern and of the concomitant myth(s) that might underpin traditional oral song. In the study of myth, as Fontenrose defines it, an oral beginning is accepted, but myth obviously has no lasting tie to orality. The associated term that has been more productive in the study of *Beowulf* has, in fact, been folktale, though none of the major figures in oral-formulaic theory has anything to say about it. Parry, for his part, in his very last words on the topic of oral poetry, dismisses terms such as "folk-literature" with the claim that any notion of "folk-," "popular," or "primitive" does nothing to advance and perhaps even retards through negativity and implied scorn our understanding of early (oral) works (Lord 1971, 470). Magoun, although he does not explore the ramifications of attaching the term "folk" to his studies, would seem in his work on *Beowulf A* and its variant (a "folk variant," lines 2009b–2176, of the first part of the poem) and *Beowulf B* (a "folk-poem" on Beowulf's death) to be connecting oral-formulaic composition with folk narrative (while also arguing for scribal management in the "soldering" of originally independent songs, thus looking back to Ettmüller's *Volkslieder*) (1958, 1963).

Folktale is as difficult to define as myth, but the term is generally agreed to denote three important features: an oral beginning, prose, and tradition. For Stith Thompson, the most important aspect of the definition is tradition, an emphasis that accords perfectly with oral-formulaic verse: "[The teller] usually desires to impress his readers or hearers with the fact that he is bringing them something that has the stamp of good authority, that the tale was heard from some great story-teller or from some aged person who remembered it from old days" (1946, 4). Though his classic study of the folktale focuses on the oral tale, Thompson acknowledges the difficulty of separating oral and written traditions, noting that "not only many influences of the folktale, but also occasionally actual versions of such tales appear in some of the earlier medieval literary classics written in the vernacular ... in all these literary treatments [among which Thompson would include *Beowulf* and the Icelandic sagas], folktales are merely taken as bases for artistic reworking" (1946, 282).

A major complication for considering folktale in relation to *Beowulf* is that differentiating folktale analyses from the long-running and wide-ranging hunt for sources and analogues is virtually impossible. The earnest effort to identify sources and analogues begins with Guðbrandur Vígfusson's connection of *Beowulf* and *Grettis saga* in 1878. Vígfusson's strongest piece of evidence is the apparent verbal parallel of the *hæftmece* (1457a), Unferth's sword Hrunting, which Beowulf brings to the fight with Grendel's mother and which fails in the fight, and the *heptisax* wielded by the giant that Grettir finds under the waterfall after defeating the *trollkona*. This connection leads scholars to consider direct influence between the two works. However, similarities are almost immediately found between Beowulf's fight with Grendel and Grettir's fight with Glámr and between the paired fights with Grendel and Grendel's mother and the *trollkona* and the giant at Sandhaugar. These identifications, which approach the idea of a story-pattern, lead to a more general search for related narrative patterns. Building on early observations by Wilhelm Grimm, the core of the story is linked to Celtic tales collected under the rubric "The Hand and the Child," a narrative paradigm that has many parallels to the first two fights of Beowulf, but that is based upon the harassment of a hall by a nocturnal monster who steals children, a hero arriving from afar, a lost arm, tracking the monster to a shared lair (a male and a female), and the hero's victory, sometimes via an arrow shot through the male's single eye.[48] Shortly after the first full study of "The Hand and the Child," in 1910, Friedrich Panzer published his massive work on "das Märchen vom Bärensohn" ("The Bear's Son Tale"). Panzer connects many tales (most of them from the nineteenth century) as developments of a core tale that informs both *Beowulf* and *Grettis saga*, including as Bear's Son heroes also Ormr Stórólfsson and Böðvarr bjarki. Panzer even includes Beowulf's fight with the dragon in his study, connecting that fight with thirty-eight (late) examples of what he considered a Bear's Son hero dying as Þórr dies after the fight with the Miðgarðsormr (1910, 294–6).[49] When R. W. Chambers includes sections on "parallels from folklore" and "Bee-wolf and Bear's Son" in the first edition of his introduction to *Beowulf* (1921) and W. W. Lawrence expends many pages on Panzer and analogues to the fight with Grendel and Grendel's mother (1928), Panzer's study becomes a mainstream part of *Beowulf* criticism; Chambers' second edition (1932) introduces "The Hand and the Child"—he notes with regret that he had overlooked Kittredge's work for the first edition—and Chambers discusses both tale-types, concluding only that correspondences between *Beowulf* and the Sandhaugar episode cannot be attributed to the long "arm of coincidence." In other words, in Chambers' opinion, the two episodes come independently from the same tale: "Panzer … proved that the struggle of Beowulf in the hall, and his plunging down into the deep, is simply an epic glorification of a folk-tale motive" (1959, 62–8, 381).[50]

Developments in the one hundred years since the introduction of "The Hand and the Child" and "The Bear's Son Tale"' to the study of the poem resolve little. The work of Antti Aarne and Stith Thompson, beginning with Aarne's 1910 catalogue to classify folktales, leads to *Beowulf*'s categorization as AT 301 or "The Three Stolen Princesses" (now ATU 301 or "The Three Kidnapped Princesses").[51] The folktale thus offers a basic narrative paradigm and possible motifs within each movement of the tale that correspond to a reasonable degree with the poem, though the movements that clearly have nothing to do with the poem or its Old Norse-Icelandic analogues also obscure their relationship:

I. *The Hero* is of supernatural origin and strength: (a) son of a bear who has stolen his mother; (b) of a dwarf or robber from whom the boy rescues himself and his mother; (c) the son of a man and a she-bear or (d) cow; or (e) engendered by the eating of fruit, (f) by the wind or (g) from a burning piece of wood. (h) He grows supernaturally strong and is unruly.

II. *The Descent.* (a) With two extraordinary companions (b) he comes to a house in the woods, or (b¹) a bridge; the monster who owns it punishes the companions but is defeated by the hero, (c) who is let down through a well into a lower world.— Alternative beginning: (d) The third prince, where his elder brothers have failed, (e) overcomes at night the monster who steals from the king's apple tree, and (f) follows him through a hole into the lower world.

III. *Stolen Maidens.* (a) Three princesses are stolen by a monster. (b) The hero goes to rescue them.

IV. *Rescue.* (a) In the lower world, with a sword which he finds there, he conquers several monsters and rescues three maidens. (b) The maidens are pulled up by the hero's companions and stolen.

V. *Betrayal of Hero.* (a) He himself is left below by his treacherous companions, but he reaches the upper world through the help of (b) a spirit whose ear he bites to get magic power to fly or (c) a bird, (d) to whom he feeds his own flesh; or (e) he is pulled up.

VI. *Recognition.* (a) He is recognized by the princesses when he arrives on the wedding day. (b) He is in disguise and (c) sends his dogs to steal from the wedding feast; or (d) he presents rings, (e) clothing, or (f) other tokens, secures the punishment of the impostors and marries one of the princesses.[52] (Aarne and Thompson 1961, 90–1)

Panzer, therefore, though it was not clear at the time, identifies a sub-type of AT 301 in "The Bear's Son Tale," though he notes as Aarne and Thompson do that several of the *Märchen* of the Grimm brothers are also closely related: *Dat Erdmänneken* (Grimm 91; a type of AT 301) and *Der starke Hans* (Grimm 166; a type of AT 650A combined with AT 301).

A major development in the field of folktale studies, the work of the Russian structuralist Vladimir Propp, first translated in 1958, leads away from *Beowulf* as a type of a particular folktale to the poem's functions as a folktale generally. The two major studies on folktale morphology and *Beowulf* appear independently in 1969 (Thomas Shippey) and 1970 (Daniel Barnes). Shippey contextualizes "the fairy-tale structure of *Beowulf*" precisely within the study of formulaicity, noting that something must lie above the level of themes and type-scenes. Propp argues that all fairy-tales are identical in structure, containing in the same sequence a selection of some thirty "functions," a feature he defines as "act[s] of a character" that are "stable, constant elements in a tale, independent of how and by whom they are performed" (1968, 21). Shippey plugs *Beowulf* into Propp's morphology and finds that "in fact the whole of *Beowulf* [that is, all three fights in three separate 'moves'] can be set out in the sigla of the 'functions,' in the right sequence, and without selection of particular incidents" (1969, 5). Importantly, Shippey reminds us that "all the 'disgressive' material and all the elegiac or moralistic material remains uncovered, so that no justice is done to the poem's thematic complexity" (1969, 5).[53] Shippey calls *Beowulf* "a fairy-tale with all the magic removed, as far as possible" and suggests that the original tale would likely have been "a story about the attack and defeat of death" (1969, 11). Barnes' conclusions are quite similar, but Barnes uses the evidence to confirm that folktale is "the germ pure and simple of the Beowulfian legend" and that the poem's three moves confirm Nist's assertion of a "triadic unity" in the three fights, an instance of folktale trebling (1970, 432–4).[54] Although Bruce R. Rosenberg (1975) points out some flaws in Barnes' logic (like Magoun's conclusion that *Beowulf* must be oral because it is formulaic, Barnes' conclusion that it must be a folktale because it can be described by a morphology is not necessarily true) and conclusions about structure, the work of Shippey and Barnes remains largely accepted, though for reasons of the rather terminal nature of such inquiry, relatively unaddressed since.[55]

The few major contributions to "The Bear's Son Tale" in the context of *Beowulf* are spread across the fifty years after Shippey and Barnes. Peter A. Jorgensen proposes a specific "two-troll variant" of "The Bear's Son Tale," a variant he finds in *Hálfdanar saga Brönufóstra* and *Gríms saga loðinkinna*, demonstrating "conscious, literary borrowing" (the direction of which is unclear) between the two sagas (1975, 42). Joaquín Martínez Pizarro, unaware of Jorgensen's work, finds among the sagas of the Hrafnistumenn evidence for Panzer's core narrative paradigm, setting out a detailed summary of how different introductions lead in the three sagas to the same fight at a lair of difficult access. Pizarro also observes what he calls "a strong contamination of motifs" from *Örvar-Odds saga* in *Orms þáttr*, which is also influenced by *Grettis saga* (1976–1977, 279): both Jorgensen and Pizarro, therefore, demonstrate the problematic nature of Old Norse-Icelandic analogues of the two-troll variety. J. Michael Stitt's modern return to the problem of "The Bear's Son Tale" summarizes 120 Scandinavian texts according to a modification of the outline originally proposed by Reidar Christiansen.[56] The "tale-type" has five movements—the villainy, the first fight, the second fight, abandonment, and resolution—and thus clearly omits the dragon fight. Stitt isolates ten examples of Jorgensen's two-troll variant, but stresses that many of the closest *Beowulf* analogues are not to be considered two-troll examples. Stitt's study is useful for collecting and breaking the examples into keyed alphanumeric summaries, and Stitt's conclusion has excellent advice for the analogue industry: "The tradition, as defined here, is simply a sequence of motifs related in structurally constant patterns. The tradition per se is essentially meaningless. Ultimately, meaning is created (or recreated) anew each time the tradition is realized in some specific narrative and social context" (1992, 94, 208). Most recently, John McKinnell counts the Bear's Son pattern among Norse tales of "meeting the other," finding a close association between Þórr story-patterns and story-patterns with human heroes. McKinnell separates *Bárðar saga Snæfellsáss*, *Orms þáttr*, and *Gríms saga loðinkinna* as "Þórr as human hero" stories from the Bear's Son examples of *Beowulf*, the various versions of the story of Bóðvarr bjarki, *Grettis saga*, and possible a pair of late Icelandic and Scots-Gaelic folktales (2005, 126–46). Finally, John F. Vickrey (2009) blends the "The Bear's Son Tale" and "The Hand and the Child" and looks for folktale "elements" outside the main narrative, in what he calls the "minor episodes" of the poem.

At the same time, *Grettis saga* remains the major focus in discussions of narrative paradigms and sources and analogues. Both Larry D. Benson and Anatoly Liberman, though as part of very different studies, reconstruct through the shared features of *Grettis saga* and *Beowulf* what a common source might have looked like.[57] Andy Orchard gathers, collates, and refines over a century of scholarship comparing the two narratives and devises a thirty-step narrative paradigm for the first two fights of the poem and then locates partial repetitions of that paradigm in five major fight sequences in the saga, the last of which places Grettir in the role of "monster" in a lair of difficult access, illustrating just how much the worlds of monsters and men overlap (2003b, 140–68). Magnús Fjalldal (1998, 2013) has been a voice of caution in these lines of inquiry, both between the poem and the saga and in the identification of the two-troll variant, but the specific narrative paradigms, which seem to have begun with Pizarro, have been expanded to introduce further analogues such as the Old Testament figures of David and Samson[58] and even possible Latin analogues to *Grettis saga* and other outlaw sagas in the *Gesta Herwardi* and related texts.[59] For the last fight of the poem, Christine Rauer develops a twenty-nine item "sequence of events" that she constructs out of sixty-three examples of medieval dragon fights (2000, 61–73), but story-patterns that account for the whole of the poem have been few.

1.5   Conclusion

If pressed to say where the story of *Beowulf* begins, one could do no better than Calvert Watkins' reconstruction of the "basic formula" of the Indo-European dragon-slaying myth: "HERO SLAY SERPENT." Watkins plugs lexical items into the formula: the verb is Proto-Indo-European *$g^w hen$- ("to strike, kill"), the ancestor (in its o-grade form) of Old English *bana*, a verb specifically used for the slaying of "a monstrous or heroic adversary"; the serpent is *$og^w hi$-/ *$ang^w hi$-/*$eg hi$- ("snake, eel") three closely related roots that have influenced one another, probably even in Indo-European. The basic formula, therefore, is *e-$g^w hen$-t $og^w him$ (he slew the serpent), where the serpent "metaphorically represents death, dissolution, and the forces of chaos" (2011, 36, 94).[60] Watkins describes how the formula develops, first of all through the possible addition of "with WEAPON" or "with COMPANION," and then as "the semantic constituents of the basic theme … undergo paradigmatic (commutational) variants," as, for example, the hero's name might be replaced by an epithet or the verb might change or the adversary might be a different beast or even another hero (1995, 302). Watkins finds in verbal parallels among Germanic dragon-slaying legends sufficient evidence for genetic relationship and notes distinctive Germanic developments of the formula:

> The Germanic innovations are only to lose the verbal root *$g^w hen$- and to develop, using inherited morphological, syntactic, and poetic means, a periphrasis with the agent noun derivative *$g^w honó$-, and to utilize the inherited *$urmi$-, rhyme-form to *$k^w rmi$- [likely a taboo replacement], for the serpent. The Indo-European asymmetry of the formula is well attested in Germanic, and the bidirectionality is perhaps more prominent in this family than any other due to the pessimistic Germanic view of "final things": Beowulf slays the Worm and is slain by him; at Ragnarök Thor will slay the Miðgarð Worm and die of its poison. (1995, 424)[61]

Geoffrey Russom shows one way the formula develops, for the original verb of Watkins' formula "appears in epithets for some famous Germanic serpent-slayers, including Sigurd Fáfnisbani … and the god Thor, known as *orms ein-bani*" (2017, 36–7). In more general terms, the basic formula develops into full narrative patterns, related orally and in writing, in poetry and in prose, in traditional and non-traditional ways, and formulaic to greater and lesser degrees.

The fact that *Beowulf* is highly formulaic, or at least contains a great degree of repetition of various kinds, can be recognized by even the most unsophisticated student of the poem. Robert P. Creed says that "*Beowulf* is a tissue of formulas" (1961, 98), and the preceding overview of scholarly approaches to formulaicity and the poem has shown that Creed's comment about half-line formulas can be reduced to the kernel that originates the poem (Watkins' basic formula) and expanded to the whole of the narrative pattern, which in turn can be broken into themes, motifs, and units such as fitts and envelope patterns right down to the half-line and even repetition of unique lexical items. The question of how to define these formulas and how to identify and describe the processes that generate them remains current, though it may be that definitive answers are impossible to devise for a tradition so distant. However, two facts are clear and have been clarified in this chapter. First of all, as Andy Orchard puts it, "the language of *Beowulf* can largely be said to be based on two opposing principles, namely repetition and variation, which essentially perform the same function: setting separate elements side by side for the purpose of comparison or contrast" (2003a, 57–8). The effect of that repetition has been made clear by Fred C. Robinson, who stresses (speaking specifically of apposition) that the device conditions the way we understand the poem by slowing the action, forcing reflection, implying rather than stating, and reminding us of the layers of meaning present in the units of the poem (1985, 60–1). Second, as John Miles Foley reminds us, we must connect all levels of the poem in our discussion of formula: "All three levels [the traditional formula, theme, and story-pattern] taken together imply a more inclusive, overarching dynamic, an interlocking system of multiformities which amounts to a way of thinking" (1981c, 263). In my view, our understanding of the poem depends upon these two facts, and the question of an oral or written tradition (or perhaps a transitional stage) is in a way irrelevant.

Recent work on the *Odyssey* by Egbert J. Bakker revisits the question of formulaic composition and originality. Bakker stresses that Parry and Lord's assertion of tradition and orality would render repetition in effect incidental except for the fact that the singer/poet must recognize a "similarity between two contexts" before producing an identical or nearly identical formula. To help interpret the repetition of formulas, Bakker proposes what he calls an "interformularity scale," on which a ubiquitous formula would be low and a formula appearing only twice would be high. If the primacy of one of the two instances of a formula is probable or even certain (think *Beowulf* and *Andreas*, for example), then that repetition is at the top of the scale (2013, 157–68). Bakker stresses the role, too, of the audience: "It is also important to observe that the continuum of increasing specificity is quintessentially cognitive: it is based on the judgment of the performer/poet and the audience as to the degree of similarity between the two contexts: the more specific a formula and/or the more restricted its distribution, the greater the possible awareness of its recurrence and of its potential for signaling meaningful repetition" (2013, 159). Though Bakker's scale is an attempt to deal with the difficulty of oral-formulaic composition and repetition, the emphasis on the degree of repetition (and, therefore, also variation) and the combined cognitive role of the poet and audience is perfectly applicable to the study of *Beowulf.*

When considering how the seemingly disparate parts of *Beowulf* might have come together at the level of overall story-pattern, we might find a general model in a recent reconstruction of the making of the *Odyssey.* M. L. West argues that Odysseus was originally known for his guile and only later became attached to the Trojan War. Two prior (and not Greek) folktales were added to Odysseus' life, "The Ogre Blinded" (AT 1137) and "The Homecoming Husband" (AT 974), the latter of which, requiring a husband to be away from home, worked well with the tradition of the Trojan War.[62] West calls this the "proto-*Odyssey*" and suggests that, within a generation or two of this foundation, the *Odyssey*-poet (a single poet) decided to turn that work into a poem meant "to emulate the *Iliad* in scale and be likewise stabilized in writing" (2014, 2). West recognizes the poet's merits and shortcomings, including among the latter that the narrative is "riddled with inconsistencies and contradictions" and, in a useful parallel with the *Andreas*-poet, that "too often he takes the easy route of reproducing or adapting verses that he or another poet [usually of the *Iliad*] has used elsewhere, without harmonizing them completely with the new context" (2014, 1).[63] West's overall observations about the poem could also describe *Beowulf:*

> We may think of the poem as an archaeological site, with items of interest buried at different depths. The upper layers represent [our single poet's] workings. He never re-laid his floor as a whole but patched over areas of it as he saw opportunities for improvement, often leaving parts of a lower

layer visible on the surface or showing through a thin covering of topsoil. Further down are [other layers that represent a] version or versions of the story that he received from others. At the bottom lies the proto-*Odyssey*. (2014, 141)

Among the poet's own additions might be the roles of Telemachos and Laertes, and West finds many different layers in the poem, all of which are instructive for our understanding of *Beowulf*, *Örvar-Odds saga*, and *The Hobbit*, including single motifs (such as Penelope's weaving and unweaving), hybrid episodes (such as the combination of *nekyia* and *katabasis* in the descent to Hades), and an overall tripartite combination of the Telemachy, the Wanderings, and the Homecoming (2014, 105, 123–5, and 94–5).

The following chapters, therefore, have a dual purpose. Each demonstrates at the level of successively larger units—from the half-line to the seed of the story and its full story-pattern—a kind of formulaic composition, where formula becomes practically a synonym for method. At the same time, that recognition of formulaic composition becomes a tool for a contemporary audience of the poem. If repetition and variation are significant and differently significant depending upon context(s), and if that repetition and variation is part of a formulaic approach to telling a story, to choosing and varying themes, to structuring a poem, a fitt, an episode, or a line, to composing lines and half-lines, and to choosing words, then any specific instance of analysis becomes also a guide to how to read—that is, how a modern audience might read—and understand the poem as a whole.

Notes

1. The summary of scholarship on formula, formulaic systems, themes, ring structure, and story-patterns is heavily indebted to earlier reviews of scholarship, reviews without which such summary would approach impossible. In particular, this chapter rests upon the efforts of Foley (1981c) and Olsen (1986, 1988), without whose work I might never have known some of the scholarship cited here. The annotated bibliographies of Short (1980) and Hasenfratz (1993) and the handbook of *Beowulf* studies edited by Bjork and Niles (1997), especially the chapter by O'Brien O'Keeffe (1997), have also been most useful. Lord's chapter on "The Formula in Anglo-Saxon Poetry," effectively a response to developments in formulaic theory, is also an excellent overview (1995, 117–36).

Throughout the book, I have also benefitted from the indispensable *Dictionary of Old English Web Corpus* (Healey 2009).

2. For a review of the early reception and criticism of *Beowulf*, see Haarder (1975, 13–110) and the somewhat idiosyncratic assessment and translation of early Germanic scholarship in Shippey and Haarder (1998).

3. On *Liedertheorie*, see also Shippey (1997, 154–60) and Shippey and Haarder (1998, 35–41).

4. Sarrazin's argument is developed over a series of works between 1886 and 1897: see Sarrazin (1886, 1888, 1892, 1897).

5. See the useful discussions in Haarder (1975, 182–4) and Olsen (1986, 559).

6. See the full discussion in Foley (1981b, 56–8) and Olsen (1986, 559).

7. The "essential idea" is not without its problems of judgment, it seems to me, for Parry notes that "the essential part of the idea is that which remains after one has counted out everything in the expression which is purely for the sake of style" (1930, 80).

8. Parry's classifications are slightly modified by Watts, who makes Sievers' verse types central to her definitions (1969, 90–1, 144).

9. For an overview of Lord's work, the impact of which, especially in the field of oral literature, cannot be overstated, see Foley (1981b, 32–51).

10. See also Rogers (1966, 89–102) for a critique of Magoun's application of Parry's definitions.

11. Here, Bonjour is commenting on Magoun (1955).

12. O'Brien O'Keeffe sees the Benson article as an important moment in the history of oral-formulaic studies in Old English: "No longer [after Benson] could the presence of identifiable formulas in Old English verse be accepted as signs of oral provenance" (1997, 100).

13. This article reprints Creed 1959 and features "Additional Remarks" responding to criticism of his original article (1968, 151–3).

14. Quirk concludes: "It should therefore be emphasized that, while formulaic utterances and habitual collocations are the necessary starting point in the study of the early alliterative poetry, they are only the starting point. The very fact that he could depend on his audience having a firm expectation of certain dependences and determined sequences involving metre, vocabulary, and grammar gave the poet his opportunity to stretch linguistic expression beyond the ordinary potentialities of prose, and to achieve a disturbing and richly suggestive poetry" (1963, 171).

15. Hainsworth also makes an important distinction between the formula as a repetition of form and a repetition of content as he investigates why there should be so many unique forms in a formulaically composed Homer.

16. This is not to say that Parry and Lord did not connect formulaic composition with the linguistic utterance, as we have seen. Parry (1932, 11–12)

equates the principles of linguistic change and conservatism in the language of oral poetry and spoken language. See also Lord (1960, 36).

17. Cassidy notes that Creed (1959, 446), too, recognizes the importance of complete syntactic units (the "syntactic entity") in the formula. Cassidy does not list all twenty-five frames.

18. Nagler (1969, 459) compares the process more specifically to language acquisition.

19. Fry (1968b) drops the word "loosely."

20. This point had, however, already been made by Diamond, who points out that meter and syntax will force the definition of formula to be different in different traditions (1959, 230).

21. The focus on meter is not new: Watts had earlier defined the formula simply as "a repeated sequence that fills one of Sievers' five basic rhythmical types," making the formulaic system "two or more phrases of a similar Sievers verse-type, syntactical pattern, and lexical significance, which may differ in an important element according to alliterative substitution, or context, or a type of narrative superfluity" (1969, 90, 144).

22. In other words, apparent examples of one formulaic system can in fact be examples of two different systems. Hutcheson would call these "interlocking formulae": listing "frequent formulaic types" by verse type, Hutcheson observes that "it is tempting to adapt Riedinger's (and Fry's) notion of a system and apply it to these interlocking formulae, except that sometimes the members of interlocking formulae that represent separate formulae do not share enough in common with each other to be grouped under the same rubric" (1995, 303 and n3). Lord would seem to suggest that this "weaving style" ("the intricate pattern of interrelationships of formulas and formulaic expressions") is "typical of oral traditional style" (1960, 122). Certainly, the effect of interlocked formulas is something to be considered outside of the circumstances of their generation.

23. Fry (1968b, 519–22). Niles makes it clear that Fry's concept of the formula is useful, but is not interpreted sufficiently rigorously (1983, 126).

24. For a full contextualization and critique of Riedinger, see Lord (1995, 124–33).

25. See also the useful response of Calvert Watkins (Kiparsky 1976, 107–11). For a discussion of Kiparsky's categories in syndetic formulas in Beowulf, see Acker (1998, 3–33).

26. The efforts of Michael Lapidge and Andy Orchard to draw attention to the formulaic methods of Anglo-Latin poets have not yet been fully integrated into the conversation (see, for example, Lapidge 1979 and Orchard 1994).

27. Wright's recent analysis of a formulaic system in Cynewulf similarly uses Niles, with Fry's definition of a system, and invokes and adapts Riedinger's concept of the formulaic set (2012, 161–3). Wright's

discussion is an excellent example of current ideas on formula and system in practice.

28. For other overviews of theme (and type-scenes), see Olsen (1986, 577–88) and Foley (1990, 329–33).

29. By *The Singer of Tales*, the definition has changed only slightly: "[A theme is] a group of ideas regularly used in telling a tale in the formulaic style of traditional song" (1960, 68).

30. For an assessment of how Lord's idea of theme changes over his career, see Clark (1995, xxii–xxxvi).

31. Lord's *Singer of Tales* comes out after the studies of Magoun and Greenfield, and Lord takes slight issue with their terminology: "I should prefer to designate as motifs what they call themes and to reserve the term theme for a structural unit that has a semantic essence but can never be divorced from its form, even if its form be constantly variable and multiform." For Lord, in *Beowulf*, themes are, for example, "repeated assemblies with speeches ... and the repeated multiform scenes of the slaying of monsters" (1960, 198–9). See also Lord (1995, 137).

32. See also above, p. 8.

33. "The regular content of this theme, then, consists not of a number of specific metrical formulas, but of a concatenation of four imagistic details" (1960, 371). As Foley puts it, "the theme in Old English became purely a sequence of ideas for those following Crowne's lead" (1990, 332).

34. To Foley's list should be added Lord's "arsenal" theme (1995, 166) and Battles and Wright's "scop's repertoire" theme, for which see below and Battles and Wright (2018).

35. For the place of responsion in traditional formulaic patterns generally, see Foley (1980b, 50). For "contiguous lexical recurrence" as a generative model outside of the concept of the formula, see Rosier (1977).

36. See Bassett (1938, 119–28).

37. Lord discusses ring composition briefly (1995, 13–14).

38. Cited in Bartlett (1935, 10–11).

39. Bartlett (1935, 26–8) notes that the *Heliand* includes similar structures.

40. Van Otterlo (1944, 1948). See also Whitman (1963, 249–84, esp. 252–6 and the four-panel foldout of the "geometric structure of scenes in the *Iliad*").

41. Niles' work on ring composition was first published as an article (1979).

42. Only the earlier article (Niles 1979, 930) includes the fuller diagram of the overall structure.

43. Quoted by Niles (1983, 161). For more on chiasmus as a figure of thought and its possible effects, see Gasché (1987, xvi–xxii).

44. See, for example, Hart (1972); Hart's complete works are listed in Kisor (2009, 43n8).

45. Howlett first advances his theory in 1974.
46. These quotations have been lightly edited to make the two patterns parallel in presentation.
47. See Foley (1981c, 276n5) for a general bibliography on story-pattern to 1981.
48. For a summary of scholarship and the story-pattern, see Scowcroft (1999, 22–3). The name of the tale comes from Kittredge (1903); see also Carney (1955) and Puhvel (1979).
49. Panzer sees Beowulf's fight with the dragon as a conflated *Sigurdtypus* and *Thortypus*, but Rauer has pointed out the difficulties with this conflation and with Panzer's examples (2000, 37–8).
50. "The Hand and the Child" discussion is added in "Recent Work on *Beowulf* to 1930" in the second edition (pp. 478–85 in the third edition of 1959). See also Lawrence, who finds Panzer's efforts to introduce the dragon fight into the tale-type less convincing (1928, 171).
51. The reformulation of the index by Uther completely reshapes the entry for AT 301 and its sub-types 301A and 301B. Uther combines all three into one entry and adds a new sub-type 301D. For ATU 301, Uther distinguishes three separate introductions (king banishes daughters; monster steals apples and is wounded and followed; exceptional hero gathers two companions, and they meet an evil dwarf/devil/giant who leads them to the underworld) before the pit entrance to the lower world and a sequence which is then mostly similar, but Uther has eliminated the sequencing of movements (2004, 176–79). Because so much scholarship is predicated on AT 301, I offer and comment on AT entries instead of ATU entries throughout.
52. The "motives" of the tale in Aarne and Thompson and then Uther, though less clearly in Uther, are adapted from Bolte and Polívka (1913–1931, II.300-1), who are working with Grimm's tales as a starting point (Grimm 91) and who cite their awareness of Panzer. Aarne's 1910 listing is brief: a detailed comparison of Aarne's starting point, Panzer, Bolte and Polívka, and the Norwegian index of Christiansen (1921) reveals striking differences and in a way demonstrates the difficulty of relying on a tale-type index.
53. See also Barnes (1970, 434).
54. In speaking of the "germ" of the legend, Barnes is quoting Klaeber's skepticism (third edition) about the central role of folktale. See Propp (1968, 74–5) on trebling. See also Chapter 6, pp. 209–10.
55. See also Gould (1985).
56. Christiansen (1921, 8–9); adapted version in Stitt (1992, 25–7, 209–10).
57. Benson (1970, 27); Liberman (1986, 380).

58. For David and Samson, see Orchard (2003a, 142–9) and Horowitz (1978).
59. Orchard (2015), with an itemized comparison of the *Gesta Herwardi* and *Grettis saga* on 19–21.
60. For another overview of "the water dragon" in Indo-European myth, see West (2007, 255–9).
61. Watkins even finds the formula in the *Nine Herbs Charm* (lines 31–5), the serpent flayed into nine bits by a kind of glory-twig (1995, 424–7).
62. See, however, Bakker's remarks on the "Returning Husband" and how the tale-type fits here and in the "Return Song" and folktale analysis (the final nine of Propp's functions) in general (2013, 13–16).
63. West explores the re-use of existing verses in detail, considering verses taken from the *Iliad* and from the *Odyssey*-poet's own verses (2014, 69–80).

References

Aarne, Antti. 1910. *Verzeichnis der Märchentypen*. Folklore Fellows Communications 3. Helsinki: Suomalaisen Tiedeakatemian Toimituksia.

Aarne, Antti, and Stith Thompson. 1961. *The Types of Folktale: A Classification and Bibliography*, 2nd revision. Folklore Fellows Communications 184. Helsinki: The Finnish Academy of Science and Letters.

Acker, Paul. 1998. *Revising Oral Theory: Formulaic Composition in Old English and Old Icelandic Verse*. New York: Garland.

Arend, Walter. 1933. *Die typischen Scenen bei Homer*. Berlin: Weidmannsche Buchhandlung.

Bakker, Egbert J. 2013. *The Meaning of Meat and the Structure of the Odyssey*. Cambridge: Cambridge University Press.

Banning, Adolf. 1886. *Die epischen Formeln im Beowulf* (Marburg diss.). Marburg: Universitäts-Buchdruckerei (R. Friedrich).

Barnes, Daniel R. 1970. Folktale Morphology and the Structure of *Beowulf*. *Speculum* 45: 416–434.

Bartlett, Adeline Courtney. 1935. *The Larger Rhetorical Patterns in Anglo-Saxon Poetry*. New York: Columbia University Press.

Bassett, Samuel Eliot. 1938. *The Poetry of Homer*. Berkeley: University of California Press.

Battles, Paul, and Charles D. Wright. 2018. *Eall-feala Ealde Sæge*: Poetic Performance and "The Scop's Repertoire" in Old English Verse. *Oral Tradition* 32 (1): 3–26.

Benson, Larry D. 1966. The Literary Character of Anglo-Saxon Formulaic Poetry. *PMLA* 81: 334–341.

Benson, Larry D. 1970. The Originality of *Beowulf*. In *The Interpretation of Narrative: Theory and Practice*, ed. Morton W. Bloomfield, 1–43. Cambridge, MA: Harvard University Press.

Bjork, Robert E., and John D. Niles (eds.). 1997. *A Beowulf Handbook*. Lincoln: University of Nebraska Press.

Bolte, Johannes, and Georg Polívka. 1913–1931. *Anmerkungen zu den Kinder- und Hausmärchen der Brüder Grimm*, 5 vols. Leipzig: Theodor Weicher.

Bolton, Whitney F. 1985. A Poetic Formula in *Beowulf* and Seven Other Old English Poems: A Computer Study. *Computers and the Humanities* 19 (3): 167–173.

Bonjour, Adrien. 1957. *Beowulf* and the Beasts of Battle. *PMLA* 72: 563–573.

Brink, Bernhard ten, and Alois Brandl. 1899. Fragment über altenglische Literatur. In *Geschichte der englischen Literatur*. Vol. 1, *Bis zu Wiclifs Auftreten*, 2nd ed. Strassburg: Trübner: 431–478.

Buttenweiser, Ellen Clune. 1898. *Studien über die Verfasserschaft des Andreas* (Heidelberg diss.). Heidelberg: E. Geisendörfer.

Carney, James. 1955. *The Irish Elements in Beowulf*, 77–128. Dublin Institute for Advanced Studies: Studies in Irish Literature and History. Dublin.

Carrigan, Eamonn. 1967. Structure and Thematic Development in *Beowulf*. *Proceedings of the Royal Irish Academy* 66: 1–51.

Cassidy, Frederic G. 1965. How Free Was the Anglo-Saxon Scop? In *Franciplegius: Medieval and Linguistic Studies in Honor of Francis Peabody Magoun, Jr.*, ed. Jess B. Bessinger, Jr. and Robert P. Creed, 75–85. New York: New York University Press.

Chadwick, H. Munro. 1912. *The Heroic Age*. Cambridge: Cambridge University Press.

Chambers, R.W. 1921. *Beowulf: An Introduction to the Study of the Poem with a Discussion of the Stories of Offa and Finn*. Cambridge: Cambridge University Press.

Chambers, R.W. 1959. *Beowulf: An Introduction to the Study of the Poem with a Discussion of the Stories of Offa and Finn*, 3rd ed. Cambridge: Cambridge University Press.

Christiansen, Reidar. 1921. *Norske Eventyr. En systematisk fortegnelse efter trytke og utrykte kilder*. Kristiania: I hovedkommission hos Jacob Dybwad.

Clark, Francelia Mason. 1995. *Theme in Oral Epic and in Beowulf*. New York: Garland.

Conner, Patrick W. 1972. Schematization of Oral-Formulaic Processes in Old English Poetry. *Language and Style* 5: 204–220.

Creed, Robert P. 1955. Studies in the Technique of Composition of the 'Beowulf' Poetry in British Museum MS: Cotton Vitellius A.xv, PhD diss., Harvard University.

Creed, Robert P. 1957. The *Andswarode*-System in Old English Poetry. *Speculum* 32: 523–528.

Creed, Robert P. 1959. The Making of an Anglo-Saxon Poem. *Journal of English Literary History* 26: 445–454.

Creed, Robert P. 1961. On the Possibility of Criticizing Old English Poetry. *Texas Studies in Language and Literature* 3: 97–106.

Creed, Robert P. 1968. The Making of an Anglo-Saxon Poem. In *The Beowulf Poet: A Collection of Critical Essays*, ed. Donald K. Fry, 141–153. Eaglewood Cliffs, NJ: Prentice-Hall.

Crowne, David K. 1960. The Hero on the Beach: An Example of Composition by Theme in Anglo-Saxon Poetry. *Neuphilologische Mitteilungen* 61: 362–372.

Diamond, Robert E. 1959. The Diction of the Signed Poems of Cynewulf. *Philological Quarterly* 38: 228–241.

Doane, A.N. 1994. The Ethnography of Scribal Writing and Anglo-Saxon Poetry: Scribe as Performer. *Oral Tradition* 9 (2): 420–439.

Ettmüller, Ludwig. 1840. *Beowulf: Heldengedicht des achten Jahrhunderts*. Zurich: Meyer and Zeller.

Fjalldal, Magnús. 1998. *The Long Arm of Coincidence: The Frustrated Connection Between Beowulf and Grettis Saga*. Toronto: University of Toronto Press.

Fjalldal, Magnús. 2013. *Beowulf* and the Old Norse Two-Troll Analogues. *Neophilologus* 97: 541–553.

Foley, John Miles. 1976. Formula and Theme in Old English Poetry. In *Oral Literature and the Formula*, ed. Benjamin A. Stolz and Richard S. Shannon, III, 207–232. Ann Arbor: Centre of Coordination of Ancient and Modern Studies, University of Michigan.

Foley, John Miles. 1980a. *Beowulf* and Traditional Narrative Song: The Potential Limits of Comparison. In *Old English Literature in Context: Ten Essays*, ed. John D. Niles, 117–136. Cambridge: D. S. Brewer and Rowman & Littlefield.

Foley, John Miles. 1980b. The Viability of the Comparative Method in Oral Literature Research. *The Comparatist* 4: 47–56.

Foley, John Miles (ed.). 1981a. *Oral Traditional Literature: A Festschrift for Albert Bates Lord*. Columbus, OH: Slavica.

Foley, John Miles. 1981b. Introduction: The Oral Theory in Context. In *Oral Traditional Literature: A Festschrift for Albert Bates Lord*, ed. John Miles Foley, 27–122. Columbus, OH: Slavica.

Foley, John Miles. 1981c. Tradition-Dependent and -Independent Features in Oral Literature: A Comparative View of the Formula. In *Oral Traditional Literature: A Festschrift for Albert Bates Lord*, ed. John Miles Foley, 262–281. Columbus, OH: Slavica Publishers.

Foley, John Miles. 1990. *Traditional Oral Epic: The Odyssey, Beowulf, and the Serbo-Croatian Return Song*. Berkeley: University of California Press.

Fontenrose, Joseph. 1974. *Python: A Study of Delphic Myth and Its Origins*. New York: Biblo and Tannen.

Fry, Donald K. 1967a. Old English Formulas and Systems. *English Studies* 48: 193–204.

Fry, Donald K. 1967b. Variation and Economy in *Beowulf. Modern Philology* 65: 353–356.

Fry, Donald K. 1968a. Old English Formulaic Themes and Type-Scenes. *Neophilologus* 52: 48–54.

Fry, Donald K. 1968b. Some Aesthetic Implications of a New Definition of the Formula. *Neuphilologische Mitteilungen* 69: 516–522.

Fry, Donald K. 1974. Cædmon as a Formulaic Poet. *Forum for Modern Language Studies* 10: 227–247.

Fry, Donald K. 1981. Formulaic Theory and Old English Poetry. In *Report of the Twelfth Congress, Berkeley 1977*, ed. Daniel Heartz and Bonnie Wade, 169–173. Kassel, Germany: Bärenreiter.

Fulk, R.D., Robert E. Bjork, and John D. Niles (eds.). 2008. *Klaeber's Beowulf*, 4th ed. Toronto: University of Toronto Press.

Gasché, Rodolphe. 1987. Reading Chiasms: An Introduction. In *Readings in Interpretation: Hölderlin, Hegel, Heidegger*, ed. Andrzej Warminski, ix–xxvi. Theory and History of Literature, Volume 26. Minneapolis: University of Minnesota Press.

Gould, Kent. 1985. *Beowulf* and Folktale Morphology: God as Magical Donor. *Folklore* 96: 98–103.

Greenfield, Stanley B. 1955. The Formulaic Expression of the Theme of "Exile" in Anglo-Saxon Poetry. *Speculum* 30: 200–206.

Griffith, Mark S. 1993. Convention and Originality in the Old English "Beasts of Battle" Typescene. *Anglo-Saxon England* 22: 179–199.

Grimm, Jacob (ed.). 1840. *Andreas und Elene*. Cassel: Theodor Fischer.

Haarder, Andreas. 1975. *Beowulf: The Appeal of a Poem*. Viborg: Akademisk Forlag.

Hainsworth, J.B. 1964. Structure and Content in Epic Formulae: The Question of the Unique Expression. *Classical Quarterly* 14: 155–164.

Hart, Thomas E. 1972. Tectonic Design, Formulaic Craft, and Literary Execution: The Episodes of Finn and Ingeld in *Beowulf. Amsterdamer Beiträge Zur älteren Germanistik* 2: 1–61.

Hart, Walter Morris. 1907. *Ballad and Epic: A Study in the Development of Narrative Art*. Harvard Studies and Notes XI. Boston: Ginn and Company.

Hasenfratz, Robert J. 1993. *Beowulf Scholarship: An Annotated Bibliography, 1979–1990*. New York: Garland Publishing.

Healey, Antonette diPaolo, with John Price Wilkin and Xin Xiang. 2009. *Dictionary of Old English Web Corpus.* Toronto: Dictionary of Old English Project.

Hieatt, Constance B. 1975. Envelope Patterns and the Structure of *Beowulf.* *English Studies in Canada* 1: 249–265.

Horowitz, Sylvia Huntley. 1978. Beowulf, Samson, David, and Christ. *Studies in Medieval Culture* 12: 17–23.

Howlett, David R. 1974. Form and Genre in *Beowulf. Studia Neophilologica* 46: 309–325.

Howlett, David R. 1997. *British Books in Biblical Style.* Dublin: Four Courts Press.

Hutcheson, B.R. 1995. *Old English Poetic Metre.* Cambridge: D. S. Brewer.

Jorgensen, Peter A. 1975. The Two-Troll Variant of the Bear's Son Folktale in *Hálfdanar saga Brönufóstra* and *Gríms saga loðinkinna. Arv* 31: 35–43.

Kail, Johannes. 1889. Über die Parallelstellen in der angelsächischen Poesie. *Anglia* 12: 21–40.

Kiparsky, Paul. 1976. Oral Poetry: Some Linguistic and Typological Considerations. In *Oral Literature and the Formula*, ed. Benjamin A. Stolz and Richard S. Shannon, III, 73–106. Ann Arbor: Centre of Coordination of Ancient and Modern Studies, University of Michigan.

Kisor, Yvette. 2009. Numerical Composition and *Beowulf:* A Reconsideration. *Anglo-Saxon England* 38: 41–76.

Kistenmacher, Richard. 1898. *Die wörtlichen Wiederholungen im Bêowulf.* Greifswald: Julius Abel.

Kittredge, George Lyman. 1903. Arthur and Gorlagon. *Harvard Studies and Notes in Philology and Literature* 8: 149–275.

Klaeber, Friedrich. 1905. Studies in the Textual Interpretation of *Beowulf. Modern Philology* 3: 235–265.

Lapidge, Michael. 1979. Aldhelm's Latin Poetry and Old English Verse. *Comparative Literature* 31: 249–314.

Lawrence, W.W. 1928. *Beowulf and Epic Tradition.* Cambridge: Harvard University Press.

Leyerle, John. 1967. The Interlace Structure of *Beowulf. University of Toronto Quarterly* 37: 1–17.

Liberman, Anatoly. 1986. Beowulf-Grettir. In *Germanic Dialects: Linguistic and Philological Investigations*, ed. Bela Brogyanyi and Thomas Krömmelbein, 353–401. Amsterdam: John Benjamins.

Lord, Albert B. 1938. Homer and Huso II: Narrative Inconsistencies in Homer and Oral Poetry. *Transactions and Proceedings of the American Philological Association* 69: 439–445.

Lord, Albert B. 1951. Composition by Theme in Homer and Southslavic Epos. *Transactions of the American Philological Association* 82: 71–80.

Lord, Albert B. 1953. Homer's Originality: Oral Dictated Texts. *Transactions of the American Philological Association* 84: 124–134.

Lord, Albert B. 1959. The Poetics of Oral Creation. In *Comparative Literature: Proceedings of the Second Congress of the International Comparative Literature Association*, Vol. 1, ed. Werner P. Friedrich, 1–6. Chapel Hill, NC: University of North Carolina Press.

Lord, Albert B. 1960. *The Singer of Tales.* Cambridge, MA: Harvard University Press.

Lord, Albert B. 1969. The Theme of the Withdrawn Hero in Serbo-Croatian Oral Epic. *Prilozi* 35: 18–30.

Lord, Albert B. 1971. Homer, Parry, and Huso. In *The Making of Homeric Verse: The Collected Papers of Milman Parry*, ed. Adam Parry, 465–478. Oxford: Clarendon Press.

Lord, Albert B. 1974. Perspectives on Recent Work in Oral Literature. *Forum for Modern Language Studies* 10: 187–210.

Lord, Albert B. 1976. The Traditional Song. In *Oral Literature and the Formula*, ed. Benjamin A. Stolz and Richard S. Shannon, III, 1–29. Ann Arbor: Center for the Coordination of Ancient and Modern Studies.

Lord, Albert B. 1980. Interlocking Mythic Patterns in *Beowulf.* In *Old English Literature in Context: Ten Essays*, ed. John D. Niles, 137–142. Cambridge: D. S. Brewer.

Lord, Albert B. 1995. *The Singer Resumes the Tale*, ed. Mary Louise Lord. Ithaca, NY: Cornell University Press.

Magoun Jr., Francis P. 1953. The Oral-Formulaic Character of Anglo-Saxon Narrative Poetry. *Speculum* 28: 446–467.

Magoun Jr., Francis P. 1955. The Theme of the Beasts of Battle in Anglo-Saxon Poetry. *Neuphilologische Mitteilungen* 56: 81–90.

Magoun Jr., Francis P. 1958. *Beowulf A*: A Folk Variant. *Arv* 14: 95–101.

Magoun Jr., Francis P. 1963. *Beowulf B*: A Folk-Poem on Beowulf's Death. In *Early English and Norse Studies*, ed. Arthur Brown and Peter Foote, 127–140. London: Methuen.

McKinnell, John. 2005. *Meeting the Other in Norse Myth and Legend.* Cambridge: D. S. Brewer.

Meyer, Richard M. 1889. *Die altgermanische Poesie nach ihren formelhaften Elementen beschrieben.* Berlin: Wilhelm Hertz.

Minchin, Elizabethan. 2001. *Homer and the Resources of Memory: Some Applications of Cognitive Theory to the Iliad and the Odyssey.* Oxford: Oxford University Press.

Müllenhoff, Karl. 1869. Die innere geschichte des Beovulfs. *Zeitschrift Für Deutsches Alterthum* 14: 193–244.

Nagler, Michael N. 1967. Towards a Generative View of the Oral Formula. *Transactions and Proceedings of the American Philological Association* 98: 269–311.

Nagler, Michael N. 1969. Oral Poetry and the Question of Originality in Literature. In *Proceedings of the Vth Congress of the International Comparative Literature Association*, ed. Nikola Banašević, 451–459. Amsterdam: Swets and Zweitlinger.

Neidorf, Leonard. 2017. *The Transmission of Beowulf: Language, Culture, and Scribal Behavior*. Ithaca: Cornell University Press.

Niles, John D. 1979. Ring Composition and the Structure of *Beowulf*. PMLA 94: 924–953.

Niles, John D. (ed.). 1980. *Old English Literature in Context: Ten Essays*. Cambridge: D. S. Brewer and Rowman & Littlefield.

Niles, John D. 1981. Formula and Formulaic System in *Beowulf*. In *Oral Traditional Literature: A Festschrift for Albert Bates Lord*, ed. John Miles Foley, 394–415. Columbus, OH: Slavica Publishers.

Niles, John D. 1983. *Beowulf: The Poem and Its Tradition*. Cambridge: Harvard University Press.

Niles, John D. 1997. Myth and History. In *A Beowulf Handbook*, ed. Robert E. Bjork and John D. Niles, 213–232. Lincoln: University of Nebraska Press.

Notopolous, James A. 1951. Continuity and Interconnexion in Homeric Oral Composition. *Transactions and Proceedings of the American Philological Association* 82: 81–101.

O'Brien O'Keeffe, Katherine. 1990. *Visible Song: Transitional Literacy in Old English Verse*. Cambridge: Cambridge University Press.

O'Brien O'Keeffe, Katherine. 1997. Diction, Variation, the Formula. In *A Beowulf Handbook*, ed. Robert E. Bjork and John D. Niles, 85–104. Lincoln: University of Nebraska Press.

Olsen, Alexandra Hennessey. 1986. Oral-Formulaic Research in Old English Studies: I. *Oral Tradition* 1 (3): 548–606.

Olsen, Alexandra Hennessey. 1988. Oral-Formulaic Research in Old English Studies: II. *Oral Tradition* 3 (1–2): 138–190.

Orchard, Andy. 1994. *The Poetic Art of Aldhelm*. Cambridge: Cambridge University Press.

Orchard, Andy. 2003a. *A Critical Companion to Beowulf*. Cambridge: D. S. Brewer.

Orchard, Andy. 2003b. *Pride and Prodigies: Studies in the Monsters of the Beowulf-Manuscript*, rev. paperback ed. Toronto: University of Toronto Press.

Orchard, Andy. 2015. Hereward and Grettir: Brothers from Another Mother? In *New Norse Studies: Essays on the Literature and Culture of Medieval Scandinavia*, ed. Jeffrey Turco, 7–59. Ithaca, NY: Cornell University Library.

Orton, Peter. 2000. *The Transmission of Old English Poetry*. Turnhout: Brepols.

Otto, Ernst. 1901. *Typische Motive in den weltlichen Epos der Angelsachsen*. Berlin: Mayer and Müller.

Owen-Crocker, Gale. 2000. *The Four Funerals in Beowulf and the Structure of the Poem*. Manchester: Manchester University Press.

Panzer, Friedrich. 1910. *Studien zur germanischen Sagengeschichte, I. Beowulf*. Munich: Oskar Beck.

Parks, Ward. 1988. Ring Structure and Narrative Embedding in Homer and *Beowulf*. *Neuphilologische Mitteilungen* 89: 237–251.

Parry, Milman. 1928. *L'Épithète traditionelle dans Homère: Essai sur un problème de style homérique*. Paris: Société d'éditions "Les belles lettres".

Parry, Milman. 1930. Studies in the Epic Technique of Oral Verse-Making. I. Homer and Homeric Style. *Harvard Studies in Classical Philology* 41: 73–147.

Parry, Milman. 1932. Studies in the Epic Technique of Oral Verse-Making. II. The Homeric Language as the Language of an Oral Poetry. *Harvard Studies in Classical Philology* 43: 1–50.

Parry, Milman. 1936. Review of *Die typischen Scenen bei Homer* von Walter Arend. *Classical Philology* 31: 357–360.

Parry, Milman. 1971a. Cór Huso: A Study of Southslavic Song. In *The Making of Homeric Verse*, ed. Adam Parry, 437–464. Oxford: Oxford University Press.

Parry, Milman. 1971b. The Traditional Epithet in Homer. In *The Making of Homeric Verse: The Collected Papers of Milman Parry*, ed. Adam Parry, 1–190. Oxford: Oxford University Press.

Pasternack, Carol Braun. 1995. *The Textuality of Old English Poetry*. Cambridge: Cambridge University Press.

Pizarro, Joaquín Martínez. 1976–1977. Transformations of the Bear's Son Tale in the Sagas of the Hrafnistumenn, *Arv* 32–33: 263–281.

Propp, Vladimir. 1968. *The Morphology of the Folktale*, trans. Laurence Scott, 2nd ed. Austin: University of Texas Press.

Puhvel, Martin. 1979. *Beowulf and Celtic Tradition*. Waterloo: Wilfrid Laurier University Press.

Quint, David. 2018. *Virgil's Double Cross: Design and Meaning in the Aeneid*. Princeton: Princeton University Press.

Quirk, Randolph. 1963. Poetic Language and Old English Metre. In *Early English and Norse Studies Presented to Hugh Smith in Honour of His Sixtieth Birthday*, ed. Arthur Brown and Peter Foote, 150–171. London: Methuen.

Rauer, Christine. 2000. *Beowulf and the Dragon: Parallels and Analogues*. Cambridge: D. S. Brewer.

Reichl, Karl. 1989. Formulaic Diction in Old English Epic Poetry. In *Traditions of Heroic and Epic Poetry II: Characteristics and Techniques*, ed. J.B. Hainsworth, 42–70. London: The Modern Humanities Research Association.

Riedinger, Anita. 1985. The Old English Formula in Context. *Speculum* 60: 294–317.

Robinson, Fred C. 1985. *Beowulf and the Appositive Style*. Knoxville, TN: University of Tennessee Press.

Rogers, H.L. 1966. The Crypto-Psychological Character of the Oral Formula. *English Studies* 47: 89–102.

Rosenberg, Bruce A. 1975. Folktale Morphology and the Structure of *Beowulf*: A Counter-Proposal. *Journal of the Folklore Institute* 11: 199–209.

Rosier, James L. 1977. Generative Composition in *Beowulf*. *English Studies* 58: 193–203.

Russom, Geoffrey. 2017. *The Evolution of Verse Structure in Old and Middle English Poetry: From the Earliest Alliterative Poems to Iambic Pentameter*. Cambridge: Cambridge University Press.

Sarrazin, Gregor. 1886. *Beowulf* und Kynewulf. *Anglia* 9: 515–550.

Sarrazin, Gregor. 1888. *Beowulf-Studien: Ein Beitrag zur Geschichte altgermanischer Sage und Dichtung*. Berlin: Mayer & Müller.

Sarrazin, Gregor. 1892. Parallelstellen in altenglischer Dichtung. *Anglia* 14: 186–192.

Sarrazin, Gregor. 1897. Neue *Beowulf*-Studien. *Englische Studien* 23: 221–267.

Schaar, Claes. 1956. On a New Theory of Old English Poetic Diction. *Neophilologus* 40: 301–305.

Schaefer, Ursula. 1997. Rhetoric and Style. In *A Beowulf Handbook*, ed. Robert E. Bjork and John D. Niles, 105–124. Lincoln: University of Nebraska Press.

Schemann, Karl. 1882. *Die Synonyma im Beowulfsliede mit Rücksicht auf Composition und Poetik des Gedichtes* (Münster diss.). Hagen: Gustav Butz.

Scowcroft, R.Mark. 1999. The Irish Analogues to *Beowulf*. *Speculum* 74: 22–64.

Shippey, Thomas A. 1969. The Fairy-Tale Structure of *Beowulf*. *Notes and Queries* 16: 2–11.

Shippey, Thomas A. 1997. Structure and Unity. In *A Beowulf Handbook*, ed. Robert E. Bjork and John D. Niles, 149–174. Lincoln: University of Nebraska Press.

Shippey, Thomas A., and Andreas Haarder (eds.). 1998. *Beowulf: The Critical Heritage*. London: Routledge.

Short, Douglas D. 1980. *Beowulf Scholarship: An Annotated Bibliography*. New York: Garland Publishing.

Stanley, Eric. 1997. Old English Poetry: "Out of the People's Warm Mouth?". *Notes and Queries* 44 (1): 6–21.

Stevick, Robert D. 1962. The Oral-Formulaic Analyses of Old English Verse. *Speculum* 37: 382–389.

Stitt, J.Michael. 1992. *Beowulf and the Bear's Son: Epic, Saga, and Fairytale in Northern Germanic Tradition*. New York: Garland Publishing.

Tatlock, John S.P. 1923. Epic Formulas, Especially in Layamon. *PMLA* 38: 494–529.

Taylor, Paul B. 1967. Themes of Death in *Beowulf*. In *Old English Poetry: Fifteen Essays*, ed. Robert P. Creed, 249–274. Providence, RI: Brown University Press.

Thompson, Stith. 1946. *The Folktale*. Berkeley: University of California Press.

Tolkien, J.R.R. 1983. *Beowulf*: The Monsters and the Critics. In *The Monsters and the Critics and Other Essays*, ed. Christopher Tolkien, 5–48. London: George Allen and Unwin.

Tonsfeldt, H. Ward. 1977. Ring Structure in *Beowulf*. *Neophilologus* 61: 443–452.

Uther, Hans-Jörg. 2004. *The Types of International Folktales: A Classification and Bibliography based on the system of Antti Aarne and Stith Thompson*. 3 vols., FF Communications no. 284–286. Helsinki: Suomalainen Tiedeakatemia.

Van Otterlo, W.A.A. 1944. *Untersuchungen über Begriff, Andwendung, und Entstehung der griechischen Ringkomposition*. Amsterdam: Noord-Hollandsche Uitgevers Maatschappij.

Van Otterlo, W.A.A. 1948. *De Ringcompositie als Opbouwprincipe in de epische Gedichten van Homerus*. Amsterdam: Noord-Hollandsche Uitgevers Maatschappij.

Vickrey, John F. 2009. *Beowulf and the Illusion of History*. Bethlehem: Lehigh University Press.

Watkins, Calvert. 1995. *How to Kill a Dragon: Aspects of Indo-European Poetics*. Oxford: Oxford University Press.

Watkins, Calvert. 2011. *The American Heritage Dictionary of Indo-European Roots*, 3rd ed. Boston: Houghton Mifflin Harcourt.

Watts, Ann C. 1969. *The Lyre and the Harp: A Comparative Reconsideration of Oral Tradition in Homer and Old English Epic Poetry*. New Haven: Yale University Press.

West, M.L. 2007. *Indo-European Poetry and Myth*. Oxford: Oxford University Press.

West, M.L. 2014. *The Making of the Odyssey*. Oxford: Oxford University Press.

Whitman, Cedric H. 1963. *Homer and the Heroic Tradition*. Cambridge, MA: Harvard University Press.

Wright, Charles D. 2012. An Old English Formulaic System and Its Contexts in Cynewulf's Poetry. *Anglo-Saxon England* 40: 151–174.

CHAPTER 2

The Half-Line Formula: *weox under wolcnum* (8a)

The opening lines of *Beowulf* have been the subject of a great deal of study. In the context of formulas and formulaic composition, how-ever, the primary studies are those of Francis P. Magoun, Jr. and John D. Niles, both of whom examine the formulaicity of the poem's first twenty-five lines. Though there are some inconsistencies in Magoun's evidence, and though Magoun at times accepts as evidence for formu-laic phrasing the repetition of a single word, his summary chart finds only twelve half-lines with no evidence whatsoever of formula.[1] His primary evidence is exact or nearly exact repetition anywhere in the Old English corpus; he also finds that five half-lines are participants in formulaic systems, admitting *Scyldes eafera* (19a) as a formulaic sys-tem even though (for obvious reasons) it is not among his repeated verses.[2] Magoun's decision to utilize the whole corpus is, in Niles' opinion "methodologically … unsound" (1983, 127) on account of the notion of tradition-dependence that develops in the years after Magoun. Further, instead of looking for exact or near-exact repetition, Niles bases his analysis on "the abstract patterns governing the con-struction of verses" (1983, 127), evidence for formulaic systems in the half-lines of *Beowulf* only. Niles concludes that thirty-three of the first fifty verses, including all five of Magoun's, are products of a formulaic system. That percentage is relatively constant for the first 500 lines of the poem, though it is worth pointing out that Niles finds thirty-six repeated verses (in the first 1000 verses, so 3.6%) that are not part of a formulaic system (1983, 127–8). Despite different approaches to a

© The Author(s) 2020
M. Fox, *Following the Formula in Beowulf, Örvar-Odds saga, and Tolkien*, https://doi.org/10.1007/978-3-030-48134-6_2

different body of evidence, the findings of Magoun and Niles are virtually identical.[3]

Fulk et al. look for verbatim repetition (ignoring particles and inflection) and find that twelve of the first fifty verses are repeated elsewhere in the poem (2008, cxiii). They further note near repetition, for example, *wilgesiþas* (23a) with *ealdgesiðas* (853b) and *swæse gesiþas* (29a, 2040a, 2518a), and accept that looking outside the poem might yield further evidence of the "traditional character" of verses (2008, cxiii). They conclude, with Magoun and Niles' individual studies, that "the formulaic nature of the poem's diction is therefore plainly not restricted to verbatim iteration of entire verses" (2008, cxiv). Andy Orchard, identifying what he calls "repeated formulas" on the basis purely of "significant parallels of phrasing" in whole lines of the poem—that is, the repetition may be broken across the caesura—finds that nine of the first twenty-five lines of the poem have "repeated formulas" (2003a, 274–5). Orchard finds no evidence in lines 3, 13, and 15, where Fulk et al. include 3a, 13b, 15a, and 15b in their evidence; the only line Orchard includes that Fulk et al. do not is line 8. The points at which Fulk et al. and Orchard disagree are informative. While Orchard admits *weox under wolcnum* (8a) on account of structures like *wan under wolcnum* (651a) and *wod under wol(c)num* (714a), Fulk et al. exclude it; however, they include, against Orchard, *þone God sende* (13b) on the basis of, I assume, half-lines such as *þe him God sealde* (1271b, 2182b), which is very close to syntactically and semantically equivalent. They also include *hu ða æþelingas* (3a) on the basis of, again, I assume, lines ending in a declined form of *æþeling*, for those are the closest repetitions in the poem (for example, 982a, 1804a, 2374a, where the last also includes a demonstrative pronoun). The only example that works across the caesura in the opening lines is *þeodcyninga þrym gefrunon* (2), which Orchard finds paralleled in *ða ic æt þearfe [gefrægn] þeodcyninges* (2694), where the repeated elements (if *gefrægn* is added correctly) are transposed.

In the poem as a whole, Orchard finds 504 examples of repeated formulas (2003a, 274–314). Breaking those parallels down by line, Orchard finds that those 504 examples are spread among just over 1200 lines and line groupings of the poem (2003a, 315–26), meaning that Orchard's data demonstrate "formulaic repetition in around 40 per cent of the lines in the poem" (2003a, 86). What Orchard provides is yet another way of approaching the data: restricting the evidence to *Beowulf*, but allowing for repetition anywhere in the poetic line and not looking for formulaic systems, Orchard still finds a staggering degree of repetition. Orchard further notes that though many half-lines are repeated verbatim, many others are subject to a reordering of elements, to synonym substitution, to part of speech substitution in "metrically equivalent words or phrases" in which the link can sometimes only be perceived by looking at a third verse or in which the only apparent link is the metrical basis of the formula (2003a, 88–9). Orchard, following Rand Hutcheson, who lists many of these, calls such verses "interlocking formulas" (Hutcheson 1995, 303–16).

I believe the notion of an interlocking formula is also useful outside of considerations of meter.[4] In that case, the repetition may not be formulaic, but interconnected systems of repetition, at the level both of word and half-line, do seem to inform our understanding of *Beowulf*. To give what should be a familiar example, Hutcheson lists *Beowulf* 103a, 1339a, and 1348a as D2* verses (PxPsx): *mære mearcstapa* (103a) and *micle mearcstapan* (1348a) should be recognized as significant repetition at least, if not formulaic in systems not based on meter, but *mihtig manscaða* (1339a) might well not be. However, *micle mansceaðan* in *Genesis A* (1269a) is the same verse-type, thus, in Hutcheson's view, connecting all three verses in *Beowulf* to the great ravagers and giant-spawn (*gigantmæcgas*; *Genesis A* 1268a) of the time just before the flood (1995, 310). Further, though, the *mihtig manscaða* (1339a) connects simply through repetition of the compound to 712a, 737b, and 2514b, all of which include the phrase *se manscaða*. The three half-lines, of which at most two are metrically identical, still significantly associate Grendel and the dragon, and interlock, I would suggest, with Hutcheson's original D2* verses.

While such a line of inquiry quickly becomes unduly complex, the important thing to keep in mind is that *Beowulf* shows evidence of many kinds of repetition, including metrical patterns, syntactic patterns, lexical patterns, and half-line patterns, and that all of these patterns can be or appear interlocked. The repetition may or may not be formulaic, depending on our definition of formula, but what remains to be seen is how a particular "formula" can be analyzed and how recognizing a formula and associated repetition can affect the way the poem is read.

2.1   THE CRITICAL BACKGROUND

The half-line *weox under wolcnum* (8a) has received an extraordinary amount of attention in analyses of formula and of the poem. Magoun (1953, 465) finds that the Old English poetic corpus contains only one near-verbatim repetition: *Genesis A* has *weox þa under wolcnum* (1702a) in its description of the growth of the tribe of Shem after the confounding of the attempt to build the Tower of Babel. Magoun also notices parallels to *Beowulf* in *wod under wolcnum* (714a), *Genesis A* in *wære under wolcnum* (1438a), and two verses in the *Phoenix*, *wridaþ under wolcnum* (27a) and *awyrde under wolcnum* (247a). Robert P. Creed introduces for *under wolcnum* alone the concept of the "complementary formula"—"formulas consisting of a short (but at least trisyllabic) prepositional phrase useful for completing a-verses"—and notes five a-verses in *Beowulf* and over a dozen others elsewhere that use it (1961, 103).[5] Ann C. Watts also picks up *weox under wolcnum*, calling it a "tag," or an "expression [that] whatever [it] might add to the stylistic tone of the poem, add[s] little or nothing to the mere march of plotted events" (1969, 148). Without calling it a system, she associates the half-line with "any phrase made up of a verb, a preposition, and *wolcnum*, in an a-verse with alliteration upon *w*" (1969, 149). Watts' description adds two half-lines from *Beowulf* to Magoun's list: *wand to wolcnum* (1119a) and *weold under wolcnum* (1770a), as well as *geworden under wolcnum* from *Advent (Christ I)* (226a) and *gewitað under wolcnum* from *Elene* (1271a). Watts later allows that the alliteration of the first word in an a-verse before *under wolcnum* might be the key feature, thus adding an array of further half-lines: *wan under wolcnum* (*Beowulf* 651a; *Dream of the Rood* 55a), *wæter under wolcnum* (*Beowulf* 1631a), *waðol under wolcnum* (*Finnsburg Fragment* 8a), and *wide under wolcnum* (*Genesis A* 1950a), though omitting Magoun's *wære under wolcnum* (*Genesis A* 1438a). To Watts, all of these verses are "tags," and "in any single formulaic system of 'tags' … at least two words, or more than one measure, in the verses should be similar" (1969, 149).[6]

In 1985, unaware of each other's work, W. F. Bolton and Anita Riedinger both comment extensively on *weox under wolcnum*. Bolton, following Frederic Cassidy's idea of a syntactical frame, proposes a much more inclusive formulaic system than Niles does. Bolton posits that the half-line comes out of a frame in which "the formula is the three-word a-verse (X Y Z) in which the first and last words (X, Z) are alliterating content-words and the second word (Y) is a preposition" (1985, 167). Further, "the formula has several features: syntactic (always three words, X and Z are content words, Y is always a preposition, Z always a noun or nominal), metrical (alliterative, confined to the a-verse), morphological (compounds and proper names predominate in Z), rhetorical (distribution is purposeful)" (1985, 169). Against Niles, therefore, Bolton would add such half-lines as *geong in geardum* (13a) and *folce to frofre* (14a) to the same formula. By Bolton's count, *Beowulf* contains 248 such formulas, and their distribution over lines 1–2199 and 2200–3182 suggests that the two parts of the poem were originally separate: his evidence from the corpus overall suggests "the longer the poem, the less frequent the formula," and the occurrences are substantially less frequent in lines 1–2199 (1985, 168).

Anita Riedinger locates *weox under wolcnum* in an *x under x* system. In Riedinger's understanding of formulas and systems, however, a system is not a formula. The formula in this case is the narrower *x under (the heavens)*, which occurs "more than a hundred times in Old English poetry" (1985, 298); because *x under (the heavens)* is a formula, the basic system takes on a general concept and a function. Recall that Riedinger's main contribution to thinking about formula is the concept of thematic function. Watts sees *weox under wolcnum* as a "tag," and Riedinger agrees that tag functions are possible. However, Riedinger feels *weox under wolcnum* belongs to the category of thematic formula, that is, formulas that "signify themes rather than ... express them, because they are dependent for their full meaning upon a context external to the semantics of the formulas themselves" (1985, 297). In turn, a half-line like *wan under wolcnum* (651a) is obviously part of the same system, but not the same formula: instead, because *wan under wolcnum* has a different thematic function, it belongs to a different formula, and that formula will allow variation so long as the verse still fits with the theme. Any group of verses, then, that shares function and system can be thought of as a set, and *weox under wolcnum* and *wan under wolcnum* belong to different sets, for reasons that we will examine below. However, the point Riedinger makes is worth repeating: formulas must be read in context and considered for connotative meaning (1985, 303).[7]

John D. Niles, limiting his search to *Beowulf*, devises a formulaic system that underlies *weox under wolcnum—X̆ under/to wólcnum*—a system that would also work for all of Magoun's and Watts' examples. Niles locates this system in *weold under wolcnum* (1770a), *wod under wolcnum*

(714a), *wand to wolcnum* (1119a), *won to wolcnum* (1374a), *wan under wolcnum* (651a), and *wæter under wolcnum* (1631a), a group in which we can see syntactic variation in the first element, which moves from finite verb to adjective to noun (1983, 132). Andy Orchard, though he never calls it a system, comments on the "X under clouds" form and the syntactic variation of "X," linking the form to all of Niles' examples with *under* (2003a, 88) and noting in his appendices (separately, that is, unconnected to examples with *under*) the form with *to* in 1119a and 1374a (2003a, 300, 319).[8]

The half-line *weox under wolcnum*, therefore, has frequently been recognized to participate in the formulaicity of *Beowulf* and, as we shall see below, others have also recognized outside of thinking about formula that its repetition may be significant both in *Beowulf* and in the corpus as a whole. The significance of the formula will be seen to reside in its alliterating content words, *weaxan* and *wolcen*, but perhaps even more importantly in the interlocked formulas to which we are led by *under wolcnum* and *to wolcnum*, particularly with the adjective *wan/won(n)*. Expressions roughly synonymous with *under wolcnum*, though not related formulaically, such as *under swegles begong* (860a, 1773a), which then links to *ofer floda begang* (1826b; varied in 362a and 2367a), also prove of interest. The formula and repetition thus bind different parts of the poem together and connect the poem thematically, sometimes leading, as Riedinger predicts (and shows), to clusters of motifs that further enrich our understanding.

2.2   Reading *weox under wolcnum* (8a)

The near-verbatim repetition noted by Magoun in *Genesis A—weox þa under wolcnum* (1702a)—given that there only two such verses in the corpus, would seem to place the formula at the high end of Bakker's interformularity scale, making the repetition significant. Riedinger would agree, seeing in these two verses a "progenitor of a distinguished line" thematic formula (1985, 299), connecting the proliferation of the good tribe of Shem after the building of the Tower of Babel with Scyld Scefing's rule and the growth of the Danes, but establishing also a temporal and thematic setting for the opening of the poem and setting up a number of parallels with the poem and events in Genesis.[9] What isolates these two verses from the other related verses is the verb *weaxan*. The verb features prominently in Genesis—God uses the imperative *weaxað/wexað* (for Latin *crescite*) to command creatures and men to multiply in Genesis I.22 and I.28 (Marsden 2008, 9–10)—giving the verses a further resonance, but other appearances of *weaxan/geweaxan* in the poem seem even more significant. Hrothgar is granted success in battle "oðð þæt seo geogoð geweox,/ magodriht micel" (until the youthful band grew, a great young host; 66b–67a), connecting his prosperity also to Scyld's (see also the *oð þæt* in line 9a) and again collapsing into one the times of creation, Shem, Scyld, and Hrothgar. When Hrothgar gives his speech to Beowulf, he begins with praise, noting Beowulf as *frofor* (1707b; compare Scyld, 7b) to his people, then transitioning abruptly to Heremod: "Ne geweox he him to willan ac to wælfealle/ ond to deaðcwalum Deniga leodum;/ … oþ þæt he ana hwearf" (he did not grow according to their desire but to slaughter and to destruction for the people of the Danes … until he wandered away alone; 1711–14). The connections to Scyld and Hrothgar are obvious, but also worth noting is that the related "slaughter" words *wælfyllo* and *wælfyl(l)* appear once each in the poem, making a set of three that connects Grendel (125a), Heremod (1711b), and the hard days the Geatish woman sees ahead at the very end of the poem (3154a). When Hrothgar moves into his more general exposition on pride, he repeats the two key words he used of Heremod to show how a man's fortunes can seem secure "oð þæt him on innan oferhygda dæl/ weaxe(ð) ond wridað" (until inside him a portion of pride grows and increases; 1740–1a). Finally, again near the end of the poem, Wiglaf prepares for the burning of Beowulf's pyre, remarking that "weaxan wonna leg" (the dark flame [shall] grow; 3115a),[10] thus juxtaposing *weaxan* and the adjective *wan/won(n)*[11] that is key to the interlocking *wan under wolcnum* formula.

The word *wolcen* appears in *Beowulf* only in the dative plural at the end of a-verses that appear to be related to the *weox under wolcnum* formula: they are all w-alliterating word (verb, adjective, or noun) plus *under wolcnum* (five times) or *to wolcnum* (twice). In the corpus as a whole, the alliterating w-word plus *under wolcnum* formula appears twenty-seven times: in *Beowulf* (5), *Genesis A* (6), *Andreas* (2), the *Dream of the Rood* (1), *Advent (Christ I)* (1), *Guthlac B* (1), the *Phoenix* (2), the *Metres of Boethius* (7), and the *Finnsburg Fragment* (1). The alliterating w-word varies widely; only *wan/won(n)* (4), *weox* (2), *woruld* (2), and *wind* (2, both in the *Metres of Boethius*) repeat. The variation *to wolcnum* appears only twice in the corpus (in *Beowulf*), and *ofer wolcnum* once (in *Exodus*, as *wand ofer wolcnum*, which thus shares a verb with

Beowulf's *wand to wolcnum*). This evidence suggests the formula was more prevalent in certain meanings such as "on earth" and "below the heavens/clouds," where the "complementary formula," to use Creed's term, might function like the biblical tag *sub sole*, for example, which is so common in Ecclesiastes. One might argue for a special significance in *Beowulf*'s *to wolcnum* (a phrase that does appear once otherwise in an Old English version of the Psalms for *ad nubes*), but only for the fact that the poet uses it twice; outside of the poem, it seems likely that the meaning "to the heavens/clouds" was rarely required. The four-fold repetition of *wan under wolcnum* with one *wan to wolcnum* out of thirty w-alliterating word preposition *wolcnum* sequences is also significant and suggests a certain thematic element to the formula.

Within the poem, the X́ *under/to wólcnum* system, to use Niles' analysis, thus generates seven a-verses. The initial effect of *weox under wolcnum* (8a) is primarily achieved by its participation in a thematic formula and echoes of *weaxan* outside the poem. Of the six other a-verses, *weold under wolcnum* (1770a) is the only one that seems to be a member of the same thematic formula:

> "Swa ic Hring-Dena hund missera
> weold under wolcnum ond hig wigge beleac
> manigum mægþa geond þysne middangeard,
> æscum ond ecgum, þæt ic me ænigne
> under swegles begong gesacan ne tealde.
> Hwæt, me þæs on eþle edwenden cwom,
> gyrn æfter gomene, seoþðan Grendel wearð,
> ealdgewinna, ingenga min;
> ic þære socne singales wæg
> modceare micle. Þæs sig metode þanc,
> ecean dryhtne, þæs ðe ic on aldre gebad
> þæt ic on þone hafelan heorodreorigne
> ofer eald gewin eagum starige.
> Ga nu to setle, symbelwynne dreoh
> wiggeweorþad; unc sceal worn fela
> maþma gemænra siþðan morgen bið." (1769–84)

So I ruled the Ring-Danes for a hundred half-years under the heavens and protected them from battle from many nations throughout this middle-earth, from ash and edge, such that I did not count any enemy under the circuit of the sky. Lo, a reversal came to me in my homeland, sorrow

after song, when Grendel, that ancient enemy, became my invader; I bore
the great grief of that seeking continually. Thanks be to the measurer, the
eternal lord, that I endured in life that I, after long struggle, should gaze
with my eyes on that bloody head. Go now to your seat, enjoy the happy
feast, now that you have been distinguished in battle; a great many shared
treasures shall there be when it is morning.

Robert P. Creed has discussed how thoroughly Hrothgar's words echo
the opening of the poem: in order, *hwæt* (1a), *monegum mægþum* (5a),
syððan ærest wearð (6b), *he þæs frofre gebad* (7b), and *weox under wolcnum*
(8a) (1961, 105). I would suggest the parallels go further and also elsewhere in the poem. First of all, I would pair *edwenden* with *oð þæt* (9a),
thus identifying Scyld's fortunes also as *edwenden*, though in the reverse
direction of bad to good. Especially given the description of Scyld's early
success, we see Scyld in Hrothgar's lack of enemies: when Hrothgar
suggests Beowulf, *wiggeweorþad*, take his seat, the poet at once echoes
weorðmyndum þah (8b) and, in effect, replaces Hrothgar with Beowulf,
especially given the next line, where *maþma gemænra* must be a repetition of *madma fela* (36b) and *madma mænigo* (41a). In a slightly more
complicated series of associations, I would also juxtapose the focus on
wig in Hrothgar's speech with *þonne wig cume* (23a) and in *mægþa geh-
wære* (25a): the gnomic statement in the middle of the proem is thus
echoed at the beginning and end of Hrothgar's speech (1770b–71a and
1783a–84a, including in the last lines the promise of *sceal*).

However, the gnomic statement (20–5) has already been echoed in
Hrothgar's fortunes (64–7a), including there the signal *wiges weorðmynd*
(65a). In fact, though Creed does note that line 1771 is repeated almost
verbatim in line 75 (1961, 102), he does not mention any further connections between Hrothgar's speech and the account of his early success
that leads to the building of Heorot (64–79). For example, our *weold
under wolcnum* is a restatement, partially lexical and partially semantic,
of *se þe his wordes geweald wide hæfde* (79), and Hrothgar's *modceare
micle* is the transformation (and, I would argue, the natural result) of
his *magodriht micel* (67a) and *medoærn micel* (69a). Further, *seoþðan
Grendel wearð*, which Creed already connected to the beginning of
the poem, is part of a broader formula that Hrothgar has already used
in this speech (1707b, 1709b, just before the passage with *geweox* discussed above) and that is prominent in Heremod's turn to the power
of fiends, a reversal that is contrasted in a confusion of pronouns (and

in a three-fold repetition) with Beowulf's positive development in the
Sigemund-Heremod digression:

> He mid eotenum wearð
> on feonda geweald forð forlacen ...
> he his leodum wearð
> eallum æþellingum to aldorceare ...
> He þær eallum wearð,
> mæg Higelaces, manna cynne,
> freondum gefægra; hine fyren onwod. (902b–15)

He [Heremod], among Jutes [or giants], was betrayed into the power of
enemies [or fiends] ... To his people, to all nobles, he became a source of
mortal care ... To all, to the race of men, the kinsman of Hygelac there
became more dear to friends; sin waded into him [Heremod].

The reversal of fortune is shown to be the same for each character, meaning that the invader, be it an embodied invader from a territory marked
as different (*under harne stan*) or the *oferhygda dæl* (portion of pride)
that enters like an arrow and grows within, is also, for all practical purposes, the same.

After Hrothgar's speech, the helmet of night brings darkness, the
host quickly rises, itself another formula (1789b–90), and the hall towers, vaulted and gold-adorned (1799b–1800a), until the black raven ...
announces the coming of dawn (1801–2a). The poet's words lead the
audience to expect yet another reversal: the darkness suggests Grendel;
the description of the hall suggests flame (81b–85); and the raven suggests battle, but none comes.[12] In the morning, Beowulf's words
announcing his desire to return home offer some of Hrothgar's words
back to him, all while further invoking the proem and Scyld (particularly
in 1826–30a: "Gif ic þæt gefricge ofer floda begang/ þæt þec ymbsit-
tend egesan þywað," etc.). Many more features could be identified—the
highly wrought structure of the original passage and how the structure
draws attention to important words and half-lines, for example—but we
see how, in the repeated use of X̣ *under/to wólcnum* in 8a and 1770a,
the poet achieves an extremely rich layering of reference. I believe *weold
under wolcnum* is part of Riedinger's "progenitor of a distinguished line"
thematic formula, yet that formula interacts with other motifs until the
theme takes on a sense of transience. Just as formulas themselves may

interlock through shared systems and, though quite differently, simply through shared lexical items, the poem in this passage is fortified by repetition of all kinds: words or word elements, alone and in clusters, half-lines, usually in clusters and even thematic echoes, all of which ask the audience to hold in mind what has passed and to be ready for what is still to come.

The remaining realizations of the X́ *under/to wólcnum* system are *wan under wolcnum*, the approach of night (651a), *wod under wol(c)num*, Grendel approaches Heorot (714a), *wand to wolcnum* (probably), the smoke of the funeral pyre in the Finn Episode (1119a), *won to wolcnum*, waves at the mere (1374a), and *wæter under wolcnum*, the bloody mere after Beowulf has emerged victorious from it (1631a), all, curiously, in the first half of the poem (Bolton 1985, 170). Of these, the second occurrence of the formula is the most rewarding to explore, and its complete context is as follows:

> Þa wæs eft swa ær inne on healle
> þryðword sprecen, ðeod on sælum,
> sigefolca sweg, oþ þæt semninga
> sunu Healfdenes secean wolde
> æfenræste; wiste þæm ahlæcan
> to þæm heahsele hilde geþinged,
> siððan hie sunnan leoht geseon meahton
> oþ ðe nipende **niht** ofer ealle,
> **scadu**helma gesceapu **scriðan cwoman**
> **wan** under wolcnum. Werod eall aras. (642–51)

Then again as before were brave words spoken in the hall, the people happy, the sound of the victory-folk, until suddenly the son of Healfdene wished to seek his evening-rest; he knew that battle was intended for that foe in the high hall for as long as they could see the light of the sun, until darkening night, the shapes of the shadows, came to circle over everything, dusky under the skies.[13] The host all arose.

The passage repeats parts of Beowulf's account of his contest with Breca, where *nipende niht* (547a, here broken over the caesura) preceded the coming of the mighty sea-beasts and the light of the sun revealed the sea-cliffs at the end of the attack (571b). Though these lines describe only the coming of night, the narrative significance of the key words of the final lines (649–51) is signaled by the repetition only fifty lines later of almost every significant content word in the beginning of Grendel's march toward Heorot: "**Com** on **wan**re **niht**/ scriðan sceadugenga" (The shadow walker came wandering in the dark night; 702b–3a). Michael Lapidge has noted that these lines are "an intentional repetition, or retroaction, of the diction describing the onset of night" (2001, 65), and we have already seen how this effect is reproduced the night after the death of Grendel's mother. The verb *scriðan*, having associated encroaching night and stalking monsters in these two passages, also describes generally the *helrunan* (163; and thus would have already perhaps, been a "retroaction" when used in line 650) and the method of locomotion of the dragon (2569) (Riedinger 1985, 302). The b-verse of the line—*werod eall aras* (651b)—is itself formulaic, appearing also after Hrothgar's speech, as we have noted (1790b) and also as the surviving Geats get up to see the wonders of their dead lord and the dragon's carcass (3030b).[14] After the repetition *on wanre niht*, the *sceotend* (shooters; 703b) who should be on guard are sleeping; in case we are slow to recognize the effect of pride, *swefeð* (the guard sleeps) and *sceoteð* (the slayer shoots from the bow) are repeated in Hrothgar's description of the sudden burgeoning of pride (1740–4). Finally, the incremental repetition in Grendel's approach to Heorot has been treated by many critics (Orchard 2003a, 189–91), and the fact that Grendel is now the subject of *wod under wolcnum* (714a) shows just how these formulas and motifs are interlocked. What is less well-known, however, is Adeline Bartlett's analysis of the structure of the passage, a structure that appears to be contained in an envelope pattern established by *on wanre niht* (702b) and *ofer þa niht* (736a) that highlights the significance of *wan* (1966, 50).

The connection of *wan under wolcnum* and *on wanre niht* is supported by a third occurrence in another formula from the system as Hrothgar describes the mere:

> Þonon yðgeblond up astigeð
> won to wolcnum þonne wind styreþ
> lað gewidru, oð þæt lyft ðrysmaþ,
> roderas reotað. (1373–6a)

From there the mingled waves rise up, dark to the heavens, when the wind stirs up hostile storms, until the air grows gloomy, the heavens weep.

In its immediate context, *won to wolcnum* most closely echoes *wand to wolcnum* (1119a), the rising smoke of Hnæf's funeral pyre. Still, the formula *wan/won(n)* preposition *wolcnum* itself only appears twice in *Beowulf*, as darkness gathers while Grendel prepares to strike and in Hrothgar's description of the mere. Anita Riedinger, however, finding *wan under wolcnum* in three other poems in the corpus, argues that, though it shares a system with *weox under wolcnum*, it in fact is another thematic formula, an "ominous darkness accompanying supernatural events formula" that is usually *wan under wolcnum*, but admits *wod under wolcnum* (714a) as "a deliberate variation" (1985, 299–302). In addition to the possibility of *wan under wolcnum* as a thematic formula, its contexts suggest a relationship between the four poems.

The three other occurrences are in the *Dream of the Rood*, *Guthlac B*, and *Andreas*. The most thematically appropriate parallel appears in *The Dream of the Rood* at the moment of Christ's crucifixion:

> þystro hæfdon
> bewrigen mid **wolcnum** wealdendes hræw,
> **scirne sciman**; **sceadu** forð eode,
> **wann under wolcnum**. **Weop eal gesceaft**,
> cwiðdon cyninges fyll. Crist wæs on rode. (52b–6)

> Shadows had covered with clouds the corpse of the Lord, that bright radiance; shadow went forth, dark under the skies. All creation wept, lamented the fall of the king. Christ was upon the cross.

Here, shadows obscure the bright body of Christ and darkness falls upon the earth as all creation laments and weeps.[15] The moment, the sudden disappearance of light, could hardly be more appropriate for the parallel. Further, the detail *weop eal gesceaft* (55b) seems also to be echoed in *roderas reotað* (*Beowulf* 1376a), a connection that suggests, verbally and via the personification of nature and the heavens, that there is a connection between Christ's crucifixion and the weather at the mere. Even the complete syntactic units as concluding half-lines, while hardly rare in Old English verse, seem here a stylistic or structural echo (*Beowulf* 651b; *DOTR* 56b). While the similarities between *Beowulf* 650–1 and 1373–6a and the *Dream of the Rood* 52b–6 are not solid evidence upon which to connect the two poems, there is one further correspondence of note.

It has long been recognized that the phrase *elne mycle* is significant in the *Dream of the Rood*, as it is repeated three times, connecting the actions of the cross, the dreamer, and Christ.[16] In the first instance, the cross reports Christ's advance: "Geseah ic þa frean mancynnes/ **efstan elne mycle** þæt he me wolde on gestigan" (Then I saw the Lord of mankind hurry with great courage that he might mount upon me; 33b–34). Beowulf, for his part, after his final boast that he will perform a glorious deed with Hrunting or die, jumps into the mere nearly as courageously:

> Æfter þæm wordum Weder-Geata leod
> **efste mid elne**, nalas andsware
> bidan wolde; brimwylm onfeng
> hilderince. Ða wæs **hwil dæges**
> ær he þone grundwong ongytan mehte. (1492–6)

> After those words, the prince of the Weder-Geats hurried with courage; not at all would he wait for an answer. The sea-surge gripped the warrior. Then it was the space of a day before he might begin to make out the bottom of the pit.

Especially as there are no other collocations of forms of the verb *efstan* with *ellen* in Old English, I would suggest that there is a connection here between *Beowulf* and *The Dream of the Rood*. In my view, though done with a light hand (unlike his borrowing from a lost vernacular version of the *Visio Pauli* for the description of the mere),[17] the poet may deliberately echo the *Dream of the Rood*, or at least a vernacular tradition of the account of Christ's crucifixion, to lend slightly more atmosphere to the scene at the mere, and to hint at the broader significance of the sequence.[18] Further, the fact that the descent took *hwil dæges* seems also to connect the passage with the final occurrences of the *wan under wolcnum* formula in *Guthlac B* and *Andreas*, where we instead find *onlonge niht* (*Guthlac B* 1287b) and *nihtlangne fyrst* (*Andreas* 834b).[19] Riedinger calls the latter a thematic formula, "a terrifying period of time prior to a battle," but only connects it to precise repetitions in *Beowulf* (528a), *Exodus* (208b), *Elene* (67b), and a second occurrence in *Andreas* (1309b) (1985, 295–6). Of course, Beowulf's last words before undertaking the fight with the dragon are similar, but by then he seems a different hero: "Ic mid elne sceall/ gold gegangan, oððe guð nimeð,/ feorhbealu frecne, frean eowerne" (I shall win gold with courage, or battle, terrible life-bale, shall take your lord; 2535b–37).[20]

If the connection between *Beowulf* and *The Dream of the Rood* may yet be felt to be somewhat circumstantial or tenuous, the formulaic web connecting *Beowulf*, *Guthlac B*, and *Andreas* can hardly be disputed. Nevertheless, the significance and direction of the relationships may be difficult to determine. The formula *wan under wolcnum* occurs in *Guthlac B* during Guthlac's protracted death scene, where *ellen* (courage) is again prominent:

	Þa se æþela glæm	
	setlgong sohte, swearc norðrodor	
1280	**won under wolcnum**, woruld miste	[*Beo* 651; *DOTR* 55]
	oferteah	
	þystrum biþeahte, þrong niht ofer tiht	[*DOTR* 52]
	londes frætwa; ða cwom leohta mæst,	
	halig of heofonum hædre **scinan**,	[*Andreas* 836]
	beorhte ofer burgsalu. **Bad** se þe sceolde	[*Andreas* 833: *bliðne bidan*]
1285	**eadig on elne** endedogor,	[*Andreas* 833; *DOTR* 34; *Beo* 1493]
	awrecen wælstrælum. Wuldres **scima**,	[*DOTR* 54]
	æþele ymb æþelne, **ondlonge niht**	[*Andreas* 834; *Beo* 1495]
	scan scirwered. Scadu sweþredon,	[*Andreas* 836; *Beo* 650; *Beo* 570b]
	tolysed under lyfte. Wæs se leohta glæm	
1290	ymb þæt halge hus, heofonlic **condel**,	[*Andreas* 835]
	from æfenglome oþþæt **eastan cwom**	[*Beo* 569b]
	ofer deop gelad dægredwoma,	[*Andreas* 190b; *Andreas* 124b-25a]
	wedertacen wearm. **Aras** se	[*Andreas* 837; *Beo* 651]
	wuldormago,	
	eadig **elnes gemyndig**, spræc to his	[*Andreas* 1001b, 1263b; *DOTR* 34; *Beo* 1493]
	onbehtþegne,	
1295	torht to his treowum gesiþe: "Tid is þæt	
	þu fere,	
	ond þa ærendu eal biþence,	
	ofestum læde, swa ic þe ær bibead,	
	lac to leofre. Nu of lice is,	
	goddreama georn, gæst swiðe fus."	
	(1278b–99)	

When the noble gleam began to set—a black northern sky, dark under the skies, wrapped the world in gloom, covered it with shadows; night pressed in upon all the adornments of the land—then the greatest light came shining clearly from the heavens, brightly over the dwellings. He who should awaited, blessed in courage, his last day, struck with death's arrows. The radiance of glory, noble around the noble one, shone all night long, clothed with brilliance. Shadows diminished, released under the air. The bright gleam was around that holy house, the heavenly candle, from the time of evening until, from the east, led over the deep, came the first hint of dawn, the warm weather-sign. The glorious champion arose, blessed, mindful of courage, spoke to his servant, the beautiful one to his true companion: "The time has come that you go and remember only that errand, quickly to undertake, as I commanded you before, the gift to the dear one. Now the spirit, out of the body, is exceedingly eager for godly joys."

The final occurrence of *wan under wolcnum* appears in *Andreas*, where it seems most likely to have been borrowed from *Guthlac B*, though the same sequence is rife with borrowings also from *Beowulf*:

	Leton þone halgan be herestræte	
	swefan on sybbe under swegles hleo,	
	bliðne bidan burhwealle neh,	
	his niðhetum, **nihtlangne fyrst**,	[*GuthB* 1287]
835	oðþæt dryhten forlet dægcandelle	[*GuthB* 1290]
	scire scinan. Sceadu sweðerodon,	[*GuthB* 1288b; *Beo* 570b]
	wonn under wolcnum; þa com	[*GuthB* 1280, *Beo* 651, 650; *GuthB*
	wederes blæst,	1293]
	hador heofonleoma, ofer hofu **blican**.	[*Beo* 222a]
	Onwoc þa **wiges heard, wang**	[*Beo* 886a; *Beo* 1413b, 2744a, 225b]
	sceawode,	
840	fore burggeatum; **beorgas steape**,	[*Beo* 222b, 1409a]
	hleoðu hlifodon, ymbe **harne stan**	[*Beo* 1358a; 887b, 1415a, 2553b,
		2744b; *Ruin* 43a]
	tigelfagan **trafu, torras** stodon,	[*Ruin* 30b; *Beo* 175b; *Ruin* 3b]
	windige weallas.	[*Beo* 572a; *Beo* 1358b, *Beo* 1374]
		(831–43a)

They [the angels] left the holy one to sleep by the road in peace, under the cover of the sky; they let him remain the entire night, unaware, near the city wall and his deadly enemies, until the Lord let the candle of day shine brightly. Shadows diminished, dark under the skies; then the weather's blast, the brilliant heavenly light, came to gleam over the dwellings. The one hard in battle awoke then, and examined the area before the city gates; steep cliffs and slopes loomed high, stone-tiled buildings and towers stood, windy walls, around a hoar stone.

The situation in *Andreas* is quite different. Andreas is transported, asleep, dawn comes, and shadows diminish before he wakes and sees the city of the Mermedonians. Riedinger argues that the thematic formula remains the same: Andreas' sudden sleep takes the place of death, and sleep is already a part of the theme's appearance in *Beowulf*, when Hrothgar's abrupt exit from the hall must signal a trip to bed (1985, 301). Otherwise, "the *Andreas*-poet often reverses traditional formulaic usage," yet, Riedinger argues, the audience would still have felt "the note of terror the author injected into this passage" (1985, 302–3). Albert B. Lord, going over the whole of Riedinger's evidence for the thematic formula, disagrees with the *Andreas* example: "There just are not enough cases in Anglo-Saxon poetry to prove that the context is *always* ominous" (1995, 127). Neither Lord nor Riedinger, however, recognizes the intense clustering of repetition in these passages, and especially in *Andreas*, where the presence of the *har stan* alone ought to be enough to strike the "note of terror."[21]

George Clark includes this passage among his examples of the "traveler recognizes his goal" theme, suggesting that though "the sequence of events and the tone are far removed from the more conventional developments of the traditional pattern," "the displacement and alteration of the recurring topics of the traditional theme sharpen the sense of wonder surrounding the episode" (1965, 654). Such a theme would account for the verbal parallels with Beowulf's arrival scene (217–24a), and Clark extends the theme also to Grendel's approach to Heorot and the *wod under wolcnum* passage (714–16a), where the poet again manipulates the theme's motifs (1965, 658). We have also seen in this passage and in *Guthlac B* some echoes of the coming of dawn scene in *Beowulf* (569b–72a), and the effect, if we accept the arguments for thematic formula and theme here, is to see how even these interlock, occasioning a meshing of motifs and vocabulary that associates poems and themes. In the case of *Andreas*, of course, the relationships seem to be settled: in a recent study, Andy Orchard concludes that the *Andreas*-poet "knows and borrows freely from a palette of poems still surviving today, including *Beowulf*, all four of the signed poems of Cynewulf, both Guthlac-poems, and the *Phoenix*" (2016, 333).[22]

2.3   OLD SAXON: *UUÁNUM UNDAR UUOLCNUN*

Though a further investigation of other instances of the alliterating w-word preposition *wolcnum* formula would lead to other connections in other poems, important evidence outside the poem might suggest a significant and separate status for *wan under wolcnum*. The most important words of the formula are attested in Old Saxon: *uuahsan* and *uuolcan*. The verb *uuahsan*, which seems to be semantically identical to *weaxan*, for it regularly translates forms of *crescere*, does not introduce any obvious formulas in Old Saxon. The closest half-line to our *weox under wolcnum* is *uuôhs undar them uuerode* (grew among the people; *Heliand* 783a), referring to Christ after Joseph and Mary have returned to Galilee. In its present tense, it forms part of the traditional compound "to wax and to wane," though reversed: *uuanod ohtho uuahsid* (wanes or waxes; *Heliand* 3629a), part of a brilliant passage in which the poet is explaining why Jericho is named after the moon, because humans wax and wane just the same way. The half-line is repeated with a different conjunction in *Homiletic Fragment I*: "Swa is nu þes middangeard mane geblonden,/ wanað ond weaxeð" (This middle-earth is now blended with evil, so it wanes and waxes; Jones 2012, 31–2a), and the formulation has a long history in English. The form *uuohsun* appears in two half-lines in the *Old Saxon Genesis, uuôhsun uuánliko* (they grew prosperously; 105a) and *uuohsun im uurisilíco* (they grew gigantically; 123a), what must be an Old Saxon envelope pattern contrasting the growth of the line of Seth with the growth of the line of Cain. The noun *uuolcan*, also semantically equivalent in Old Saxon, generally translating *nubes*, appears frequently at the end of a-verses, such as in *uueros uuiðer uuolcan* (men, near the clouds; *Heliand* 3118a). Variation similar to what we have seen in Old English is also apparent, for in the verses announcing the birth of Christ, the darkness splits into two and light comes shining from the sky *uuánum thurh thiu uuolcan* (gleaming through the clouds; *Heliand* 392a) before the angels come down, speak to the horse-guards, and wend their way back up through the clouds (*uundun thurh thiu uuolcan*; *Heliand* 415a), again an envelope pattern, this time varying between adjective and verb, similar to forms we have seen in *Beowulf* (*wan* and *wand*). The *Heliand* also has precisely repeated half-lines with *uuânum* in *uuânum te thesero uueroldi* (shining into this world; 168a, 447a, 687a), which describes births of John and Christ, then the coming of day after the wise men have found Christ.

In 1878, Eduard Sievers listed *uuânum undar uuolcnun* (649a) among his *systematischer Teil*, in possible formulas sorted by preposition (*undar*), even though the half-line, so far as I have been able to find, only occurs once in Old Saxon (1878, 480). Within Old Saxon, Sievers links the half-line to *uuânum thurh thiu uuolcan* (392a), suggesting he understands how the formulaic system might work. The formula appears as the wise men are seeking Christ: "Thô gengun eft thiu cumbal forð/ uuânum undar uuolcnun" (Then again the sign came forth, gleaming under the clouds; *Heliand* 648b–49a). It is worth noting that the two major manuscripts of the *Heliand* have different readings at this point. The reading here is from M, the ninth-century Munich manuscript; C, the possible Anglo-Saxon manuscript of the tenth century, has instead *uuânum undar thiu uuolcan*, suggesting, perhaps, a scribe familiar with the prior formula (392a, 415a). Robert L. Kellogg, looking for formulas in the *Heliand* 630–52a across all related traditions, connects the *Heliand* 649a with *Beowulf* 651a and 1374a, though he does not consider if they are semantically equivalent (1965, 71).[23] Finally, to go back to *uueros uuiðer uuolcan* (men, near the clouds; *Heliand* 3118a), this half-line introduces Christ on the Mount of Transfiguration, and the passage confirms the Old Saxon adjective *uuânam* means "brilliant, shining, gleaming" (Tiefenbach 2010, 439; the passage contains the adverb *uuânamo* [3127a]); the Old Saxon equivalent of Old English *wan/ won(n)* would be Old Saxon *wan(n)* "dark," "lacking," with a short vowel (Tiefenbach 2010, 440; Berr 1971, 429). *Wann* may appear, for example, in *Heliand* 5766b as the guards wait by Christ's tomb through the night, though the word is again different in C (*uuanom nahton*, as opposed to editorial *uuânamon nahton*, which is usually rendered "brilliant nights"). In other words, *uuânum undar uuolcnun* may be quite a different formula from *wan under wolcnum*, perhaps neither semantically identical nor to be counted with Riedinger's thematic formula. However, the Old Saxon evidence for alliterating w-word preposition *uuolcan* half-lines suggests a very similar formulaic system, and the difficulty of Old English *wan/won(n)* further hints at a possible confusion of formulaic expressions across Old Saxon and Old English.

2.4   Conclusion

Though a detailed investigation of every half-line in *Beowulf* would certainly not yield the rich results we have seen for *weox under wolcnum*, a recognition of the principles of formulaic composition and an eye for lexical and semantic repetition can lead in many different directions. Some kind of alliterating w-word preposition *wolcnum* formula would seem without doubt to have existed, and the narrower "complementary" *under wolcnum* formula is extremely productive. Though products of the same formulaic system do not necessarily tell us anything more than how common a system might have been, certain repetitions seem to have some thematic import, even if they cannot clearly be proven to have been thematic formulas. In this case, *weox under wolcnum* clearly connects the opening of the poem to the world of Genesis, if not to *Genesis A* itself, and the complementary formula, expanded to include both *under* and *to wolcnum*, is important within the poem, offering, as it were, suggestions to the reader of where to look for further clusters of formulas and repetition, where to find clues for how the poet signals and strengthens the themes of the poem. Outside the poem, *wan under/to wolcnum* associates *Beowulf* with the *Dream of the Rood*, *Guthlac B*, and *Andreas*, and awareness of those connections (and the clusters around them) helps us to understand different poetic approaches to traditional formulas and themes. Finally, evidence from Old Saxon suggests that the processes we have considered are very much parallel in a related tradition, even to the point of apparently identical formulas, but that thematic formulas are not necessarily consistent across traditions.

Notes

1. Magoun's own summation says thirteen half-lines are "not matched wholly or in part elsewhere" (1953, 449).
2. I am assuming that the listing of 5b among his repeated verses is an error for 6b, as 5b has no indication of being a formula on Chart I (Magoun 1953, 450, 464–5).
3. See, however, the discussion of Duggan on the difficulty of extrapolating and comparing formulaic data within and across poems and traditions (1973, 16–21).
4. See also Chapter 1, p. 40n22.
5. Creed's analysis is in a way supported by Howlett's analysis of the proem, for he sees after the three-line opening two elaborate "verse paragraphs"

(4–11, 12–19). The first is chiastic and breaks 8a and 8b to complete the pattern. At the center is (A) *weox* (B) *under wolcnum* (B') *weorðmyndum* (A') *þah* (1997, 506–7).

6. Watts considers *to* an "unimportant substitution" for *under* (1969, 149).

7. See Chapter 1, pp. 13–14.

8. Liuzza also briefly notes an *X under wolcnum* formula, calling it "one of the poet's ready-made metrical packages" (2013, 20).

9. The connections are fully explored in Chapter 3.

10. See Fulk et al. on issues with translation and emendation in this passage (2008, 268).

11. I have translated *wan/won(n)* as "dark" throughout, but the (color-)term remains a difficult one (see Lerner 1951, 248–9; Barley 1974; Earl 1979, 96–8; Bragg 1985 for 1982; Breeze 1997; North and Bintley 2016, 276–7).

12. Michael Lapidge locates this scene in the poem's reversal (*edwenden*) theme, showing how the sequence of reversals builds expectation in the audience that something bad is coming (2001, 63–7).

13. The intended sense of 646b–651a is extremely unclear; the text has often been emended to include a *ne* in 648. See Fulk et al. (2008, 156n646b).

14. The formula appears twice in *Exodus* (Irving 1953, lines 100b, 299b), in the former instance amid a cluster of familiar images of day and night, not long after the "dægscealdes hleo/wand ofer wolcnum" (the protection of the day-shield moved over the sky; 79b–80a) as God draws a layer of protection between the burning sun and Moses' people. I am ignoring Irving's emendation to *dægsceades* (Irving 1953, 74).

15. Michael Swanton calls this lament a "commonplace of contemporary literature" and lists correspondences (1987, 119).

16. Swanton notes the three-fold repetition of *elne mycle* and that *DOTR* 34a is parallel to *Beowulf* 1493a and *Christ in Judgment* 451a (1987, 112). Elsewhere, I have noted that "the poet, through the repetition of such phrases as *elne mycle* (34a, 60a, 123a) and *mæte werede* (69b, 124a) to describe Christ, the cross, and the dreamer, in the first instance, and Christ and the dreamer in the second, affirms the fundamental similarity of nature and will between Christ and man" (2007, 40–1).

17. See Chapter 3, p. 87 and Chapter 4, pp. 130–4.

18. The other main connection to Christ is the word *non* (nine, the ninth hour of the day; 1600a), for it is *circa horam nonam* (around the ninth hour; Matthew XXVII.45–50) that Christ calls out to God and dies.

19. However, that it should take *hwil dæges* to reach the bottom of the mere may be demanded by the inherited narrative paradigm of the monster fights. See Orchard (2003b, 140–68).

20. *Ellen* appears in many other important contexts: see, most significantly, *Beowulf* 1–3 and the *Wanderer* 112–14a.
21. See Chapter 4, pp. 123–39. The link to *The Ruin* is noted by North and Bintley, who comment that the "description in lines 839-43 capture[s] Mermedonia as the shell of a Roman city with gate, towers and walls, now in decline ... The Mermedonians are portrayed more as squatters than as master builders" (2016, 255).
22. Anita Riedinger places the *Andreas*-poet in a transitional period: "[The poet] helps break up oral-formulaic tradition and ... reveals some characteristics of a literate mind acting upon the product of the oral mind that lies behind the tradition" (1989, 183).
23. On Old Saxon formulas generally, see also Capek (1970) and Haferland (2010).

REFERENCES

Adeline Courtney Bartlett. 1966. *The Larger Rhetorical Patterns in Anglo-Saxon Poetry*. New York: AMS Press Inc.
Barley, Nigel F. 1974. Old English Colour Classification: Where Do Matters Stand? *Anglo-Saxon England* 3: 15–28.
Behaghel, Otto, and Burkhard Taeger (eds.). 1996. *Heliand und Genesis*, 10th ed. Tübingen: Max Niemeyer.
Berr, Samuel. 1971. *An Etymological Dictionary to the Old Saxon Heliand*. Berne and Frankfurt: Herbert Lang & Co., Ltd.
Bolton, Whitney F. 1985. A Poetic Formula in *Beowulf* and Seven Other Old English Poems: A Computer Study. *Computers and the Humanities* 19: 167–173.
Bragg, Lois. 1985 for 1982. Color Words in *Beowulf*. *Proceedings of the Patristic, Mediaeval, and Renaissance Conference* 7: 47–55.
Breeze, Andrew. 1997. Old English *wann* "dark; pallid": Welsh *gwann* "weak; sad, gloomy". *American Notes and Queries* 10 (4): 10–13.
Capek, Michael J. 1970. A Note on Formula Development in Old Saxon. *Modern Philology* 67 (4): 357–363.
Clark, George. 1965. The Traveler Recognizes His Goal: A Theme in Anglo-Saxon Poetry. *Journal of English and Germanic Philology* 64 (4): 645–659.
Creed, Robert P. 1961. On the Possibility of Criticizing Old English Poetry. *Texas Studies in Language and Literature* 3: 97–106.
Doane, A.N. (ed.). 2013. *Genesis A: A New Edition, Revised*. Tempe, AZ: Arizona Center for Medieval and Renaissance Studies.

Duggan, Joseph J. 1973. *The Song of Roland: Formulaic Style and Poetic Craft.* Publications of the Center for Medieval and Renaissance Studies. Berkeley: University of California Press.

Earl, James W. 1979. The Necessity of Evil in *Beowulf. South Atlantic Bulletin* 44: 81–98.

Fox, Michael. 2007. Origins in the English Tradition. In *The Oxford Handbook of English Literature and Theology*, ed. Andrew W. Hass, David Jasper, and Elisabeth Jay, 35–53. Oxford: Oxford University Press.

Fulk, R.D., Robert E. Bjork, and John D. Niles (eds.). 2008. *Klaeber's Beowulf*, 4th ed. Toronto: University of Toronto Press.

Haferland, Harald. 2010. Was the Heliand Poet Illiterate?, trans. Valentine A. Pakis. In *Perspectives on the Old Saxon Heliand*, ed. Pakis, 167–207. Morgantown, VA: West Virginia University Press.

Howlett, David R. 1997. *British Books in Biblical Style.* Dublin: Four Courts Press.

Hutcheson, B.R. 1995. *Old English Poetic Metre.* Cambridge: D. S. Brewer.

Irving, Edward Burroughs, Jr. (ed.) 1953. *The Old English Exodus.* New Haven: Yale University Press.

Jones, Christopher A. (ed. and trans.). 2012. *Homiletic Fragment I.* In *Old English Shorter Poems: Volume 1, Religious and Didactic*, ed. and trans. Jones, 120–123. Cambridge, MA: Harvard University Press.

Kellogg, Robert L. 1965. The South Germanic Oral Tradition. In *Franciplegius: Medieval and Linguistic Studies in Honor of Francis Peabody Magoun, Jr.*, ed. Jess B. Bessinger, Jr., and Robert P. Creed, 66–74. New York: New York University Press.

Lapidge, Michael. 2001. *Beowulf* and Perception. *Proceedings of the British Academy* 111: 61–97.

Lerner, L.D. 1951. Colour Words in Anglo-Saxon. *The Modern Language Review* 46: 246–249.

Liuzza, Roy (ed. and trans.). 2013. *Beowulf*, 2nd ed. Peterborough, ON: Broadview.

Lord, Albert B. 1995. *The Singer Resumes the Tale*, ed. Mary Louise Lord. Ithaca, NY: Cornell University Press.

Magoun Jr., Francis P. 1953. The Oral-Formulaic Character of Anglo-Saxon Narrative Poetry. *Speculum* 28: 446–467.

Marsden, Richard (ed.). 2008. *The Old English Heptateuch and Ælfric's Libellus de ueteri testamento et nouo*, vol. 1, EETS o.s. 330. Oxford: Oxford University Press.

Niles, John D. 1983. *Beowulf: The Poem and Its Tradition.* Cambridge: Harvard University Press.

North, Richard, and Michael D. J. Bintley (eds.). 2016. *Andreas: An Edition.* Liverpool: Liverpool University Press.

Orchard, Andy. 2003a. *A Critical Companion to Beowulf.* Cambridge: D. S. Brewer.

Orchard, Andy. 2003b. *Pride and Prodigies: Studies in the Monsters of the Beowulf-Manuscript*, rev. paperback ed. Toronto: University of Toronto Press.

Orchard, Andy. 2016. The Originality of *Andreas.* In *Old English Philology: Studies in Honour of R. D. Fulk*, ed. Leonard Neidorf, Rafael J. Pascual, and Tom Shippey, 331–370. Cambridge: D. S. Brewer.

Riedinger, Anita. 1985. The Old English Formula in Context. *Speculum* 60: 294–317.

Riedinger, Anita. 1989. *Andreas* and the Formula in Transition. In *Hermeneutics and Medieval Culture*, ed. Patrick J. Gallacher and Helen Damico, 183–191. Albany: State University of New York Press.

Roberts, Jane. 1979. *The Guthlac Poems of the Exeter Book.* Oxford: Clarendon Press.

Swanton, Michael (ed.). 1987. *The Dream of the Rood*, rev ed. Exeter: Exeter University Press.

Tiefenbach, Heinrich. 2010. *Altsächsisches Handworterbuch.* Berlin: De Gruyter.

Watts, Ann C. 1969. *The Lyre and the Harp: A Comparative Reconsideration of Oral Tradition in Homer and Old English Epic Poetry.* New Haven: Yale University Press.

Werner, L.D. 1951. Colour Words in Anglo-Saxon. *Modern Language Review* 46: 246–249.

CHAPTER 3

The Fitt Formula: Genesis and Fitt 1

The half-line *weox under wolcnum* is a particularly rich way to begin thinking about *Beowulf* and formulas and plays an important role in the unity and thematic consistency of the earliest lines of the poem. The half-line appears in the first unnumbered fitt (lines 1–52) and, at least for some scholars, is therefore also part of the poem's first digression or episode. The identification and significance of fitts and digressions and episodes, however, is not without problems. The fitt divisions of the poem, first of all, are indicated differently by the two scribes of the poem and also seem to have been subjected to an unfinished attempt to correct them by a later reader of the manuscript who noticed the absence of Fitt 24 (Kiernan 1996, 265). Several critics have suggested that the fitt divisions were for one reason or another not part of the exemplar from which the two scribes were working, either because they had not been previously numbered or because they were earlier (perhaps authorial) and missing from the (intermediate) version of the poem the scribes were copying (Kiernan 1996, 269; Fulk et al. 2008, xxxv; Orchard 2003a, 96). What we are left with, then, are 42 fitts (numbered 1–23 and 25–43, though partially corrected) and an unnumbered introduction.[1] Andy Orchard would say that "some clear patterns seem to emerge from a consideration of the surviving fitt divisions" (2003a, 93) for many of the fitts begin with an *X maðelode* formula (10 fitts) or with a connective *Þa* (11 fitts), and Constance B. Hieatt notes envelope patterns of various complexity in ten different fitts (1975); Fulk et al. note that fitts often end with maxims, clearly summative passages, or the conclusions

© The Author(s) 2020

M. Fox, *Following the Formula in Beowulf, Örvar-Odds saga, and Tolkien*, https://doi.org/10.1007/978-3-030-48134-6_3

of digressions (2008, xxxv). In contrast, Orchard points to oddities in the distribution of the openings across the two parts of the poem, and Fulk et al. conclude that "while much of the sectioning does seem artful, certain other of the poem's divisions may justly be called arbitrary and inappropriate" (2008, xxxv), meaning that readings of the poem based substantially on fitt divisions are difficult to make, even though some intricate arguments have been made for the structure of the poem on the basis of the fitt numbers and for complex patterns linking across fitts.[2]

At the opening of the poem, however (indeed, until line 1629), the fitt numbering seems in order, and other evidence points to coherent and unified fitts.[3] In fact, the structure of the opening three fitts, that is, the introduction and Fitts 1 and 2, would seem to suggest that lines 1–188 were to be seen as a tripartite unit. For example, each of the first three fitts begins with an eleven-line introduction that is clearly marked as separate from the rest of the fitt. The introduction sums up the career of Scyld Scefing with *Þæt wæs god cyning* (11b); Fitt 1, with its *Þa ... Þa* (53a–64a) structure, distinguishes Hrothgar's career from his ancestors'; and Fitt 2 has a clear *Gewat ... neosian ... gewat ... neosan* (115–25) envelope pattern. Each fitt also has a closing passage, either a kind of maxim (introduction), a summing up of the giants' feud with God (Fitt 1), or an almost homiletic observation that many have felt breaks the narrative frame of the poem (Fitt 2). The evidence could be multiplied with more specific details, as we will partly see below, but Fitt 3 has a completely different kind of structure.[4]

In terms of digressions and episodes, the background to which will be considered more fully in the following chapter, most readers of the poem take the whole of the introduction (1–52) as the first episode, even though Adrien Bonjour, in treating the section separately, notes its peculiarity (1950, 1), and Hans-Jürgen Diller would exclude it because, coming at the beginning of the poem, the fitt has no narrative from which to digress (1984, 82). The first fitt, in turn, has usually been taken to include three episodes or digressions, the lines on the fate of Heorot (82b–85), the scop's creation song (90b–98), and the concluding lines on Cain's offspring and punishment (107b–114, usually, depending on how 104b–7a is read).[5] However one counts episodes and digressions, Fitt 1 is the first section of the poem to establish how the poet will break from the main narrative to introduce material that looks forward and backward (prolepses and analepses), both inside and outside (homodiegetic and extradiegetic) the main narrative of the poem

(Lapidge 2001). Because of the episodes and digressions, further, Fitt 1 also offers a first look, on a fairly small level, at how the poet deals with time, which is a key feature of the poem as a whole, though particularly in terms of its episodes and digressions.[6] John D. Niles makes two key points about time: first of all, "almost no other feature of the poem's composition distinguishes it so clearly from the narrative mode of the folktale or the heroic lay as does its handling of the dimension of time"; second, in terms of how it works, "the hero is set into a complex net of temporal interdependencies that range from the beginning of Creation ... to the day of the final dissolution of time" (1983, 179).[7] That handling of time is connected to formulaic composition at the level of the half-line in the way that elements are juxtaposed, from the level of words to the overall narrative structure. In the second half of the poem, these "separate strokes," as Tolkien would call them, are used to insert, piece-by-piece and out of chronological sequence, the details of the feud between the Swedes and Geats,[8] but the pattern appears first on a small scale in Fitt 1.

3.1   READING FITT 1

Malcolm Godden observes that the Old Testament was "the major influence on Old English literature," singling out *Beowulf* as "in many ways the most imaginative response to the Old Testament" because of the ways that the poem "draws on biblical stories of creation, of Cain and the giants to form part of its mythic structure" (1991, 206–7). J. R. R. Tolkien first made this point, arguing that the scriptural allusions to Cain and to the giants and their war with God are central, for the connections between scripture and northern myth are "the precise point at which an imagination, pondering old and new, was kindled"; in other words, "new Scripture and old tradition touched and ignited" and a poem was born. In fact, Tolkien suggests that the *Beowulf*-poet "brought probably *first* to his task a knowledge of Christian poetry, especially that of the Cædmon school, and especially *Genesis*" (1983, 26). The Old Testament motifs in the poem have also been suggested to have obvious thematic importance: "Cain's story warns 'Thou shalt not kill,' the Flood cautions against resisting God's will, and the Creation passage elaborates the theme 'the world belongs to the Lord!'" (Klaeber 1996, 51).[9] Virtually every major study to consider biblical influence on the poem isolates the same three or four passages—creation (90b–8); Cain and the giants' war against God (106–14); Cain alone (1261b–66a); and the giants' war against God as depicted on the hilt (1687–93)—even though the creation passage need not be specifically scriptural. Most readers of the poem would now accept that the passages are simply too completely woven into the fabric of the poem to be dismissed as interpolations.[10] However, within this critical acceptance of the unique place of Genesis as a source of *Beowulf*, the scriptural structure of Fitt 1 of the poem has never precisely been enumerated.

The prologue (1–52) of the poem sets the stage for the retelling, in Fitt 1, of Genesis I–XI. The prologue establishes Scyld Scefing as the founder of the Danish royal line and does so in language that is suggestive:

> [Scyld Scefing]
> weox under wolcnum, weorðmyndum þah,
> oð þæt him æghwylc þara ymbsittendra
> ofer hronrade hyran scolde,
> gomban gyldan. Þæt was god cyning. (8–11)[11]

Scyld Scefing waxed under the clouds, prospered in honours, until each of those near-dwellers over the whale-road should obey him, should pay him tribute. That was a good king.

The alliterating w-word preposition *wolcnum* formula, which, as we have seen, is significant in the poem as a whole,[12] here connects the success of the founder of the Danish royal line with *Genesis A*'s description of the growth of the tribe of Sem/Shem after the interruption of the building of the Tower of Babel:

> Weox þa under wolcnum and wriðade
> mægburh Semes, oð þæt mon awoc
> on þære cneorisse cynebearna rim,
> þancolmod wer,[13] þeawum hydig. (1702–5)[14]

The tribe of Sem/Shem waxed then under the clouds and grew, until a man was born among that family, that count of noble children, a thoughtful man, mindful of custom.

In the midst of all the language of birth and growth that connects Genesis (and *Genesis A*) with the beginning of the prologue and the new generations of Danes at the opening of Fitt 1, the poet also specifically connects Scyld Scefing with Hrothgar (and thus Hrothgar with events around the time of the building of the Tower of Babel), through a masterful redeployment of similar vocabulary:

> Þa wæs Hroðgare heresped gyfen,
> wiges **weorðmynd**, þæt him his winemagas
> georne **hyrdon**, oðð þæt seo geogoð **geweox**,
> magodriht micel. (64–7a)

Then was success in battle given to Hrothgar, honour in warfare, so that his retainers obeyed him eagerly, until that young host grew, a great warband.

The poet further binds Fitt 1 through a kind of envelope pattern in the repetition of *longe þrage* (54b and 114a; connecting the rule of Beow with the duration of the giants' struggle against God and perhaps hinting at Grendel's structural role by repeating *þrage* in almost the precise middle of the fitt)[15] and given that indisputable structure, the fact that the offspring of Healfdene are four who *in worold wocun* (60a) and that the *untydras* that *onwocon* (111)[16] also seem to be four, presented in a syntactically similar way ("eotenas ond ylfe ond orcneas,/ swycle gigantas" [112–13a])[17] is also worth noting: there are parallels in the worlds of men and monsters.[18]

In order of biblical verses, I would suggest that we see reference in Fitt 1 to creation (90b–98), to the temptation in Eden (the serpent in paradise; 100b–101a), to Cain's killing of Abel (106–8), to the giants who struggle against God (111–14), to the Flood (114), and to the building of the Tower of Babel (67b–85) and the wasteland that remains afterward (103–4). In other words, Genesis I, III, IV, VI, X, and XI can all be argued to be at least referred to in Fitt 1. Not surprisingly, a completely different approach to the opening of the poem shows similar results: J. B. Bessinger, Jr., has found parallels to every verse in *Cædmon's Hymn* near the beginning of the poem (67b–182b), most often in Fitt 1 (1974, 95–6).[19] Given that the certain sources of or influences on the poem are very few, this cluster of Old Testament/Christian echoes is extremely important. The poet nearly presents these events in their biblical order, moving only the possible reference to the building of the Tower of Babel to the beginning of the sequence:

                        Him on mod bearn
þæt healreced hatan wolde,
medoærn micel men gewyrcean
þon[n]e yldo bearn æfre gefrunon,
ond þær on innan eall gedælan
geongum ond ealdum swylc him God sealde,
buton folcscare ond feorum gumena.
Ða ic wide gefrægn weorc gebannan
manigre mægþe geond þisne middangeard,
folcstede frætwan. **Him on fyrste gelomp,**
ædre mid yldum, þæt hit wearð eal gearo,
healærna mæst; scop him Heort naman
se þe his wordes geweald wide hæfde.
He beot ne aleh: beagas dælde,
sinc æt symle. Sele hlifade,
heah ond horngeap; heaðowylma bad,
laðan liges— ne wæs hit lenge þa gen
þæt se ecghete aþumsweoran
æfter wælniðe **wæcnan** scolde. (67b–85)

It occurred to him in his mind that he should command men to build a
hall, a great mead-hall, which the children of men should ever hear of, and
that he should distribute there to young and to old all that which God
gave him, except the people's portion and the lives of men. Then I heard
the work ordered among many nations throughout this earth, to decorate
the folkstead. It came to pass quickly in time that it was all ready, the best
of halls; he created the name Heorot for it, he who widely had the power
of his word. He did not forget the promise: he distributed rings, treasure
at the feast. The hall towered, high and horn-gabled; it awaited surging
war, hostile flame—it was longer yet before the edge-hate between those
who had sworn oaths after deadly slaughter should awaken.

Within the poem, the passage is artfully connected to the prologue,
the first part of the fitt, and Hrothgar's speech much later in the poem.
The alliteration and syntax of *medoærn micel* connects the hall immediately to its primary occupants, the *magodriht micel* (67a), establishing
almost a causal relationship between the establishment of the great host
and the need for a great mead-hall. Hrothgar's vow to distribute wealth
in the hall and its fulfillment connect this passage to the gnomic statement that forms the central passage of the prologue (20–25); the many
nations who hear the call to work (75a) echo the many nations sub-
dued by Scyld Scefing (5a)[20]; and the power of Hrothgar's word recalls

Scyld's decisions about his own funeral (30a). The full line *manigre mægþe geond þisne middangeard* (75) is repeated almost verbatim by Hrothgar (1771), amid a cluster of repetitions and parallels to the opening eleven lines of the poem, including the "complementary formula" *under wolcnum* (1770a), as we have seen (Creed 1961, 105).[21] Even the passage itself has a balance of parallelism and chiasmus, with the two sections beginning *him on mod bearn* and *him on fyrste gelomp* having parallel remarks on the command to build and the bestowing of the name and the promise to distribute and act of distributing treasure with a floating comment on the command to build the hall and the rapid execution of the command (68–9 and 77–8a).

The identification of Heorot with Babel is at no point absolute. Specific references to the Tower in the OE *Heptateuch* or *Genesis A* refer to it in different terms: the tower is *ane burh* (or *ceastre*) and *ænne stypel* or a *torr* to be constructed *to beacne* (Marsden 2008, 28, 29).[22] The *Andreas*-poet, in fact, seems to have borrowed *heah ond horngeap* to describe the *tempel dryhtnes*.[23] However, the motivation that it should be ever heard of by men is precisely scriptural (*uton mærsian urne namon*) and is always associated with the tower (and even by the *Andreas*-poet with the *tempel dryhtnes*); the use of *hlifian* (standing high or towering), the later note that the hall was so high (or so bright, perhaps on account of the gold) that its light shone over many lands (*lixte se leoma ofer landa fela*; 311),[24] the way the notion occurs to Hrothgar (with its "faint" suggestion of pride[25]), the collaborative effort of many peoples in its construction, and the immediate reversal of fortune all suggest a situation analogous to the building of the tower. Without doubt, there are other things going on here: Panzer has suggested that the speed with which Heorot is built has a parallel in one of his versions of "The Bear's Son Tale"[26]; Hrothgar creates almost by his "word" (associating him with God rather than Nimrod, and these parallel associations are much amplified at other points in the poem); Klaeber long ago pointed out the biblical echo in *yldo bearn* and its variants (*filium hominum*)[27]; and the establishment of Heorot is later in the fitt likened more to the establishment of Eden, where men *dreamum lifdon* (99b), a moment of bliss so closely juxtaposed to the creation sequence that we cannot but think of Adam and Eve in paradise and, afterward, the envious onlooker of the apocryphal tradition. Across the poem as a whole, of course, much in this passage about the building of Heorot connects Hrothgar's monument with Beowulf's, the barrow by the sea at the end of poem, a monument that will *heah hlifian* (2805a) and that will be *wide gesyne* (3158b).

Other features of the poem also suggest a Heorot/Babel connection. While we must recognize that the genealogy presented at the beginning of the poem may be read at least two different ways[28]—that is, the poet at once seems to refer to the tradition of Scef as the extra-biblical ark-born son of Noah (a direct Scef-Scyld-Beow line, as in Æthelweard's Latin *Chronicle*, conflated with the Sceaf as ark-born son of Noah that we see in the *Anglo-Saxon Chronicle* B, C, and D and perhaps Asser's *Vita Ælfredi regis Angul Saxonum*)[29] and to the tradition in which Heremod is the ruler before Scyld (the *grim cyning* who brought misery to the Danes, as Hrothgar later reports, with several generations between Scef and Heremod)—the presentation of time is at least worth considering. When we are introduced to the dragon's treasure, we hear the Lay of the Last Survivor, then we hear that the dragon held that hoard for three hundred winters (2278–80a). When the rule of kings is specifically enumerated in the poem, a king rules for fifty winters: Beowulf (2208b–9a, 2732b–3a) and Hrothgar both rule for fifty winters, and Hrothgar says so himself, in highly suggestive language that echoes other parts of the poem, as we have seen: "Swa ic Hring-Dena hund missera/ weold under wolcnum!" (So for a hundred half-years I ruled the Ring-Danes under the clouds; 1769–70a). Even the anti-rulers seem to abide by the fifty-year principle, as things go well for Grendel's mother in the mere for fifty years as well (1498b). If we accept that fifty years makes a reign, give or take small differences and twelve-year periods of harassment, then the generations that are explicit in the poem, even though we must skip from Danes to Geats—(Noah)-Scef-Scyld-Beow(ulf)-Healfdene-Hrothgar-Beowulf—make the action of the poem take place three hundred years after the Flood. What, then, does the dragon represent, and who is the Last Survivor? If we doubt that the poet intended such a scheme, remember the days of Noah, as, for example, reported in *Genesis A*:

> þa nyttade Noe siððan
> mid sunum sinum sidan rices
> þreohund wintra þisses lifes,
> freomen æfter flode and fiftig eac
> þa he forð gewat. (1598–1601c)

Then Noah[30] enjoyed after that with his sons the broad kingdom for three-hundred winters of this life, free men after the Flood, and fifty more besides, before he went forth.

Of course, Nimrod is not the sixth generation after Noah, but he is rather the fourth—Noah, Cham, Chus, Nimrod—but the longevity of that part of Noah's family is not precisely enumerated. In the poem's first, most explicit, genealogy, then, Nimrod is of the same generation as Beo(w)(ulf), as he is in Æthelweard's *Chronicle*. At the very least, juxtaposing the apparent chronology and genealogies of the poem with scriptural genealogy is suggestive. Slightly less convincing, perhaps, but still worth mentioning, is the collective significance of the three-hundred-year reign of the dragon, the fifty-year reigns of kings and monsters, and the 30-fold strength of Beowulf and Grendel: surely every contemporary audience member of the poem would have known the dimensions of the ark, given here as God gives orders to Noah in *Genesis A*: "Þu þær fær gewyrc fiftiges wid,/ ðrittiges heah [and] þreohund lang/ elngemeta" (You shall make there a ship, fifty ells wide, thirty ells high, and three hundred ells long; 1307–9a).

If Nimrod and the Tower of Babel[31] are accepted as part of the poet's system of allusions in Fitt 1, then those references should be extended. The most enigmatic and suggestive of these is in *Solomon and Saturn II*:

> [SALOMON CVÆÐ:]
>   Wat ic ðæt wæron Caldeas
> guðe ðæs gielpne ond ðæs goldwlonce,
> mærða ðæs modige, ðær to ðam moning gelomp
> suð ymbe Sanere feld. Sæge me from ðam lande
> ðær nænig fyra ne mæg fotum gestæppan.
> SATVRNVS CVÆÐ:
> Se mæra was haten <mere>liðende
> weallende wulf, werðeodum cuð
> Filistina, freond Nebrondes.
> He on ðam felda ofslog . xxv .
> dracena on dægred, ond hine ða deað offeoll,
> forðan ða foldan ne mæg fira ænig,
> ðone mercstede, mon gesecan,
> fugol gefleogan, ne ðon ma foldan nita.
> Ðanon atercynn ærest gewurdon
> wide onwæcned, ða ðe nu weallende
> ðurh attres oroð ingang rymað.
> Git his sweord scinað swiðe gescæned,
> ond ofer ða byrgenna blicað ða hieltas. (29b–46)[32]

[Solomon said:] I know that the Chaldeans were so boastful in battle, gold-proud, and pleased with their deeds that a warning came to them, south around the field of Sennaar. Tell me about that land where no man may set his feet. Saturn said: The great one was called sea-travelling, the surging wolf, known to the people of the Philistines, a friend of Nimrod. He on that field slew 25 dragons at daybreak, and death then took him; for that reason no man may seek that border-stead, no bird may fly there, no more than any beasts of the earth. From there the poisonous race first was widely awoken, those which now, surging, through the breath of poison, make roomy the entrance. Still his sword shines, very polished, and the hilt gleams over the graves.

The passage has several echoes of Fitt 1 and *Beowulf* as a whole. First of all, the setting is clearly that of Genesis XI and, therefore, at least associated temporally with the building of Heorot. The Chaldeans are *goldwlanc* just as Beowulf is as he prepares to return to the Geats (*guðrinc goldwlanc*; 1881a): the compound appears only twice in the poetic corpus. The pride of the Chaldeans invites a warning (*moning*), which comes suddenly. The dragon-slayer is a friend of Nimrod; he is at least metaphorically called a wolf, if that is not to be seen as a proper name; he seems accomplished in feats that take place at sea; he slays twenty-five dragons before himself falling dead; his deeds seem related in some way to a place of utter desolation that gives birth to the poisonous races[33] and that cannot be visited by birds, beasts, or men; and the sword shines over the graves all around the land, a light, a beacon, and a warning. Daniel Anlezark has pointed out several of these parallels, including the striking fact that the next lines from Solomon in the poem have to do with the foolishness of undertaking feats at sea, a sentiment that seems closely related to Unferth's abuse of Beowulf.[34]

The field at Sennaar and the mere of Grendel and his mother (as presented in *Solomon and Saturn II* and *Beowulf*) have quite a few similarities, and their similarities have been traced to a classical tradition of "poisoned places."[35] Even here, in Fitt 1, the poet gives a brief description of the mere after the building of Heorot:

> Wæs se grimma gæst Grendel haten,
> mære mearcstapa, se þe moras heold,
> fen ond fæsten; fifelcynnes eard
> wonsæli wer weardode hwile. (102–5)

The grim spirit was called Grendel, the infamous border-stepper, he who ruled the moors, the fen, and the fastness; the wretched man occupied the yard of the monster-race for a time.

The abode of monsters in the first two-thirds of the poem is also linked to hell through the *Visio Pauli* and Blickling Homily XVI, where it seems most likely that both the homily and *Beowulf* draw upon a lost vernacular version of the *Visio Pauli*.[36] In *Beowulf*, the waste place has wolf-slopes (1358a), is unknown in its depths to anyone (1366b–7), is avoided by the hart (1368–72), has *nicorhusa fela* and *wyrmcynnes fela* (1411b; 1425b), *saedracan* (1426a), *nicras* (1427b), *wyrmas ond wildeor* (1430a), *saedeor monig* (1510b), and the *brimwylf* (1599a and perhaps 1506a) herself, Grendel's mother. Blickling XVI has a reduced cast of monsters, containing only *niccra eardung ond wearga* and fiends in the likeness of nicors, seizing souls like greedy wolves. The *Visio Pauli* is difficult to deploy as a possible source because of its many different redactions, but *Redactio* II is highly reminiscent of the scene at the mere: there are many water monsters, and the monsters issue from a source that connects the *Visio* also to Beowulf's final opponent. In a lightless place where the world-river Oceanus flows is also a seething, fiery river:

> Et draco igneus in medio loci et habens in collo eius capita tria et mille dentes, et unusquisque dens quasi gladius acutus et oculi quasi gladii acuti; semperque aperto ore stabat ut absorberet animas. Et erat nomen eius Bachimach. Et ab eo procedebant serpentes et rane et omnia genera uermium. (Silverstein 1935, 156)

> And there was a fiery dragon in the middle of that place with three heads and a thousand teeth and each tooth was sharp like a sword and its eyes were sharp like swords; and it stood always with an open mouth that it might swallow souls. And its name was Bachimach. And out of it issued serpents and frogs and all species of worms.

Of the redactions that have been specifically connected with England and Ireland, *Redactio* IV (which is most likely to be English) has a similar scene, with a terrifying river, "in quo multe bestie dyabolice erant quasi pisces in medio maris, que animas peccatrices devorant sine ulla misericordia quasi lupi devorant oves" (in which were many hellish beasts, like fish in the depths of the sea, that devoured the souls of sinners without any mercy, as wolves devour sheep; Brandes 1885, 76).

What has not often been noted, however, in the terrifying scene at the mere, is the exegetical tradition of the waste of Babylon. To give just one example of how richly imagined that landscape can be, Jerome's commentary on Isaiah XIII.20–2 is worth quoting in full:

Nec ponet ibi tentoria Arabs; nec pastores requiescent ibi. Sed erunt ibi bestiae, replebuntur domus eorum draconibus et habitabunt ibi struthiones, et pilosi saltabunt ibi. Et respondebunt ululae in aedibus eius, et sirenae in delubris uoluptatis.

In tantum Babylon uastata erit atque deserta, ut ne ad pascua quidem armentorum et pecorum utilis sit. Non enim tendet ibi Arabs Saracenusque tentoria, nec pastores post uestigia gregum fessi labore quiescent, sed inter parietinas et angustias ueterum ruinarum habitabunt Siim: quod soli LXX bestias transtulerunt. Alii ipso nomine quod apud Hebraeos scriptum est, uolentes genera daemonum intellegi uel phantasmata. *Et replebuntur,* inquit, *domus,* ut nos diximus, *draconibus:* ut Aquila transtulit, typhonibus; ut Symmachus ohim, ipsum uerbum Hebraicum exprimens. LXX uero et Theodotio clamores uel sonitus interpretati sunt. Quodque sequitur: *Pilosi saltabunt ibi,* uel incubones, uel satyros, uel siluestres quosdam homines, quos nonnulli fatuos ficarios[37] uocant, aut daemonum genera intellegunt. Pro ululis quoque omnes ipsum uerbum Hebraicum iim, soli LXX onocentauros transtulerunt. Sirenae autem thennim uocantur, quas nos aut daemones aut monstra quaedam, uel certe dracones magnos interpretabimur, qui cristati sunt et uolantes. Per quae omnia uastitatis et solitudinis signa monstrantur, quod tanta sit depopulatio urbis quondam potissimae, ut prae multitudine daemonum ac bestiarum nullus in eam audeat pastorum, id est deserti appetitor intrare. Didicimus a quodam fratre Elamita, qui de illis finibus egrediens, nunc Hierosolymis uitam exigit monachorum, uenationes regias esse in Babylone et omnis generis bestias murorum eius tantum ambitu coerceri. (Adriaen 1963, 165–6)

The Arab shall not pitch his tent there, nor shall shepherds rest there. Rather, *bestiae* [beasts] shall rest there, and their houses shall be filled with *dracones* [dragons]; *strutiones* [ostriches] shall live there, and *pilosi* [hairy ones; satyrs] there shall dance. And *ululae* [owls] shall answer in its houses, and *sirenae* [sirens] in the luxurious palaces.

So much will Babylon be laid waste and deserted that it will not be useful for the grazing of cattle and sheep. The Arab and the Saracen shall not make camp there, nor shall shepherds, made weary by labour on the trail of their herds, rest there. Rather, among the old walls and difficult places of ancient ruins shall dwell SIIM, which only the Septuagint translates *bestiae*: others, by that word which is written among Hebrews, wish us to understand the races of demons, or perhaps phantasms. "And they shall fill," it says, "the houses," as we said, "with *dracones*": as Aquila translates, "with *typhones*,"[38] as Symmachus translates, OHIM, expressing that in a Hebrew word; which by the Septuagint and by Theodotion are interpreted as *clamores* [loud shouts; echoes] or *sonitus* [resoundings]. What follows, "*pilosi* shall dance there," is understood as either *incubones* [*incubi*, but also, spirits that guard buried treasure], or satyrs, or certain forest-dwelling men, that some call the fools of the fig-trees, or as the races of demons. For *ululae*, also, only the Septuagint translated "onocentaur." THENNIM, indeed, are called *sirenae*, which we shall interpret either as *daemones* or *monstra*, or, certainly, great *dracones*, which are crested [plumed; tufted] and flying. Through all of these things are shown signs of devastation and solitude, that so great might be the ravaging of the city once most powerful that not one of the shepherds, that is, not one who desires a solitary place, on account of the multitude of *daemones* and *bestiae*, shall dare to enter into it. We have learned from a certain brother Elamitas, who, departing from those territories, now leads the life of a monk in Jerusalem, that there are royal hunts in Babylon, and that beasts of every kind are confined only by the circuit of its walls.

After the construction of Heorot/Babel, two fates await: flame and Grendel and his ilk. The quick articulation of these fates, though they are themselves reminiscent of the Christian tradition, interrupts the narrative before the poet continues to the song of the scop. This "creation song" has no real parallels with other Christian sources, and it has long been recognized to echo Iopas' "song" in the *Aeneid*, meaning that it is not (but for the context) particularly scriptural. This sequence retrospectively explains Grendel's hostility and establishes or characterizes that Danes as "almost aware" of the one God of the poet/audience. Characteristic of the poem as a whole—and this fitt in particular—is the abrupt reversal, the *edwenden* that Michael Lapidge has discussed at length (2001, 63–4). The scop's song is again in an envelope: the *hlud dream* that enrages Grendel (86–9a) leads into the song, and everyone "dreamum lifdon,/ eadiglice, oþ þæt an ongan/ fyrene fre(m)man" (lived in joy, happily, until one began to perform evil deeds; 99b–101a). In this repetition of *dream*, an important theme in the poem is established, for most of the other occurrences of the word in the poem (in compounds or otherwise) relate to Cain's or to Grendel's lack of joy (721a; 850b; 1264b; 1275a), while the others appear in the context of Beowulf's arrival at Heorot and the restoration of joy in the hall (497b), his arrival home (2014–16a), and Wealtheow's desire that Beowulf preserve joy for her sons (1226a–7). Significantly, the only other occurrences in the

poem refer to Heremod, who "ana hwearf,/ mære þeoden mondrea-
mum from" (wandered alone, that well-known lord, away from the joys
of men; 1714b–15) and "dreamleas gebad/ þæt he þæs gewinnes weorc
þrowade,/ leodbealo longsum" (endured joyless, that he suffered the
trouble of that conflict, a long-lasting bale to the people; 1720b–22a),
thus connecting him to Cain and the depredations of Grendel. In terms
of Genesis, too, to take just the example of *Genesis A*, the presence and
absence of "dream" is hugely important: the angelic hosts have it and
have it confirmed after the expulsion of the rebels (12b; 81b), and the
rebel angels do not (40a; 56b). God prepares a joyless *witehus* through
his command as their reward (*grim lean*), in a manner that anticipates
the reward of the Flood (*Beowulf* 114b). Further, the world before creation in *Genesis A* is *idel and unnyt* (106b) and "joyless" (108b), precisely echoing Heorot in its terrorized state, which happens abruptly like
all the transitions in the poem as a whole: "Swa rixode ond wið rihte
wan,/ ana wið eallum, oð þæt idel stod/ husa selest" (So he [Grendel]
ruled and fought against right, one against all, until the best of houses
stood empty; 144–6a). In case the audience misses the connections in
Fitt 1 ("oþ þæt an ongan/ fyrene fre[m]man"), the links are made more
clearly in Fitt 2 ("ana wið eallum, oð þæt idel stod/ husa selest"), and
the echoes of the creation sequence appear a third time when Beowulf
announces his understanding of the situation in Heorot to Hrothgar,
linking the *idel ond unnyt* hall with the disappearance of light (411–
14).[39] At the end of the poem, Wiglaf announces that the Geats will
wander *idel* (2888a), and the treasure is returned to the earth, "eldum
swa unnyt swa hyt (æro)r wæs" (to men as useless as it was before;
3168), a split repetition that is among the best evidence of the *Beowulf*-
poet's genius in interweaving episodes and themes.

The inhabitants of Heorot live in joy, therefore, until *an ongan/ fyrene
fre(m)man* (one began to perform wretched deeds; 100b–101a), and the
reversal of fortune is similarly presented when the dragon appears, making the connection between the two very clear (2210b–11). Living with
joy, blessedly, happily, suggests Eden, particularly because this observation
comes on the heels of the scop's song. The poem does not even make
it particularly clear that the song has ended: as the passage is structured,
it seems equally possible to read lines 99–101 as part of the song of the
scop (the Christian audience might) and as the transition to the introduction of Grendel (which would happen, therefore, in line 102). In any case,

Heorot/Eden is at least suggested, making Hrothgar a kind of God figure, making Grendel a kind of serpent/devil figure, making the narrative
seem a little more than just a narrative about one specific hall in Denmark.

3.2   CONCLUSION

Though I have suggested a thorough retelling of Genesis I–XI in Fitt 1
of the poem, it remains a fact that the only three parts of Genesis that are
certainly mentioned in the poem (and mentioned twice) are the killing
of Abel by Cain (106–8, 1255b–65a), the giants who struggled against
God (111–14, 1688b–89a), and the Flood (114; maybe 1260–1b [the
cold currents Grendel's mother is forced to inhabit after Abel's murder];
and 1689b–93, the inscription on the hilt that so puzzles Hrothgar).
Those lines cover Genesis IV, Genesis VI, and Genesis X. In these specific references, the poet explains the origin of Grendel and his ilk and
the general nature of evil and monstrosity.[40] Fitt 1's explanation of the
origin of *fǣhð* (109a) has also been connected by Constance B. Hieatt
(1975, 260) to a larger chiastic structure of repetition, most clearly the
aftermath of the feud with the dragon in Fitts 41 (2948b, 2999a) and
42 (3061b), but also to the renewal of strife after the fight with Grendel
(1380a) and the feuds facing the Danes (2028b). The story of present
conflict is contextualized within an ancient struggle of good and evil,
though there seems to be some confusion here about what kinds of conflict are happening: we have men against men, and men against monsters. In Augustinian terms, we seem to see the city of man (Cain, the
monsters) versus the city of God (Abel) as well as the city of man against
itself, particularly by the end of the poem.[41]

Especially if the other allusions to Genesis are accepted, the biblical
structure of the fitt provides a sense of temporal setting in the generations after the Flood. It suggests, as other aspects of the poem do, that
history is cyclical, that narrative patterns repeat, and the tone of the fitt
guides the narrative toward symbolism and allegory, though I would not
suggest that this is the poet's primary intention.[42] If we return to thinking about the presentation of time, we can now see just how complex the
poet's construction of Fitt 1 is and what associations the poet's handling
of chronology evokes. The fitt moves closer to textual time through
the histories of Beow and Hrothgar, relates the building of Heorot in a
way that at once juxtaposes it with the post-diluvian construction of the
Tower of Babel, and then magnificently collapses all of time into lines

82b–98, working in reverse from a proleptic look at Heorot's burning (which looks forward to the dragon and last days), through Grendel's joyless suffering, to creation at the beginning of time. The beginning of Grendel's reign is juxtaposed with temptation in Eden (the loss of joy), and the fitt seems to flash forward to the devastation after the razing of the tower, again juxtaposed with the land around Heorot, before ending with a chronological presentation of Cain's killing of Abel, the giants' struggle with God, and the Flood. Fitt 1, in other words, accomplishes at the level of the single fitt what the poet does with narrative structure and time in the poem as a whole, introducing the episodic and digressive narrative and its functions.

John Miles Foley, as we saw in Chapter 1, links formula and theme as combinations of form and content, where the formula is the product of metrical template plus traditional vocabulary and the theme is the product of episodic impulse plus traditional actions (1976, 226).[43] The notion of traditional actions as episodic content makes sense from an oral-formulaic point of view, but if the definition were slightly modified to make theme an episodic or digressive impulse plus thematic relevance or a repetition of central themes, we might have a definition that works more specifically for the poem (although that would not at all exclude "traditional actions"). Foley's notion of "initialization" and "termination" are also most useful here, for the boundaries of, for example, his "scourging" theme in *Andreas*, in that case set by repetition of "stave-roots," are fully chiastic, again showing the interaction of different levels of formula. Foley further observes that initialization and termination may be seen as markers of temporal transition, signaling "interfaces" between Eliade's sacred and profane time, where the former is primarily what we see in Fitt 1, "circular … reversible and recoverable, a sort of eternal mythical present."[44] Introducing thematically relevant content through episodes and digressions, as Foley points out in different words, has the effect of presenting that content alongside everything to which it is related: in Fitt 1, if the tradition of the wasteland after the devastation of Babylon is evoked here, and the later description of the mere further suggests that it is, then it and Heorot's surroundings (the mere) take their place in sacred time beside all other poisoned places in a way that very much affects the way we read the poem.[45]

Without doubt, too, the narrative is made in Fitt 1 to resonate more with a Christian audience: that audience sees how "God" controls even the pagan world and "knows" what the Danes (and Geats) do not. In other words, in narratological terms, this fitt establishes clearly an extradiegetic level of narrative where, for example, Hrothgar is God, speaking and making promises precisely as God does.[46] In contrast, as we have seen, Hrothgar is also Nimrod, in the same way that Heorot is at once Eden and the Tower of Babel, proximate to the waste of Babylon. Heorot is also a tomb, Beowulf's barrow at the end of the poem. Beowulf becomes Adam; Beowulf is Nimrod, who, after all, is described in *Genesis A* as the ruler of the *yrfestole*: "he moncynnes mæste hæfde/ on þam mældagum mægen and strengo" (he had the greatest might and strength of mankind in those days; 1631–2)[47]; Beowulf is a friend to Hrothgar, standing in relation to Nimrod as the surging wolf of *Solomon and Saturn* II, himself ultimately responsible for the wasteland of the Geats.

NOTES

1. See Orchard (2003a, 94–5) and Kiernan (1996, 268) for tables of the fitts and how they are marked.
2. See, for example, Carrigan (1967), Howlett (1974; 1997, 504–40), and Owen-Crocker (2000, 133–57).
3. "All of the fitt numbers in *Beowulf* preceding line 1629 in the tenth gathering, from I to XXIII, are in perfect order, and have not been tampered with in any way" (Kiernan 1996, 265).
4. Carrigan, too, sets aside lines 1–188 as the poem's "exordium," suggesting that *wihte gewendan* (186a) "both expresses the plight of the Danes and hints at the central structural principle of the poem's exordium: reversal" (1967, 6).
5. Diller would exclude the lines on the fate of Heorot on the basis that they contain no sequence of events (1984, 82).
6. However, Robinson observes that in the first three lines of the poem "the poet initiates the theme of present time confronting past time" and that "this emphasis on the contrasting time periods is maintained by various devices throughout the remainder of the poem" (1985, 28).
7. See also the observations of Leyerle (1967, 13) and Chapter 1, p. 24. Albert B. Lord would say: "Fact is present in the epic, but relative chronology in the catalogue is confused. Time is telescoped. The past of various times is all assembled into the present performance ... Oral epic presents a composite picture of the past" (Foley 1981, 46).
8. See Chapter 6, p. 196.

9. The central role of the Flood has been argued recently by Anlezark: "The Flood constitutes a mythical underpinning of the action in the poem, which, like Genesis itself, fuses mythical and historical perspectives" (2006, 18).

10. Orchard comments: "There seems no getting rid of the poet's clear references to the biblical tales of Cain and Abel (lines 107-10 and 1261b-1265a) and the subsequent story of the Flood (lines 1260-1b and 1688b-1693) without doing irreparable damage to the transmitted text" (2003a, 131).

11. All quotations from the poem are from Fulk et al. (2008). All translations are my own.

12. See Orchard (2003a, 274–5, 313) and Chapter 2.

13. The manuscript has *pancolmod wer*, which Doane (2013) now emends to *pancolmod þare* (referring thus to Thare, father of Abraham).

14. All quotations from *Genesis A* (I have silently added some capitalization and punctuation) are from Doane (2013); all translations are mine.

15. Such a structure has been called a "double envelope," in which "the central repetition divides the overall envelope into two parts, enclosing separate but parallel developments—in this case, Danish prosperity as against the resentment of the exiled monster" (Hieatt 1975, 250).

16. Hieatt draws attention to *onwoc* (56b), *wocun* (60a), *wæcnan* (85b), *onwocon* (111b), and the progression of objects for the different forms of the verb (1975, 250).

17. One could argue, however, that this is really three specific races, three Germanic words gathered under the Latin (via Greek) *gigantas* that makes specific the link to Genesis VI.4.

18. Howlett devotes many pages to counting lines and words and analyzing the structure of both the prologue and Fitt 1, and he includes this observation about the four children of Healfdene and the four types of monsters (1997, 505–14).

19. Bessinger notes that the parallels have "one stunning climactic adaptation, the work of a master," and that is that the "we should praise God" at the opening of the hymn becomes the *herian ne cuðon* (182b) of the Danes (1974, 97).

20. In fact, each of the first three units of the poem has a parallel scene. In Fitt 2, word of Grendel's activities spreads to the "sons of men" (149b–54a).

21. See Chapter 2, p. 56.

22. Genesis XI.4; *Genesis A* 1666b.

23. See Brooks (1961, ll.666–69a).

24. The half-line *lixte se leoma* is repeated in the moment that Grendel's mother falls (1570a), a wonderful nod at once to the reestablishment of joy in the hall and the ever-looming flame that shall yet consume it.

25. See Shippey (1969, 6).
26. The story is Panzer's Variant 114, in which a king and his sons come to a valley of gold. The eldest son begs for a house there, and the king, despite his misgivings, gathers builders from the city who are to erect an estate in just three days. Midnight of the first night, however, brings a terrible noise, and the problems thus begin (Panzer 1910, 96ff; the connection to *Beowulf* is made on 257n1, as pointed out in Klaeber 1996, 119).
27. Klaeber (1996, 42).
28. Even the name Scyld Scefing points to two different traditions, a martial "Shield" and an agrarian "Sheaf," or, as Tolkien puts it, the "heraldic and the mythical": "[The poet] was blending the vague and fictitious warlike glory of the eponymous ancestor of the conquering house with the more mysterious, far older and more poetical myth of the mysterious arrival of the babe, the corn-god or the culture hero his descendant, at the beginning of a people's history" (2014, 138–9). The separate traditions of Scyld and the interweaving of genealogies are techniques of layering that Quint has recently identified also in Virgil's treatment of Dido: "Virgil self-consciously layers his own invented story of Dido over the older 'true' story of the founding queen of Carthage, a demonstration of how later history rewrites the past but also (here criticizing, on its own terms, the earlier story of a chaste Dido) an explanation of the demographic limitations that eventually doomed the Carthaginian empire" (2018, xiv).
29. Asser has "Seth" where we would expect "Scef" and "Seth" also where we would expect him as the son of Adam. The most relevant passages are gathered in Garmonsway et al. (1968, 118–19). For all the texts related to Scyld and Scef and a discussion of their importance across all the works in which they appear, see Bruce (2002).
30. Noah is 600 years old when the Flood comes (Genesis VII.6), but lives another 350 years after the Flood (Genesis IX.28).
31. Genesis does not openly state that Nimrod is responsible for the building of the tower, though the connection is widely accepted (much like the fall of the angels and Satan's role in the temptation in Eden). In Wulfstan's *De falsis deis*, for example, we find: "Nembroð ond ða entas worhton þone wundorlican stypel æfter Noes flode" ("Nimrod and the giants built that strange tower after Noah's flood"); Bethurum (1957, XII.8–9). On the tradition, see Menner (1938, 335–42).
32. Anlezark (2009). I have silently emended Anlezark's capitalization of *wulf*; the translation is mine.
33. See Chapter 4, p. 109 and p. 145n35, on the significance of poison in the context of the dragon fight.
34. Anlezark notes some interesting parallels in language between *Solomon and Saturn II* 47–51 and *Beowulf* 508–12: "This range of coincidence

[which includes some other excellent points of correspondence] gives weight to a possible connection between Wulf and Beowulf" (2011, 239).

35. For a lengthy comparison of the two poems and a discussion of the tradition of "poisoned places," see Anlezark (2007).

36. The relationship between the three works seems to rest with the analysis of Wright: "If no single one of these details proves that the *Beowulf*-poet drew independently on the *Visio S. Pauli*, the cumulative weight of the parallels I have listed (none of which occurs in Blickling XVI) supports the presumption that he did" (1993, 136). For more on the *Visio Pauli*, Blickling XVI, and *Beowulf*, see Chapter 4, pp. 130–4.

37. This was emended in early editions to *faunos ficarios* (figgy-fauns), which, though it appears in no manuscripts, does make sense here and perhaps ought to be what is understood by "fools of the fig-trees." See, for example, the *Liber monstrorum* I.5 (from Isidore's *Etymologiae* VIII.ix.87), in which the *fauni* are *siluicolae (homines)* (Orchard 2003b, 260). The fauns are half-human and half-goat.

38. This could be "typhoons," "whirlwinds," or it could be related to the giant Typhoeus (Typhon) of classical mythology, whose name becomes synonymous with "gigantic monster" and who is the father of many monstrous hybrids with his half-snake, half-woman spouse Echidna. Most significant among them is probably Scylla, and Echidna is probably also the mother of the Sphinx. Kaske has linked Grendel's mother to the monsters of classical tradition, particularly sirens (1971, 421–31); see also Orchard on Typhoeus and sirens, both of which figure in the *Liber monstrorum* and have different ties to the poem (2003b, 94, 100).

39. One might be tempted to consider *The Wanderer* in this context as well: the *eald enta geweorc* being laid waste by the *ielda scieppend* and becoming *idel* (85–7) and the earth itself becoming empty (110). Liuzza, in fact, has connected *The Wanderer* with the original "ruin" of the Tower of Babel and suggested how the episode is "elegant[ly] elaborate[ed]" in *Genesis A* (2003, 1).

40. Menner would connect the Tower of Babel to other apocryphal traditions of the origin of the monstrous races: "The scattering of evil spirits throughout the world after the destruction of the Tower of Babel is strangely reminiscent of ... the belief that the demons and monsters of the world were the evil descendants of Cain" (1938, 337).

41. See further Chapter 4, pp. 146–7n50.

42. Thus, while I would not suggest the poem be read allegorically in any sustained way, I find the poem does not disagree with some allegorical readings. For example, consider the view of Goldsmith: "In the history of one man's battles, the poet also creates an image of the battle of mankind

sub specie aeternitatis. When one reflects on the story in this way, Heorot recalls Babylon; the giants in the waters, the proud of the earth cast down into the depths of hell; the dragon's gold, the glory of the world with its *calix aureus Babylon*; the great dragon enlarges into the Ancient Enemy himself, whose poison has infected humankind, and who is *auctor mortis* as God is *auctor uitae*" (1970, 144). Anlezark has argued that the Flood is part of the "pattern of water and fire running through the *Beowulf*": "These two elements, inseparable in the medieval imagination from the twinning of ancient Flood and future apocalypse, are presented in the poem as a mythic backdrop against which Beowulf's own struggles must be understood" (2006, 19).

43. See also Chapter 1, pp. 19–20.
44. Eliade (1959, 70), cited in Foley (1976, 227, n. 26). Eliade, of course, is contrasting the "religious man" and the "nonreligious man"; the latter will feel different "temporal rhythms," but the former experiences (and these words work well for *Beowulf*) "intervals of time that ... have no part in the temporal duration that precedes and follows them, that have a wholly different structure and origin" (1959, 71).
45. As Foley puts it in his *Andreas* example, "the impression of form upon content (of the episodic impulse upon traditional actions) places the three scourgings in the sacred time continuum that contains all mythic scourgings" (1976, 227-9).
46. That is, Hrothgar's promises to Beowulf (660b–61 and 949b–50) echo very closely God's promise to Adam and Eve in Eden (Genesis II.16–17) as paraphrased in *Genesis B* (235–6), and, to a lesser extent, God's promise to Noah in *Genesis A* (1532–33a) that, among other things, the Flood will not come again (Fox 2007, 44).
47. Orchard has made this connection between Nimrod and Beowulf on the basis of their respective positions as the strongest men of their days (2003a, 167).

REFERENCES

Adriaen, Marcus (ed.). 1963. *S. Hieronymi presbyteri commentarorium in Esaiam*, CCSL 73–73A. V.xiii.20–22. Turnhout: Brepols.
Anlezark, Daniel. 2006. *Water and Fire: The Myth of the Flood in Anglo-Saxon England*. Manchester: Manchester University Press.
Anlezark, Daniel. 2007. Poisoned Places: The Avernian Tradition in Old English Poetry. *Anglo-Saxon England* 36: 103–126.
Anlezark, Daniel. 2009. *The Old English Dialogues of Solomon and Saturn*. Anglo-Saxon Texts 7. Cambridge: D. S. Brewer.

Anlezark, Daniel. 2011. All at Sea: Beowulf's Marvellous Swimming. In *Myths, Legends, and Heroes: Essays on Old Notes and Old English Literature in Honour of John McKinnell*, ed. Daniel Anlezark, 225–241. Toronto: University of Toronto Press.

Bessinger, Jess B., Jr. 1974. Homage to Caedmon and Others: A Beowulfian Praise Song. In *Old English Studies in Honour of John C. Pope*, ed. Robert B. Burlin and Edward B. Irving, Jr., 91–106. Toronto: University of Toronto Press.

Bethurum, Dorothy. 1957. *The Homilies of Wulfstan*. Oxford: Clarendon Press.

Bonjour, Adrien. 1950. *The Digressions in Beowulf*. Oxford: Basil Blackwell.

Brandes, Herman (ed.). 1885. *Visio S. Pauli: ein Beitrag zur Visionslitteratur mit einem deutschen und zwei lateinischen Texten*, 75–80. Halle: Max Niemeyer.

Brooks, Kenneth R. (ed.). 1961. *Andreas and the Fates of the Apostles*. Oxford: Clarendon Press.

Bruce, Alexander M. 2002. *Scyld and Scef: Expanding the Analogues*. New York: Routledge.

Carrigan, Eamonn. 1967. Structure and Thematic Development in *Beowulf*. *Proceedings of the Royal Irish Academy* 66: 1–51.

Creed, Robert P. 1961. On the Possibility of Criticizing Old English Poetry. *Texas Studies in Language and Literature* 3: 97–106.

Diller, Hans-Jürgen. 1984. Contiguity and Similarity in the *Beowulf* Digressions. In *Medieval Studies Conference, Aachen, 1983*, ed. Wolf-Dietrich Bald and Horst Weinstock, 71–83. Frankfurt: Peter Lang.

Doane, A.N. (ed.). 2013. *Genesis A: A New Edition, Revised*. Tempe, AZ: Arizona Center for Medieval and Renaissance Studies.

Eliade, Mircea. 1959. *The Sacred and the Profane: The Nature of Religion*, trans. Willard R. Trask. New York: Harcourt, Brace, and World.

Foley, John Miles. 1976. Formula and Theme in Old English Poetry. In *Oral Literature and the Formula*, ed. Benjamin A. Stolz and Richard S. Shannon, III, 207–232. Ann Arbor: Centre of Coordination of Ancient and Modern Studies, University of Michigan.

Foley, John Miles. 1981. Introduction: The Oral Theory in Context. In *Oral Traditional Literature: A Festschrift for Albert Bates Lord*, ed. Foley, 27–122. Columbus, OH: Slavica.

Fox, Michael. 2007. Origins in the English Tradition. In *The Oxford Handbook of English Literature and Theology*, ed. Andrew W. Hass, David Jasper, and Elisabeth Jay, 35–53. Oxford: Oxford University Press.

Fulk, R.D., Robert E. Bjork, and John D. Niles (eds.). 2008. *Klaeber's Beowulf*, 4th ed. Toronto: University of Toronto Press.

Garmonsway, G.N., Jacqueline Simpson, and Hilda Ellis Davidson. 1968. *Beowulf and Its Analogues*. London: J. M. Dent and Sons.

Godden, Malcolm. 1991. Biblical Literature: The Old Testament. In *The Cambridge Companion to Old English Literature*, ed. Malcolm Godden and Michael Lapidge, 206–226. Cambridge: Cambridge University Press.

Goldsmith, Margaret E. 1970. *The Mode and Meaning of Beowulf.* London: The Athlone Press.

Hieatt, Constance B. 1975. Envelope Patterns and the Structure of *Beowulf. English Studies in Canada* 1: 249–265.

Howlett, David R. 1974. Form and Genre in *Beowulf. Studia Neophilologica* 46: 309–325.

Howlett, David R. 1997. *British Books in Biblical Style.* Dublin: Four Courts Press.

Kaske, R.E. 1971. *Beowulf* and the Book of Enoch. *Speculum* 46: 421–431.

Kiernan, Kevin. 1996. *Beowulf and the Beowulf Manuscript*, rev ed. Ann Arbor: University of Michigan Press.

Klaeber, Friedrich. 1996. *The Christian Elements in Beowulf*, trans. Paul Battles. *OEN Subsidia* 24. Kalamazoo: Medieval Institute Publications.

Lapidge, Michael. 2001. *Beowulf* and Perception. *Proceedings of the British Academy* 111: 61–97.

Leyerle, John. 1967. The Interlace Structure of *Beowulf. University of Toronto Quarterly* 36: 1–17.

Liuzza, Roy. 2003. The Tower of Babel: *The Wanderer* and the Ruins of History. *Studies in the Literary Imagination* 36 (1): 1–35.

Marsden, Richard (ed.). 2008. *The Old English Heptateuch and Ælfric's Libellus de ueteri testament et nouo*, vol. 1: Introduction and Text, EETS os 330. Oxford: Oxford University Press.

Menner, Robert J. 1938. Nimrod and the Wolf in the Old English *Solomon and Saturn. JEGP* 37 (3): 332–345.

Niles, John D. 1983. *Beowulf: The Poem and Its Tradition.* Cambridge: Harvard University Press.

Orchard, Andy. 2003a. *A Critical Companion to Beowulf.* Cambridge: D. S. Brewer.

Orchard, Andy. 2003b. *Pride and Prodigies: Studies in the Monsters of the Beowulf-Manuscript*, rev. paperback ed. Toronto: University of Toronto Press.

Owen-Crocker, Gale. 2000. *The Four Funerals in Beowulf and the Structure of the Poem.* Manchester: Manchester University Press.

Panzer, Friedrich. 1910. *Studien zur germanischen Sagengeschichte, I. Beowulf.* Munich: Oskar Beck.

Quint, David. 2018. *Virgil's Double Cross: Design and Meaning in the Aeneid.* Princeton: Princeton University Press.

Robinson, Fred C. 1985. *Beowulf and the Appositive Style.* Knoxville, TN: University of Tennessee Press.

Shippey, Thomas A. 1969. The Fairy-Tale Structure of *Beowulf. Notes and Queries* 16: 2–11.

Silverstein, Theodore (ed.). 1935. *Visio Sancti Pauli: The History of the Apocalypse in Latin together with Nine Texts.* London: Christophers.

Tolkien, J.R.R. 1983. *Beowulf:* The Monsters and the Critics. In *The Monsters and the Critics and Other Essays*, ed. Christopher Tolkien, 5–48. London: George Allen and Unwin.

Tolkien, J.R.R. 2014. *Beowulf: A Translation and Commentary.* London: HarperCollins.

Wright, Charles D. 1993. *The Irish Tradition in Old English Literature*, CSASE 6. Cambridge: Cambridge University Press.

CHAPTER 4

The Digressive Formula:
The Sigemund-Heremod Digression

Observing that J. R. R. Tolkien's 1936 Sir Israel Gollancz Memorial Lecture at the British Academy on the monsters and the critics of *Beowulf* changed the course of *Beowulf* scholarship has become common. Tolkien's well-known complaint, of course, was that the poem, though the object of much worthy scholarly attention, was nevertheless "poor in criticism, criticism … directed to the understanding of a poem as a poem" (1983, 5). Responding directly to those (and primarily, in fact, to W. P. Ker and R. W. Chambers) who might assess the weakness of the poem as its tendency to place "irrelevances in the centre and the serious things on the outer edges" (Ker 1904, 252–3; qtd. in Tolkien 1983, 11), Tolkien uses the image of a man who inherits a field full of stones from an old hall. The man decides to build a tower using some old stones from the field, but his friends, upon seeing the tower, do not bother even to climb it before proclaiming their recognition of the old stones and pushing the tower over to look for clues about their origin. Some even forget the stones completely, and dig underneath where the tower had been: "They all sa[y]: 'This tower is most interesting.' But they also sa[y] (after pushing it over): 'What a muddle it is in!'" (1983, 8). The observation of R. W. Chambers helps to identify some of these stones, for Chambers comments that "the folk-tale is a good servant, but a bad master: it has been allowed in *Beowulf* to usurp the place of honour, and to drive into episodes and digressions the things which should be the main stuff of a well-conducted epic." To use Tolkien's allegory, then, one set of stones could be the folktale, the core narrative of the monsters and the monster-fights that will be addressed in the next chapter, and another could be the "episodes and digressions," material like the allusion to the story of Ingeld, which Chambers feels is a story "old heroic poets" would not have sold "for a wilderness of dragons" (1925, xxvi; qtd. in Tolkien 1983, 11–13).[1]

Since Tolkien's lecture, many of these other stones have continued to live an existence somehow separate from the poem and usually under the description given to them by Chambers, as "episodes and digressions," even if early theories that these interruptions in the main flow of the narrative were evidence of the piecing together of originally separate lays have been largely dismissed.[2] Klaeber's third edition, while admitting the unity of the poem, hardly gives an enthusiastic account of the incorporation of this material, and he still sees the episodes and digressions as "subjects of intensely absorbing interest" that "serve as foil to a story which in itself is of decidedly inferior weight" (1950, liii–lv). At the same time, Adrien Bonjour attempted to survey all the material in the poem that might be considered digressional or episodic, for, in his words, "it is perhaps no exaggeration to say that few other features are more characteristic of the *Beowulf* than the use of numerous digressions and episodes" (1950, xi). Bonjour attempts to distinguish episodes and digressions by the degree to which the main narrative breaks (an episode is "a real whole," yet "merged in the main narrative," whereas a digression is "more of an adjunction and generally entails a sudden break in the narrative"; 1950, xi), but his distinction is not precisely maintained even in his own book. Hans-Jürgen Diller reduces the whole category to "digression" and offers this definition: "A digression is a piece of text which interrupts the chronological progress of the surrounding story or argument by telling or summarizing sequences of events outside the main story. The topic is not identical with that of the surrounding text" (1984, 73).[3] More useful, perhaps, is to recall our modified definition in the previous chapter, effectively grouping episodes and digressions together as an unspecified theme, where the episodic or digressive impulse is the form and the content is a thematic relevance or repetition. At the same time—and this is true for the Sigemund-Heremod digression, but especially true for what Bonjour would call allusions instead of episodes, like the burning of Heorot and the reference to Hama—the episodic and digressive material relies on the audience to fill in gaps in content and meaning. Elizabeth Minchin's study of Homer and memory, though again conducted in the context of the oral tradition, is relevant to these stories embedded within story:

If speakers can assume that other people have access to the same scripts as their own, it will not be necessary to provide microscopic detail of the action sequence they are referring to or of every causal connection within it. They can leave it to the audience to refer to the script which has been invoked and, therefore, to fill in the intervening steps, the causal connections, which make discourse coherent. (2001, 13–14)

Minchin's view of how the audience "fills in the intervening steps" provides process and agency for Foley's idea of the "sacred time continuum" and theme.[4]

Bonjour identifies perhaps nineteen episodes and digressions, and the number of such passages, now generally known only as digressions, has today settled around twenty-eight, encompassing about 700 lines or over 20% of the poem as a whole (Fulk et al. 2008, lxxxiv–vi; Bjork 1997, 201). Tolkien's view of the poem's unity was supported by Bonjour[5] and later by John Leyerle, who states emphatically that "there are no digressions in *Beowulf*" (1967, 13). The most recent editors of the poem suggest that the "critical consensus" is now "that the episodes and digressions are integral to an aesthetic mode unlike that admired in the classical and neoclassical traditions" (Fulk et al. 2008, lxxxv). Bonjour divides the digressions into three main categories: "digressions concerning episodes of Beowulf's life and Geatish history," "historical, or legendary, digressions not connected with Beowulf and the Geats," and "digressions of a biblical character" (1950, ix). The final category is distinctive, and we have already seen how the *scop*'s song of creation (90b–98) and references to Cain and the giants' struggle with God before the Flood (107b–114; 1261b–65a; 1688b–93) are digressions that are central to the understanding of the poem as a whole. The digressions concerning episodes of Beowulf's life and Geatish history are mainly found in the second half of the poem (one notable exception being the Unferth episode), but an episode such as Hygelac's Frisian raid demonstrates just how sophisticated these breaks from the main narrative can be. Details of the raid are given in four separate passages, one in the first half of the poem and three in the second, and appear proleptically and analeptically in three different voices (the narrator, Beowulf, and Wiglaf).[6] Such digressions often give "useful information, particularly about chief characters" (Fulk et al. 2008, lxxxv), but Catherine Karkov and Robert T. Farrell note that historical digressions and instructional gnomes—another substantial category of content in the poem—often work together to link specific historical examples to the universal, to the eternal, and to what ought to be (1990, 306).[7] For obvious reasons, the historical or legendary digressions not connected with Beowulf and the Geats cluster in the first half of the poem. That part of the digressive material that comes from heroic legend, as Arthur Brodeur points out, is only found in the first part of the poem, and Brodeur suggests that the material, which certainly includes the story of Sigemund, "serves as enrichment or adornment, or affords characterization by way of compliment or contrast, or drives home a specific point, or—in Tolkien's words—gives the 'sense of perspective, of antiquity with a greater and yet darker antiquity behind'" (1960, 133). Indeed, the principle of contrast is a feature often noted in the digressions and episodes, and Fulk, Bjork, and Niles further classify that contrast as linked to "human deportment in the face of *edwenden* [reversal]," a key feature also of the poem as whole (2008, lxxxv).[8] Finally, Ward Parks proposes we read the digressions not only for their relationship to the rest of the poem, but also for how they constitute "the visible impingement of interperformativity upon performance," the effects of a series of performative acts (1989, 32).[9]

The Sigemund-Heremod digression introduces us to the compositional processes of the scop. The scop has sung before—we have heard a song of creation and we have heard the long Finn episode—but here we seem to see a song being composed, to witness the interlacing of characters and themes that is characteristic of the entire poem.[10] Klaeber suggests that the digression, at least as it begins with the story of Sigemund, is designed to raise Beowulf "to the rank of pre-eminent Germanic heroes" (1950, 158); and Bonjour feels that the whole is "definitely intended to praise Beowulf" (1950, 47). Robert E. Kaske, although arguing for a specific thematic message, opines that "it seems hardly open to question … that the basic theme of the whole Sigemund-Heremod passage is the contrast between Sigemund, who preserved his fame by continuing deeds of prowess and courage, and Heremod, who lost his fame when his prowess and courage somehow died" (1959, 490). Scott Gwara feels that the passage, more specifically, "predicts Beowulf's destiny by describing two possible paths for the potential *wrecca* that Beowulf represents" (2008, 59); and Mark Griffith complicates earlier readings of the digression by suggesting that the positive comparison of Beowulf to Sigemund is wholly problematic (1995, 40). For now, the assessment of Constance B. Hieatt will suffice: the

Sigemund-Heremod digression "establishes a thoroughly complex set of exact parallels and contrasts intertwining all three characters and including direct comparisons between Sigemund and Heremod" (1984, 175). As we shall see, the digression also does much more.

4.1   BACKGROUND

Andy Orchard has observed that *Beowulf* contains over seventy named characters, almost half of whom appear only once (2003a, 169). Names such as Hama and Thryth, if Thryth is even the correct form of the name, have left almost no trace outside of the poem, although the same could be said for the poem's hero. Though the characters of the Sigemund-Heremod digression are more familiar to a modern audience, better known outside of the poem, in fact, than Beowulf himself, what an Anglo-Saxon audience might have known of Sigemund (named twice), Fitela (named twice), Wæls (named once), and Heremod (named once in the digression, twice in the poem) is difficult to reconstruct. Although readers generally refer to Old Norse sources for relatively full accounts of the Völsungs and their dragon-slayer, Sigurðr, son of Sigmundr, some earlier sources have been suggested. In a connection Jesse L. Byock calls "highly conjectural," the legend of Sigurðr has been linked to the Germanic chieftain Arminius and the Battle of Teutoburg Forest (9 CE), a battle in which Arminius destroyed three Roman legions led by Quintilius Varus (1990, 22–4).[11] Gregory of Tours' *Historia Francorum* has much more intriguing evidence of a King Sigimund of the Burgundians (he ruled from 516–523) who, caught up in a dispute between his son and his new wife (his son's step-mother, therefore), is persuaded to oversee the strangling of his son, drunk with wine; Sigimund afterward laments his actions bitterly, and a dispute between in-laws ensues (Krusch and Levison 1951, III.5–6; Finch 1965, xxxiv–v). The *Historia* has also been suggested to have an early version of Sigurðr in the Frankish king Sigibert (535–575), a king who marries the Visigoth Brunhilda, which is really the only parallel to the Völsung legend besides more familial strife (Krusch and Levison 1951, IV.23–51; Byock 1990, 24–5).[12]

Even the early Norse sources fail to illuminate the digression in any substantial way.[13] Perhaps the earliest reference (second half of the ninth century?) to any part of the story is in Bragi Boddason's *Ragnarsdrápa*, in verses preserved in Snorri Sturluson's *Skáldskaparmál*:

Þá er forns Litar flotna
á fangboða ǫngli
hrøkkviáll of hrokkinn
hekk Vǫlsunga drekku. (Faulkes 1998, I.50)

When on the hook of the old Lit's men's [giants'] fight-challenger [Thor]
hung the coiling eel [Midgard serpent] of the Völsungs' drink [poison]
coiled. (Faulkes 1987, 106)

Other early evidence comes from related verses of the tenth century, as
both Sigmundr and Hermóðr receive gifts from Óðinn, and both, along
with Sinfjötli, seem to be honored guests in Valhöll, for in similar passages in *Eiríksmál* (just after 954) and *Hákonarmál* (probably just after
960, and no doubt modeled after the former), old heroes are sent by
Óðinn to greet newcomers to the hall:

Sigmundr ok Sinfjötli,
rísið snarliga
ok gangið í gǫgn grami,
inn þú bjóð,
ef Eiríkr séi;
hans es mér nú vón vituð. (*Eiríksmál* 5; Jónsson 1912–15, BI.165)

Sigmundr and Sinfjötli, rise quickly and go meet the king; invite him in if
it is Eiríkr; he it is I hope for now.

Hermóðr ok Bragi,
kvað Hroptatýr [Óðinn],
gangið í gǫgn grami,
þvít konungr ferr,
sás kappi þykkir,
til hallar hinig. (*Hákonarmál* 14; Eyvindr 1912–15, BI.59)

Hermóðr and Bragi, said Hroptatýr, go meet the king, because a king who
is thought a champion comes to the hall.

Though, as Roberta Frank reports, no Norse skald alludes to Sigurðr's
"dragon fight, dragon-heart roast, sword, horse, Brynhildr, Rhine gold
or any of that before the last half of the tenth century, and in most cases
not until the early eleventh" (1981, 130), we do then find the poet

Þórfinnr munnr (c. 1030) mentioning, somewhat obliquely, the dragon fight and possibly the roasting of the dragon's heart:

> Geisli stendr til grundar
> Gunnar jarðar munna;
> ofan fellr blóð á báðar
> benskeiðr, en gramr reiðisk.
> Hritisk hjǫrr í brjósti
> hringi grœnna lyngva,
> en folkþorinn fylkir
> ferr við steik at leika. (*Lausavísur* 1)

The sunbeam of the land of Gunnr [a sword] sticks in the ground of the mouth; blood falls down on both wound-ships, and the warrior becomes angry. The sword shakes in the breast of the ring of green heathers [a serpent[14]], and the valiant king goes to play at roasting meat. (Adapted from Whaley 2012, 845)

Scenes from Sigurðr's portion of the legend appear with relative frequency in English and Manx sculpture, but again only in the late tenth and eleventh centuries (Frank 1981, 130–1).[15] A possible eleventh-century depiction from Winchester of Sigmundr biting off the she-wolf's tongue has also been identified (Biddle 1966, 329–32 and Plate LXIIa).[16]

Later, fuller, sources of the Völsung legend start to appear after the middle of the twelfth century, certainly, and most abundantly in the thirteenth century. In Middle High German, *Das Nibelungenlied* was written probably not later than 1204, but the epic poem has a different tone from the Norse material and divergent content. *Das Nibelungenlied* reads more like a chivalric romance: Sigemund is mentioned only as the father of Siegfried, who is said to be the strongest warrior of all time, to have killed a dragon and bathed in its blood, so treating his skin that no weapon might bite it, and to have won single-handedly the treasure of the Nibelungs and a cloak of invisibility (the *Tarnkappe*) from the dwarf Alberich. The dragon fight and the winning of the gold happen outside of the main narrative, perhaps demonstrating just how well-known the dragon fight already was.[17] The other major poetic source is the *Poetic Edda* (1150–1250?), which contains some eighteen lays on the Völsung material.[18] The *Poetic Edda* was likely a source for the author of *Völsunga saga* (1260–1270), and Snorri Sturluson's *Prose Edda* (1220–1241?)

preserves much of the story, primarily in an extended explanation of the kenning *otrgjǫld* ("otter-payment" for "gold"). Other significant versions of the story occur in *Þiðreks saga af Bern* (again probably in the mid-thirteenth century, in which the story of Theodoric the Ostrogoth [493–526] has the story of the Völsungs woven into it)[19] and the fourteenth-century frame story known as *Nornagests þáttr*, which contains passages from the *Prose Edda* and evidence of knowledge of the *Poetic Edda* and a lost *Sigurðar saga*.[20]

The key features of the Völsung story for the purposes of understanding the Sigemund-Heremod digression are found most fully in *Völsunga saga*. Snorri hardly mentions the early history of the Völsungs, noting only the family immunity (Sigmundr) and resistance (Sigurðr and Sinfjötli) to poison (an observation that introduces the verse from Bragi, quoted above).[21] The genealogy of the Völsungs, as it is traced in the saga, originates the line with Óðinn three generations before Völsungr (OE Wæls), the eponymous ancestor of the Völsungs.[22] Sigmundr is the eldest son of Völsungr and Hljóð, who is a daughter of Hrímnir the giant, and thus Sigmundr is descended on the one hand from Óðinn, and on the other from giants, a fact that is clearly significant in the context of the poem. Sigmundr has a twin sister, Signý, and the two of them are foremost among Völsungr's children. Sigmundr is an Odinic hero: at the wedding feast of his sister, Óðinn buries a sword in a tree and only Sigmundr can pull it out. Signý's husband wants the blade, but Sigmundr refuses to give it up, initiating a feud. The proud Völsungs enter a sure trap, and Völsungr falls while all his sons are captured by Siggeir, his son-in-law. Signý begs that they be put in the stocks, rather than immediately killed, and Siggeir is all too happy to oblige. An old she-wolf (*ylgr*) appears and eats one every night, before, when Sigmundr is the last left, Signý devises the stratagem of smearing Sigmundr's face with honey. When the wolf licks his face, Sigmundr seizes the tongue with his teeth, and the stocks split. Sigmundr escapes and lives as an exile, but Signý tries to help by sending her sons to him. None proves fitting. Signý assumes the shape of a sorceress and sleeps with her brother to conceive Sinfjötli (OE Fitela), making Sigmundr both his father and his uncle. Sinfjötli is hardy enough, and the two men live many years as outlaws and wolves before exacting their revenge. Later, Sinfjötli has a significant verbal duel that is similar in structure to the Unferth/Beowulf episode.[23] Of Sigmundr, the saga observes: "Sigmundr konungr … þykkir verit hafa inn mesti kappi ok konungr í fornum sið" (King Sigmundr

… is thought to have been the greatest champion and king in ancient times; Jónsson 1954b, 134); Sigmundr dies when Óðinn comes for him in battle.

The main facts of Sigurðr's dragon fight are found without major variation in *Reginsmál* (background), *Fáfnismál* (the fight itself), *Skáldskaparmál*, and *Völsunga saga*. In a case of mistaken identity, Loki kills an otter, but the otter turns out to be Otr, the brother of Reginn and Fáfnir. The father of the boys, Hreiðmarr, demands compensation for the killing, and Loki robs a dwarf named Andvari of all his gold, including a last ring upon which Andvari pronounces a curse. Naturally, this bothers Loki not a whit; he dutifully passes on the curse to Hreiðmarr when the gold is handed over. Now, Otr's brothers, Reginn and Fáfnir, demand a share of the gold. When Hreiðmarr refuses, Fáfnir kills him (Reginn reports in *Völsunga saga* that Fáfnir alone does the killing, but Snorri says both brothers were involved). Fáfnir refuses to share the treasure with Reginn. Fáfnir takes his father's helmet of terror (*ægishjálmr*), constructs a lair for himself, and settles in with his cursed gold, now in the form of a serpent (*ormr*).

Reginn fosters Sigurðr, thus standing in for his absent father. Reginn encourages Sigurðr to attack Fáfnir, repairing Sigmundr's sword (*Völsunga saga*)[24] or apparently making a new one (*Reginsmál*; *Skáldskaparmál*), called Gram either way, that he might do so. Each of the accounts of the dragon fight includes the following details: Sigurðr digs a pit or a trench and stabs up at Fáfnir from below; Reginn wants Fáfnir's roasted heart, but Sigurðr tastes it first, comes to understand the language of birds, and listens to their advice to kill Reginn; Sigurðr loads the treasure on his horse, Grani. *Fáfnismál* and *Völsunga saga* add quite a bit of detail, with *Völsunga saga* adding some unique details: Sigurðr expresses doubt about the size of the dragon and Reginn's plan to dig the ditch, and an old man (Óðinn?) appears to advise Sigurðr to dig some extra channels for the blood to run off. Both *Fáfnismál* and *Völsunga saga* incorporate a focus on Fáfnir's poison, with both including a long, riddling dialogue between Sigurðr and the mortally wounded Fáfnir, a dialogue in which, most importantly, Fáfnir twice passes on the curse on the treasure. In fact, as if to emphasize the significance of the dragon's poison and the cursed treasure, both are mentioned twice, in parallel. Finally, like his father, Sigurðr is foremost among champions and chieftains, known in all languages north of Greece for as long as the world might last (Jónsson 1954b, 164).[25]

The tradition that the poet invokes when he, in apparent contrast to Sigemund, mentions Heremod is much more difficult to trace. Heremod appears in several genealogies, including the *Anglo-Saxon Chronicle* for the year 855, and always precedes Scyld, not too many generations after Sceaf/Scef, the ark-born son of Noah. Thus, the *Anglo-Saxon Chronicle*, MS C, Asser's *Vita Ælfredi*, the Norse *Langfeðgatal*, and Snorri's *Prose Edda* all include Heremod/Hermóðr before a Scyld/Skjǫldr, though only the Anglo-Saxon sources trace the line back to Scef and Noah.[26] In Æthelweard's chronicle, Heremod does not appear (the line begins with Scef arriving from across the sea, and his son is Scyld), and in William of Malmesbury's *De gestis regum Anglorum*, Heremodius becomes the father of Sceaf. The confusion about this part of the gene-alogy is reflected in the poem's treatment of Scyld and Heremod, as we have seen, but the genealogies tell us little about how an audience might have understood the Sigemund-Heremod digression. A pas-sage in *Gylfaginning* is similarly difficult to interpret: Hermóðr, son of Óðinn, is sent to Hel to retrieve Baldr, but the test for all creation to weep is foiled, apparently by Loki, and Hermóðr is unsuccessful (Faulkes 1987, 46–8).[27] The connection of this Hermóðr, apparently a god, with the king of the genealogies is, as Chambers reports, "obscure" (1967, 90n2).[28] Even more unlikely is a connection originally made by Klaeber to the Armóðr of *Egils saga einhenda*, a character famous only for having been killed in the tub by Starkaðr the Old. In *Nornagests þáttr*, Starkaðr (right after being bested by Sigurðr) instead kills King Áli in the tub; this Áli would appear to be the Danish king Olo (Oli), plotted against and killed in the tub by Starcatherus because of his cruel and tyrannical rule. Curiously, Olo has such piercing eyes that, even though he is lying helpless in the tub, Starcatherus cannot approach until Olo covers his face; Sigurðr's death scene contains precisely the same motif as Guttormr comes to kill him (Klaeber 1950, 162–4; Saxo 2015, viii.6.2–3; Jónsson 1954b, 190).

In the absence of extra-textual references to Heremod's career, the information that *Beowulf* itself supplies is vital to understanding his pres-ence in the poem. The latter part of the digression (901–15) relates how Heremod fails to live up to the expectations of his people and becomes *to aldorceare*, as his *hild*, *eafoð*, and *ellen* diminish. Heremod had clearly become a common negative exemplum among the Danes, as Hrothgar next mentions his reign in his admonitory speech to Beowulf[29]:

> Ne wearð Heremod swa
> eaforum Ecgwelan, Ar-Scyldingum;
> ne geweox he him to willan ac to wælfealle
> ond to deaðcwalum Deniga leodum;
> breat bolgenmod beodgeneatas,
> eaxlgesteallan, oþ þæt he ana hwearf,
> mære þeoden mondreamum from.
> Ðeah þe hine mihtig God mægenes wynnum,
> eafeþum stepte ofer ealle men,
> forð gefremede, hwæþere him on ferhðe greow
> breosthord blodreow, nallas beagas geaf
> Denum after dome; dreamleas gebad
> Þæt he þæs gewinnes weorc þrowade,
> leodbealo longsum. (1709b-22a)

Heremod was not so [*frofor/help*; a comfort/help] to his people, to the sons of Ecgwala, the Ar-Scyldings; he did not mature for them as a delight, but as slaughter and death for the people of the Danes. Enraged, he killed his table companions, his close warriors, until he went alone, famous chief, from the joys of men, although mighty God had exalted him with the pleasures of strength, with might, over all other men. Still, in his heart he cultivated a blood-thirsty spirit; not at all did he give rings to the Danes on account of glory; he lived joyless, suffered pain for this strife, long-lasting people-bale.

Though he had been exalted over all men by God, Heremod, it seems, grew covetous and killed his *beodgeneatas* and *eaxlgesteallan* before being turned out to wander alone. From this speech, we learn that Heremod was in fact leader of the Scyldings and must, therefore, in accordance with what the genealogies tell us, be placed before Scyld in the Danish line. As Chambers says, "the way in which Heremod is referred to would fit in very well with the supposition that he was the last of a dynasty ... and that it was the death or exile of Heremod which ushered in the time when the Danes were without a prince" (1967, 89).

In Saxo Grammaticus, the father of Scyld (Skyoldus) is not Heremod, but Lotherus, even though the career of Lotherus is appropriate to Heremod's role in *Beowulf*:

Sed nec Lotherus tolerabiliorem regem quam militem egit, ut prorsus insolentia ac scelere regnum auspicari uideretur. Siquidem illustrissimum quemque uita aut opibus spoliare patriamque bonis ciuibus uacuefacere probitatis loco duxit, regni emulos ratus quos nobilitate pares habuerat. Nec diu scelerum impunitus patrie consternatione perimitur, eadem spiritum eripiente, que regnum largita fuerat.

Lother, on the other hand, played the king as intolerably as the soldier, immediately inaugurating his reign with arrogance and crime; he reckoned it a measure of virtue to deprive all his most distinguished subjects of life and wealth and to clear his country of fine citizens, imagining that his equals in birth must be rivals to his throne. Nor did he remain long unpunished for his enormities; he perished in a rebellion of the nation, which snatched away his life as it had formerly bestowed the realm. (Saxo 2015, I.ii.2, pp. 22–3)[30]

In Saxo's reference to *insolentia ac scelere*, one is tempted to see the alliterating pair *fæhðe ond fyrene* (137a, 153a, 879a, 2480a),[31] or at least the blunt *hine* (presumably Heremod) *fyren onwod* (915b), and the focus on the plundering of life and wealth accords more closely with what Hrothgar reports of Heremod's career. In Saxo, too, we learn that Lotherus violently seized power from his brother, Humli (thus the reference to Lotherus' careers as soldier and as king), the kind of familial misbehavior that receives much attention in the poem and that we have seen among the Völsungs.

There are only a few places where the names Sigemund and Heremod can be found in close proximity to one another,[32] and there is little indication what, in the minds of an Anglo-Saxon audience, their relationship might have been (if, in fact, one had existed prior to the minstrel's lay). Perhaps the most tantalizing clue to the stories of Sigemund and Heremod is a single verse in *Hyndluljóð*:

> Biðjum Herjaföðr [Óðinn] í hugum sitja,
> hann geldur og gefur gull verðungu;
> gaf hann Hermóði hjálm ok brynju,
> en Sigmundi sverð að þiggja. (*Hyndluljóð* 2; Briem 1985, 499)

> Let's ask the Host-father [Odin] to sit in good cheer;
> he grants and gives out gold to the worthy;
> he gave Hermód a helmet and corselet,
> and to Sigmund a sword to keep. (Orchard 2011, 250)

Both Sigmundr and Hermóðr receive gifts from Óðinn, and both, along with Sinfjötli, seem to be honored guests in Valhalla, as we saw in the passages from *Eiríksmál* and *Hákonarmál*.

The question remains: why is it Sigemund who slays the dragon in *Beowulf* and not his son, as in all the other sources?[33] First, the *Beowulf*-poet may have had the story right or may have mistaken or misheard his source in transferring the deed to Sigemund.[34] The problem with any such explanation, however, has been pointed out by Andy Orchard: "[T]he setting and manner of Sigemund's otherwise unattested dragon-fight is precisely that of Beowulf's own, fought against a creature from a cave beside the sea" (2003a, 108–9).[35] Far more likely is the suggestion that the poet deliberately transferred the fight to Sigemund, for a few possible reasons. The most convincing of these is that the poet was keen to highlight the uncle/nephew relationship, which is extremely important in the poem as a whole, as we shall see. Less convincing, but still possible, is the aptness of the name: Orchard has also demonstrated just how suitable the name Sigemund ("victory-hand") is at this moment, just after Beowulf has torn off Grendel's arm (2003a, 105, 173).[36] A final distant possibility is that the poet intended to praise a Sigemund about whom next to nothing is known, perhaps the Sigemund who appears among the genealogies of the East Saxon kings (contextual evidence would place this Sigemund in the very early eighth century).[37] In the same way that we have seen the poet adjust the logic of his genealogies and the temporal setting of the poem, I believe the poet here adjusts the Völsung legend better to suit the career of Beowulf, somewhat parallel to how deeds accrue to Odysseus because they fit his character and the narrative (West 2014, 7–13).

4.2   READING THE SIGEMUND-HEREMOD DIGRESSION

In order to appreciate as much as possible the function of the digression in the poem, quoting it in full is necessary. Without listing every parallel, I have attempted to demonstrate how and where the digression interacts with itself, with the rest of the poem, and with the Old English corpus by encoding those relationships in the text. Bold text is used for words significant within the passage; italicized text is for words significant in the poem as a whole; and underlined text is for words significant in the corpus outside *Beowulf*, though I have limited this to a particular set of circumstances. A majuscule "x" is used to indicate manuscript punctuation.

Hwilum heaþorofe hleapan leton,	[867b, 916a]
865 on *geflit faran* *fealwe mearas*,	[855b; 916b-17a]
ðær him foldwegas fægere þuhton,	
cystum cuðe. **Hwilum** cyninges þegn,	[923a; *uncuþ*: 876b, 1410b, 2214a; 864a, 916a]
guma gilphlæden, gidda gemyndig,	
se ðe **eal fela** ealdgesegena	[883a]
870 *worn gemunde*, word oþer fand	[2114b]
soðe gebunden; secg eft ongan	
sið Beowulfes snyttrum styrian,	[877b, 908a, 1971a, 2532b, 2541b]
ond on sped wrecan spel gerade,	
wordum wrixlan; *welhwylc gecwæð*,	[366a; 987b]
875 þæt he fram Sigemunde[s] secgan hyrde	
ellendædum, *uncuþes fela*,	[900a; 867a, etc.]
Wælsinges gewin, wide *siðas*,	[872a, 908a]
þara þe gumena bearn gearwe ne wiston,X	
fæhðe ond fyrena, buton Fitela mid hine,	[137a, 153a, 2480a]
880 þonne he swulces hwæt secgan wolde,	
eam his nefan, swa hie a wæron	[1117a, 2170b]
æt niða gehwam nydgesteallan;X	
hæfdon *eal fela* **eotena cynnes**	[869a, 2511b; 902b]
sweordum gesæged. Sigemunde gesprong	
885 *æfter deaðdæge* *dom* unlytel,X	[187a; 954b, 1720a, 2820b (*soðfæstra dom*)]
syþðan <u>wiges heard</u> wyrm acwealde,	[*Andreas* 839a]
hordes hyrde. He <u>under harne stan</u>,	[1415a, 2553b, 2744b, etc.]
æþelinges bearn ana geneðde	[910a, 1408b, 2597a, 3170a; 145a, 425b, 433a, 1714a, 2498a, 2533b, 2541a, 2643b, 2657b, 2876a; 1656b, 2511b]
frecne **dæde**, ne wæs him Fitela mid;X	[1359a, 1378a, 1691a, 2250a, 2537a, 2689a; 876a, 900a]
890 hwæþre him gesælde, ðæt þæt swurd *þurhwod*	[915b; 1567b]
wrætlicne wyrm, þæt hit on wealle ætstod,	
dryhtlic iren; **draca morðre swealt**.X	[2782b]
Hæfde aglæca **elne** gegongen,	[3b, 876a, 900a, 1493a, 2861b]
þæt he beahhordes *brucan moste*	[2241a, 3100b]
895 *selfes dome*: sæbat gehleod,	[2147b, 2776a]
bær on bearm scipes beorhte frætwa,	[35, 214, 2775]
Wælses eafera; **wyrm hat gemealt**.X	[892b, 1608a, 1615a, 2628a]
Se wæs *wreccena* wide mærost	[1137b, 2613a, (109b, etc.)]

ofer werþeode, *wigendra hleo,*	[429b, 1972b, 2337b]
900 **ellendædum** *–he þæs ær onðah–*	[876a, etc.; 8b]
siððan Heremodes hild sweðrode,	
eafoð ond ellen. **He mid eotenum**	[602a, 2349a; 905b, 913b; *eotenas.*
wearð	112a, etc.]
on feonda geweald forð forlacen,	[808a]
snude forsended. Hine sorhwylmas	
905 lemedon to lange; **he his leodum wearð,**	[902b, 913b]
eallum æþellingum to aldorceare;X	[913b]
swylce oft bemearn *ærran mælum*	[2237a, 3035a]
swiðferhþes *sið* snotor ceorl monig,	[872a, 877b]
se þe him bealwa to bote gelyfde,	
910 þæt þæt *ðeodnes bearn geþeon scolde,*	[888a, etc.; 900b, etc.]
fæderæþelum onfon, folc gehealdan,	
hord ond hleoburh, hæleþa rice,	
eþel Scyldinga. He þær **eallum wearð**	[902b, 905b, 906a]
mæg Higelaces, manna cynne,	
915 freondum gefægra; hine fyren **onwod.**X	[890b]
Hwilum flitende **fealwe** stræte	[864a, 867b; 865b]
mearum mæton. (864-917a)	[865b]

Sometimes, where the paths seemed fair to them, and were known to be choice, those brave in battle allowed their bay horses to gallop and race in competition. Sometimes, a servant of the king, a man full of high language, mindful of songs, who remembered a great number of old stories, found other words, faithfully bound; the man afterwards began to retell with experience the exploit of Beowulf, and with skill to utter an apt tale, to alternate words. He related everything that he had heard said about the brave deeds of Sigemund: many unknown things, the struggles of the Wælsings, broad journeys, feud and crimes, things that the children of men did not at all know, except Fitela who was with him, when he would say something of such, the uncle to his nephew. They were always thus, at every battle, companions in need; they had laid low with swords a great number of the race of the giants. After his death-day, no small glory accrued to Sigemund, because the one brave in battle killed a serpent, keeper of a hoard. He, son of a noble, risked the daring deed alone under the hoar stone:[38] Fitela was not with him. Still it befell him that the sword pushed through the wondrous serpent until it stood fixed in the wall–noble iron; the dragon died from that assault. The attacker had, with courage, brought it about that he might enjoy the ring-hoard at his own judgment. He, son of Wæls, loaded a sea-boat, bore into the bosom of the ship bright treasures: the serpent melted in its own heat.

He[39] was the most widely renowned of adventurers, protector of warriors, over the nations, for his brave deeds—he had prospered in this—after the fight, strength, and courage of Heremod diminished. He, among Jutes [or giants], was betrayed into the power of enemies [or fiends], quickly killed. Surging sorrows oppressed him too long. To his people, to all nobles, he became a source of mortal care; likewise, often, in earlier times, many a wise man bemoaned the exploit of the strong-minded one, those men who had counted on him as a remedy for evils, that the lord's son should prosper, take after fatherly nobility, rule the people, the hoard and the stronghold, the kingdom of men, the homeland of the Scyldings. To all, to the race of men, the kinsman of Hygelac there became more dear to friends; sin waded into him. Sometimes, those competing measured the dusky street with horses.

In general, the "artfulness" of the passage is immediately apparent.[40] The repetition of *hwilum* (864a; 916a) and the echoes in general of the beginning of the digression at the end signal what has traditionally been called an "envelope pattern." What makes this different from a simple envelope such as *Dryhtsele dynede ... Reced hlynsode* (767–70)[41] is, at first glance, the internal repetition of *hwilum* (867b). Orchard, therefore, connects this with the well-known *com ... com ... com* pattern (702b–727) in Grendel's approach to Heorot, calling it "incremental repetition" (2003a, 78–9). The effect here, however, rather than the building terror of Grendel's approach, is to juxtapose the two activities: sometimes they race horses, and sometimes they listen to the scop, and the sense of ritual or at least expected and customary behavior is reinforced by other *hwilum* passages (2016b–24a; 2107–13a). As they listen to the scop, they hear about Beowulf (through the exempla, then, of Sigemund and Heremod), then, in a summative parallel structure, again about Beowulf before a contrastive half-line about Heremod. Adeline Bartlett (1966, 20–2) expands the passage to 853–917a, noting in it a double envelope pattern and noting a further envelope in 837–41a (*Ða wæs on morgen ... guðrinc monig ... wundor sceawian*) and 917b–20a (*Ða wæs morgenleoht ... scealc monig ... searowundor seon*). Constance B. Hieatt demonstrates that the pattern could be extended to the whole of Fitt 13, noting how *tirleases trode* (843) is echoed by *tryddode tirfæst* (922a), even while *cystum gecyped* (923a) looks back to the central *cystum cuðe* (867a). Hieatt's summary of the fitt's overall structure is worth quoting in full:

The double envelope pattern starts with a key cluster: *Đa wæs* (A) in the *morgen* (B) *monig* men (C) who viewed the *wundor* (D), and saw the *tirleases trode* (E); riding on *mearum* (F) they raced (*flitan, geflit*) (G) *fealwe* (H) horses on paths *cystum cuđe* (I). Between clusters A to E and F to I is an interlude describing the way in which Beowulf was praised; after the second cluster comes the Sigemund passage, praising him in a different way. Thereafter, all nine elements of the envelope are repeated, in the order GHFABCDEI, establishing at least one contrast as well as various parallels, since Hrothgar is as *tirfæst* as Grendel is *tirleas*. (1975, 251–2)

The sophistication of the passage and the fitt as a whole is further demonstrated by the parallel and chiastic structures within it and outside it. As David Howlett shows, for example, part of the deeds of Sigemund is told in parallel (878–887a; 888–894a) and a larger structure from 876–900 (beginning and ending with the repetition of *ellendædum*) is chiastic (1997, 517–19).[42] Yvette Kisor, evaluating Howlett and adding important observations of her own, notes that the "Lay of Sigemund," appearing in Fitt 13, contains two parallel passages of thirteen lines (874b–887; 888–900) and is followed by thirteen lines on Heremod (901–13a), all while the 88 lines of the fitt have a Golden Section at 870b, *word oþer fand* (2009, 59–60). Looking outside the passage, Thomas E. Hart (1972, 20–5) finds an intricate chiastic interlace between lines 871–900 and lines 2283–2313, events right after the theft of the cup.

The digression proper, however, might be said to be divided into five sections: the first and fifth are brief descriptions of the racing of horses (864–67a; 916–17a); the second introduces the king's thane and poet (867b–74a); and the two central passages treat of Sigemund and Heremod, respectively, though how to divide these two passages is perhaps not quite clear.

The opening and closing of the digression are, as we have seen, clearly marked. That the horses initially race on paths that seem fair and are *cystum cuđe* further links the introduction not only to the many unknown things that the poet relates (*uncuþes fela*, 876b), but also to the great distribution of *cuđ/uncuđ* in the poem, including the specific contrast, no doubt, with the *uncuđ gelad* on the approach to the mere (1410b) and to the dragon's lair (2214a). If warrior and poet are not sufficiently linked[43] by the repetition of *hwilum*, the characterization of the scop as one who remembers *eal fela ealdgesegena* (869)—itself a hugely significant line for its resemblance to a pen trial in London, British Library, Harley 208 (*hwæt ic eall feala ealdesæge*; N. R. Ker 1957, no. 229, 304)[44]—and of Sigemund and Fitela as a pair who have laid to rest *eal fela eotena cynnes* (883) might further suggest such a link. Slightly different is the repetition of *worn gemunde* (870a; 2114b), which looks outside the digression to link the scop and Hrothgar, who, apparently, can relate a *syllic spell* (2109b) like a scop, as we learn in a brilliant, condensed three-fold repetition of *hwilum* (2107a; 2108b; 2109b).

The purpose of the passage is also suggested by the poet's choice of words: we move from the *sið Beowulfes* (872a) to the *wide siðas* (877b) of the Wælsinges to the *swiðferhþes sið* (908a), the exploits of Heremod, the strong-minded one. From the expedition of Beowulf, the poet moves on to the *ellendæda* of Sigemund, and of course the very mention of *ellen* (3b, but also 893b) and verbs of hearing, saying, and asking ought to remind us of the people-kings of the spear-Danes at the opening of the poem. The poet again uses *ellendæd* in the transition to Heremod (900a), an effect that serves to demonstrate that both Sigemund and Heremod had promising early careers, as of course has Beowulf. Curiously, *ellendæd* appears only on two other occasions in the corpus, both times in circumstances of loss: what is to be lost after eating from the tree of death in *Genesis B* (484b) and what the followers of Holofernes will have no more after his beheading in *Judith* (273a). Further, though I am not aware of any serious suggestions to read the passage this way—Tolkien (1982, 59) and Griffith (1995, 15) mention the possibility—I accept the manuscript punctuation here as significant (after 897b) and read the demonstrative pronoun *se* (898a) as referring to Heremod: the referent for *se* will appear in line 901a. This ought not to seem a jarring transition, for the shift from Heremod to Beowulf in 913b is hardly better signaled, and indeed the confusion of pronouns in this passage and elsewhere in the poem is an oft-mentioned technique of the poet, meaning the ambiguity may well be deliberate. Thus, lines 898–902a could also read: "He [Heremod] was the most widely renowned of exiles, protector of warriors, over the nations, for his brave deeds—he had prospered in this earlier–afterwards, the fight, strength, and courage of Heremod diminished."[45]

This same effect of the blurring of distinctions between Sigemund and Heremod may be achieved by the similar epithets used for each, *æpelinges bearn* (888a) and *þeodnes bearn* (910a), a technique that also reaches outside the digression to the repeated use of *æpelinga bearn* to refer to

Beowulf at the mere (1408b)—though this has been suggested to be a plural, the singular verb suggests this is meant only to refer to Beowulf—and the certainly plural *æþelinga bearn* also appears, negatively and neutrally, in the final third of the poem (2597a; 3170a) for the retainers who flee and the twelve who ride around Beowulf's tomb, respectively. The difficulty of distinguishing characters in their epithets and pronouns (and the identifications of Beowulf and the monsters he fights) is a key feature of the poem, and one that is often achieved through patterned repetition. The technique is not new: David Quint has shown how Virgil, for example, through chiastic patterning (of pronouns), "doubles" Aeneas and Turnus to such an extent that the effect becomes "vertiginous": though perhaps the effect is not so strongly felt in Beowulf, Quint's conclusion is startling appropriate: "Aeneas kills a series of versions of himself" (2018, xv, 5–12).

Characters in the passage are also connected by the verb *þurhwadan*, the word that is used to describe the piercing of Sigemund's dragon (890b), Beowulf's slash at the neck of Grendel's mother (1567b), and, perhaps more importantly here, with slight variation, the invasion of sin into Heremod—*hine fyren onwod* (915b)—demonstrating at once the similarity and the difference of the outcomes for the dragon, Heremod, and Grendel's mother. The fact that Heremod passes *on feonda geweald* (903a), a phrase used of Grendel just a few lines before (808a), affirms such a reading; N. F. Blake, in fact, would say that lines 902b–5a are completely about Heremod's suffering in hell (*on feonda geweald*), among the giants who mostly arrived earlier (*mid eotenum*), tormented by surging flames (*sorhwylmas*) forever (*to lange*).[46]

In the section on Heremod, there are several further connections with other parts of the digression, including the reference again to *eotenas* (902b; be they here giants or Jutes, this again contrasts Heremod with Sigemund and Fitela),[47] which also looks back to the introduction of the kin of Cain (112a, etc.) and ahead to the discovery of the sword in the lair of Grendel's mother (*ealdsweord eotenisc*; 1558a). Tellingly, the same description is used of Eanmund's sword, passed to Weohstan, and then to Wiglaf, which seems likely to be the cause of renewed Swedish/Geatish hostilities (2616a) and of the sword Eofor uses to kill Ongentheow (2979a). Further, three lines in the section, as we have seen, are a formula ending in *weard* (902b; 905b; 913b) that will be echoed by Hrothgar: the first describes Heremod's personal end; the second the fate of his people, and the third, introduced simply with the pronoun *he*, sets up the expectation that the final instance will also refer to Heremod, but instead marks the brief reintroduction of Beowulf into the digression as the poet observes that he, unlike Heremod, became more dear to friends. The subversion of expectation, a fairly common technique of the poet, has also been seen in the use of *oþ þæt* to signal reversals, as in the appearance of the black raven the night after the death of Grendel's mother. As Michael Lapidge as shown, the audience, hearing *oþ þæt hrefn blaca* (1801a) as night falls after the defeat of Grendel's mother, would be expecting something worse than the happy announcement of morning (2001, 66–7). Later, when the part of Hrothgar's speech about Heremod begins *Ne wearð Heremod swa* (1709b), the poet signals that the following words will inform what we have learned of Heremod in the digression. The digression, therefore, connects Heremod with Cain, Grendel, Sigemund, Beowulf, and general models of poor kingship, thus contrasting Heremod with Scyld, Hrothgar, and Beowulf, each described as a *god cyning* in the poem (11b; 863b; 2390b). Heremod might be described as the *Deor*-poet sums up the reign of Eormanric: *þæt wæs grimm cyning* (23b; That was a bad king).

The digression, however, though it rewards close reading as an isolated digression on Beowulf and his possible futures, is connected verbally and thematically with the rest of the poem in ways we have not yet mentioned. How this is done could be related at length, but I will focus only on a few major features, saving the most intricate and interesting for last. The first is the relationship of Sigemund and Fitela (*eam his nefan* [881a]) as uncle and nephew. Regardless of what the Anglo-Saxon audience might have been expected to know of Völsung history, it needs to be stated that the poet mentions only this relationship. If the more sordid part of their relationship (as father and son, as we have seen), their many years together as wolves, and their killing of Signý's children are hinted at in the *uncuþes fela* (876b), all we know for certain is that the audience was reminded that the pair is uncle and nephew. The uncle–nephew connection is enormously important in the poem, as many critics have acknowledged,[48] standing as a positive example of the relationship, with Hygelac and Beowulf, and, figuratively, with Beowulf and Wiglaf,[49] but against the negative example of Hrothgar and Hrothulf, and perhaps also that of Hnaef and his unnamed nephew, the son of Hildeburh, who burns with him at the hall of Finn. One might also think here of the brothers Eanmund and Eadgils as they rebel against Onela and look forward to what might happen in Freawaru's marriage to Ingeld. Thinking outside the poem, there is an interesting inversion in Sigurðr's slaying of Fáfnir, as Fáfnir, as the brother of Reginn, is in effect an uncle to Sigurðr after his fosterage by Reginn. Further, in terms of the conflict between the offspring of Cain and the line of Abel (or Seth),[50] one might think of Grendel and the monstrous races generally as nephews to the "good" races with whom they are at odds.

The second major thematic element is the bright treasure that Sigemund bears into the heart of a ship: this treasure echoes the burial of Scyld (34–6b), the loading of Beowulf's ship for the journey to Denmark (213b–15a), and Wiglaf's trip in the dragon's barrow (2773–76a) verbally, but thematically the role of treasure and hoards in the poem as a whole, including the *dom* that determines them (895a [Sigemund]; 2147b [Beowulf]; 2776a [Wiglaf]). In this passage, and throughout the poem as a whole, it seems to me to have been the poet's intention often to direct the audience's understanding of the poem through sequential associations that force a continuous rethinking of what has gone before. Michael Lapidge, though he focuses more on macrocontexts and episodes that are repeatedly narrated in the poem, usefully relates this process to Michael Riffaterre's notion of "retroaction," "namely the process by which a reader is induced to reflect on what has proceeded, so that the text becomes the object of progressive discovery, of a dynamic of perception which is constantly changing" (2001, 67–8), as we have seen in the context of the coming of darkness and Grendel with *weox under wolcnum*.[51] The funeral of Scyld and the treasure loaded into the ship are echoed as Beowulf sails to Denmark, suggesting he is, in a way, Scyld come again from across the water to the Danes in their time of need. When Sigemund defeats a dragon and loads a ship with treasure, he enters the same category of positive heroes. However, at the same time, the treasure now becomes associated with the dragon's hoard and Sigemund, which retroactively, at least slightly, begins to muddy the audience's conception of the valence of the three heroes, especially as our knowledge of Heremod grows. Beowulf's apparent choosing of his rewards connects his gifts from Hrothgar (or at least his relationship to that wealth) to Sigemund's reward for slaying the dragon. Next, the Last Survivor enters the conversation, and the unnamed character seems to stash the hoard and die with it, connecting him both with the treasure and with the dragon. Retroactively, we add the Last Survivor especially to what we remember of Scyld and Beowulf at the beginning of the poem. Next, Beowulf's lap is loaded with treasure, again echoing Scyld and now echoing Beowulf's departure for Denmark. Wiglaf chooses the treasure, however, adding Wiglaf to the chain of associations running through Scyld, Beowulf, and Sigemund. However, the audience's opinion of the treasure shifts markedly, for this treasure, connected with all the other wealth in the poem, is cursed (3051–7) and destined to be returned to the earth, as useless to men as always (3166–8), at the funeral of Beowulf, who now parallels also the Last Survivor, calling into question everything positive about Scyld, Sigemund, Beowulf, Wiglaf, material reward, and treasure in general. Further, such a rapid overview omits a mass of further associations with, for example, the kin of Cain and material goods, the *enta geweorc*, the Flood, and the Völsung legend (the curse and Fáfnir's apparent transformation into a dragon).[52] To complicate matters further, each such thematic element and its nexus of associations is then interlaced with others, such as, in this case, the four funerals of the poem, models of kingship, earthly transience, and, as we shall see next, isolation.

We have already seen how the poet uses *sið* to connect the careers of Beowulf, Sigemund, and Heremod within the passage. This word is important outside the passage as well, particularly as it appears in close proximity to *an/ana*: a key feature of the *sið* of a hero seems to be that it be undertaken alone. And so, preparing to fight the dragon, Beowulf remarks: "Nis þæt eower sið,/ ne gemet mannes, nef(ne) min anes" (That is not your exploit, nor is it fitting for any man, except me alone; 2532b–3), and in case the audience misses the point, the poet then adds just a few lines later that Beowulf "strengo getruwode/ anes mannes; ne bið swylc earges sið!" ([Beowulf] trusted in the strength of one man; such is not the exploit of the cowardly!; 2540b–1). In fact, lines 887b–889 of the digression demonstrate the poet signaling as insistently as possible that we recognize the significance of these words. Much more could be said about *an/ana*, but I might here simply add that Grendel's struggle is characterized as *ana wið eallum* (one against all; 145a) early in the poem: as many have remarked on shared strength and epithets for heroes and monsters, so are their exploits in some ways similar.[53] The verb *neðan* or *geneþan* appears with moderate frequency in the poem, and one might particularly note that this is how Beowulf assesses his own early career toward the end of the poem: "Ic geneðde fela/ guða on geogoðe" (I ventured many battles in my youth; 2511b–12a), where the *fela guða* might also be said to echo *fela* and *ealfela* in the digression.

4.3   *Under harne stan* (887b)

By far the most interesting phrase in the digression, however, is *under harne stan* (887b), which describes where Sigemund engages his dragon. The *har stan* appears three other times in the poem: in line 1415a, as a marker at the mere, and in lines 2553b and 2744b with reference to the dragon's barrow in Beowulf's final fight. The immediate effect of this repetition is obvious: Sigemund's dragon, Grendel, Grendel's mother, and Beowulf's dragon are linked; the abodes of monsters are *under harne stan*. Further, the exploits of Sigemund and Beowulf become the same sorts of fights against the same sorts of beings. The great deeds of the heroes Sigemund and Beowulf are harmonized, and this may help to explain the common objection that the poet's praise of Beowulf, connecting Sigemund's successful fight to Beowulf's unsuccessful one, has to contain implicit criticism. Looking only at the two dragon fights, one might agree with Kenneth Sisam's observation that "to remind the audience of Sigemund's more complete success was not the happiest way of praising Beowulf" (1965, 4n2).[54] However, Beowulf wins two fights with creatures who issue from beyond the *har stan* before losing the third; surely even Sigemund did not attempt this thrice.[55] The final mention, in 2744b, comes from the tongue of Beowulf himself, who, in his dying wish, directs Wiglaf *under harne stan* to gather some of the treasure. Though the passage is not complicated by the presence of a living dragon or monster, this may further represent the passing of the hero's mantle from Beowulf to the young Wiglaf.

Although the general effect of the four-fold repetition of *har stan* is relatively straightforward, examining the phrase in context expands its significance. First of all, *under harne stan* has the appearance of possibly being part of a formula or formulaic system. In the poem, the only variation is in the preposition, which is *ofer* once (1415a), though that variation is for logical reasons. I am unable to discover or imagine a formulaic system of sufficient specificity to generate *under/ofer harne stan*, except the rather obvious ability to vary the preposition, which does not seem flexible enough to be a system. Within the poem, then, the repetition seems to be just that, and the similar contexts in which the phrase appears suggests a very specific function. The next appearance after the digression is *ofer harne stan*, which is part of the description of the mere as Beowulf approaches, a description that must be paired with Hrothgar's earlier remarks on that horrible place:

Hie dygel lond
warigeað, wulfhleoþu, windige næssas,   [*Andreas* 841a; *Andreas* 843a]
frecne fengelad, ðær fyrgenstream   [889a, etc.; cf. Blickling XVI]
1360   under næssa genipu niþer gewiteð,   [Blickling 16; Blickling XVI]
flod under foldan. Nis þæt feor heonon
milgemearces þæt se mere standeð;
ofer þæm hongiað hrinde bearwas,   [Blickling XVI; Blickling XVI]
wudu wyrtum fæst wæter oferhelmað.
(1357b-64)

They [Grendel and his mother] occupy a secret land, wolf-slopes, windy bluffs, a terrible fen-path, where the mountain stream, under the mists of the bluffs, goes downward, the flood under the earth. It is not many mile-markers from here that the mere stands. Frost-covered trees hang over it; a wood fast with roots overshadows the water.

Ofereode þa *æpelinga bearn*   [888a, 910a, 2597a, 3170a]
steap stanhliðo, stige nearwe,   [*Andreas* 840b; *Andreas* 841a]
1410   enge anpaðas, *uncuð gelad,*   [*cuð*: 867a; *uncuð*: 876b, 1410b, 2214a]
neowle næssas, *nicorhusa fela*;   [422a, 575a, 845b, 1427b, Blickling XVI]
he feara sum beforan gengde
wisra monna *wong sceawian,*   [2744a, *Andreas* 839b]
oþ þæt he færinga fyrgenbeamas
1415   *ofer harne stan* hleonian funde,   [887b, 2553b, 2744b, Blickling XVI,
                                                    Andreas 841b]
wynleasne wudu; wæter under stod   [Blickling XVI]
dreorig ond gedrefed. (1408-17a)

The son of nobles traversed the steep, stony slopes, narrow ways up, tight solitary paths, an unknown way, precipitous bluffs, many a dwelling place of *nicors*. He, one of a few wise men, rode ahead to examine the land, until he suddenly found mountain trees leaning over the hoar stone, a joyless wood. Underneath, the water was bloody and agitated.

1425   Gesawon ða æfter wætere   [869a, 876b, 883b]
          wyrmcynnes fela,
sellice *sædracan sund cunnian,*   [892b, 2211b, etc.; 508b]
swylce on næshleoðum *nicras*   [422a, 575a, 845b, 1411b, Blickling
          licgean,   XVI]
ða on undernmæl oft bewitigað
sorhfulne *sið* on seglrade,   [872a, 877b, 908a, etc.]

1430   *wyrmas* ond wildeor. Hie on weg   [897b]
        hruron
        bitere ond *gebolgne*; bearhtm   [709a, 723b, 1539b, 1713a, 2220b,
        ongeaton,   2304a, 2401b, 2550b]
        guðhorn galan. (1425-32a)

Then, on the water, they [the men] saw many of the serpent race and
strange sea-dragons exploring the sea, as well as, on the headland slopes,
nicors lying, who in morning often undertake a sorrowful exploit on the
ocean, serpents and wild beasts. They [the beasts] fell away, bitter and
enraged; they heard a bright sound, a battle-horn sing.

The description at the mere recalls the Sigemund-Heremod digression
in several key ways. The parallel of *frecne fengelad* (1359a) and *frecne
dæde* (889a) suggests that the path leads to a place where a dragon fight
might happen; the deployment of *frecne* as an adjective in the poem supports this view, for it otherwise appears in the context of the mere a few
lines later (1378a), the suffering of the giants (1691a), and the dragon
(2689a). Most significantly, the Last Survivor laments that *(f)eorhbeal(o)
frecne* (2250a) has taken his people, and this is precisely the phrase
Beowulf uses in his boast that he will fight alone or die (2537a), thus
again making it a reference to the dragon and paralleling the destruction
of the two peoples.[56] The other echoes of the digression serve to link
Beowulf with Sigemund and Heremod (1408b), to invoke the pattern
of *cuð/uncuð* in which the digression participates and which is important in the poem as a whole (1410b), to call attention to the similarity
in setting of the mere and of Sigemund's dragon fight (1415a; 1425b;
1426a; 1430a), and to compare and add the earlier deeds of Beowulf,
Sigemund, Fitela, and Heremod to this one (1429a). The other important connection here to the digression, although it happens retroactively, is a verbal echo of the description of Heremod in Hrothgar's
speech. *Bolgenmod* (1713a), Heremod kills his close companions; the
beasts of the mere are similarly enraged (1431a), and the other characters of the poem who feel that kind of anger are Beowulf (709a [*bolgenmod*]; 1539b; 2401a; 2550b), Grendel (723b), and the dragon (2220b;
2304a).[57]

The *har stan* reappears as Beowulf approaches the dragon:

2550	Let ða of breostum, ða he *gebolgen* wæs,	[709a, 723b, 1431a, 1539b, 1713a, 2220b, 2304a, 2401b]
	Weder-Geata leod word ut faran,	
	stearcheort styrmde; stefn in becom	
	heaðotorht *hlynnan under harne stan*.	[2558b; 887b, 1415a, 2744b, Blickling XVI, *Andreas* 841b]
	Hete wæs onhrered, hordweard oncniow	
2555	mannes reorde; næs ðær mara fyrst	
	freode to friclan. From ærest cwom	
	oruð aglæcean ut of stane,	
	hat hildeswat; *hruse dynede*. (2550-58)	[767a, 770b, 1317b]

Then, from his breast, when he was enraged, the prince of the Geats let words fly out, the stark-hearted one stormed; his voice, clear in battle, began to roar inside, under the hoar stone. Hate was stirred up, the hoard-guardian recognized the voice of a man; there was not more time to ask for friendship. First came the breath of the enemy from out of the stone, hot battle-sweat; the earth resounded.

In the second passage, the poet repeats the envelope pattern that is so effectively used in the fight with Grendel. Where we there hear that the *dryhtsele dynede* (767a) and then *reced hlynsode* (770b), here Beowulf's voice roars (*hlynnan*; 2553a), and the earth itself resounds (*hruse dynede*; 2558b), thus creating a kind of chiastic structure between the two envelopes. The poet again invokes the theme of rage (2550b), here connecting Beowulf for the last time with the sort of rage by which his opponents and Heremod have been motivated.

Finally, as Beowulf lies dying, he sends Wiglaf to explore the hoard:

	Nu ðu lungre geong	
	hord *sceawian under harne stan*,	[840b, 1413b, 2402b, 3032b, *Andreas* 839b; 887b, 1415a, 2553a, Blickling XVI, *Andreas* 841b]
2745	Wiglaf leofa, nu se *wyrm* ligeð,	[897b, 1430a]
	swefeð sare wund, since bereafod.	
	(2743a-46)	

Now go quickly and explore the hoard under the hoar stone, dear Wiglaf, now that the worm lies, sleeps sorely wounded, deprived of treasure.

Although the most important feature of this passage must be the anoint-ing of Wiglaf as Beowulf's heir, the repetition of *harne stan* (2744b) and *wyrm* (2745b) also connect the passage to the digression and the mere. The verb *sceawian* in its infinitive form appears six times in the poem, with reference to Grendel's tracks leading away from Heorot (840b), the scouting of the path to the mere (1413b), the dragon (2402b), the hoard (2744a), and Beowulf's dead body (3032b), a final *wundor* that subtly speaks both to how the Geats view their king and how the poet wants to suggest the audience might view the hero.[58] Were we to look outside *Beowulf* for the *har stan*, we would find three other poetic occurrences, in *Andreas, The Ruin*, and *Riddle 40*:

	Sceadu sweðerodon,	
	wonn under wolcnum; þa com wederes	[*Beo* 651a, 1374a; *DOTR* 54b-55a]
	blæst,	
	hador heofonleoma, ofer hofu blican.	[*Beo* 222a]
	Onwoc þa wiges heard, wang sceawode	[*Beo* 886a; *Beo* 1413b, 2744a, 225b]
840	fore burggeatum; beorgas steape,	[*Beo* 222b, 1409a]
	hleoðu hlifodon, ymbe harne stan	[*Beo* 1358a; *Beo* 887b, 1415a, 2553b, 2744b]
	tigelfagan trafu, torras stodon,	
	windige weallas. Þa se wis\<a\>oncneow	[*Beo* 1358b]
	þæt he Marmedonia mægðe hæfde	
845	siðe gesohte, swa him sylf bebead,	[*Beo* 872a, 877b, 908a, 2532b, 2541b]
	þa he him fore gescraf, fæder	(*Andreas* 836b-46)
	mancynnes.	

Shadows disappeared, gloom under the skies; next, a blaze came gleam-ing from the air, bright heaven-light, over the dwellings. The one hard in battle awoke then, and surveyed the field before the city gates; high cliffs and slopes towered up, around the hoar stone stood tile-adorned build-ings, towers and windy walls. Then the wise one perceived that he had in his expedition reached the nation of the Mermedonians, as the father of mankind himself had commanded, when he assigned the journey to him.

	Stanhofu stodan, stream hate wearp
	widan wylme; weal eall befeng
40	beorhtan bosme, þær þa baþu wæron,

hat on hreþre. Þæt wæs hyðelic.
Leton þonne geotan [.......]
<u>ofer harne stan</u> hate streamas
un[...............]
45   [o]þ þæt hringmere hate [.......
............] þær þa baþu wæron.
Þonne is [..................
.......]re. Þæt is cynelic þing
hu s[e ....] burg [..].   (*The Ruin* 38–49)

Stone dwellings stood, the stream hotly cast forth a broad current, and a
wall encircled all in its bright bosom where those baths were, hot at its
centre. That was the way it should be. They let hot streams gush forth over
the hoar stone ... until the round mere hotly ... where those baths were.
Then is ... That is a royal thing, how the ... city ...

Hefigere ic eom micle þonne <u>se hara stan</u>
75   oþþe unlytel leades clympre,
leohtre ic eom micle þonne þes lytla wyrm
þe her on flode gæð fotum dryge.   (*Riddle* 40 74–7)

I am much heavier than the hoar stone or the massive clump of lead; I am
much lighter than the little worm, which moves across the water here with
dry feet.

The scene in *Andreas* is the arrival of the hero in the land of the
Mermedonians.[59] The passage as whole has an incredible cluster of
borrowings from *Beowulf,* borrowings that make it clear that the
Andreas-poet was consciously copying *Beowulf* in the composition of
this section of the poem. The *Andreas*-poet borrows from three sections of *Beowulf:* the arrival in the land of the Danes (217–226a), the
fall of night before the Danes rush out of Heorot to leave Beowulf alone
(649–51a), and Hrothgar's description of and Beowulf's arrival at the
mere (1357b–1379; 1408–17a). An audience familiar with *Beowulf*
would no doubt feel a frisson of fear at the appearance of the *har stan,*
but the passage indicates how intimately the *Andreas*-poet knew *Beowulf,*
which of course has already been shown[60]; still, the sophistication of his
borrowing is worth seeing here. Recall, too, that the disappearance of
darkness in the passage is very closely connected not only to the falling
darkness of *Beowulf* (649–51a), itself a neat inversion on the part of the

Andreas-poet, but also to Christ on the cross in *The Dream of the Rood* (52b–6), as we saw in relation to *weox under wolcnum*.

The next occurrence is in the *The Ruin*, though unfortunately at the conclusion of the poem where we have only fragments of lines. The connection between the *har stan* and *enta geweorc* is perhaps most obvious in this poem, and it seems that the *Andreas*-poet might also have been incorporating stock descriptions of Roman ruins in the first glimpse of Mermedonia, as *The Ruin* and *Andreas* share some fairly unusual Old English words, such as *torras* (*Andreas* 842b; *Ruin* 3b) and *tigel* (*Andreas* 842a; *Ruin* 30b) as well as the *har stan*. This would further suggest such a connection for the *enta geweorc* of *Beowulf*, and in fact, Emily Thornbury (2000) has argued that the poet likely fused elements of Roman architecture and indigenous burial mounds in the difficult to resolve description of the dragon's lair (particularly the *stanbogan* [2545a], exactly the point at which we might note that a stream bursts forth from the barrow [2545b–6] as in *The Ruin* and the mere scene). The final poetic occurrence of the *har stan* is in *Riddle 40*, the answer to which is assumed to be "creation." The context suggests something of the size and permanence of the stone, as well, perhaps, as a sense of wonder about it, especially in the contrast to the worm or bug that moves across the water without getting wet. Outside of *Beowulf*, then, the formula undergoes a further variation in preposition in *Andreas*, where *ymbe harne stan*, though I believe clearly a literary borrowing, is at a very high end of the interformularity scale (to use Bakker's term). *Ofer harne stan* in *The Ruin* is difficult to evaluate, but both *Andreas* and *The Ruin* would seem to add new semantic features to the repetition, associating the *har stan* with (perhaps) past civilizations of dubious morality, though the specific feature of cannibalism is shared in *Beowulf* and *Andreas*. The *har stan* in *Riddle 40* seems more closely connected to some prose examples than these poetic occurrences, as we will see.

When we come to prose, we come to Blickling Homily XVI: *ofer harne stan* (1415a) is part of a long-recognized and often-quoted series of parallels between the conclusion of Blickling Homily XVI and the description of Grendel's mere. Again, we are at the high end of the interformularity scale:

Ac uton nu biddan þone heahengel Sanctus Michahel ond ða nigen endebyrdnessa ðara haligra engla þæt hie us syn on <u>fultume</u> wið <u>helsceaðum</u>. Hie wæron þa halgan on onfenge manna saulum. Swa Sanctus Paulus wæs geseonde on norðanweardne þisne middangeard, þær ealle wætero niðergewitað, ond he þær geseah ofer ðæm wætere sumne harne stan, ond wæron norð of ðæm stane awexene swiðe hrimige bearwas. Ond ðær wæron þystrogenipo; ond under þæm stane wæs niccra eardung ond wearga. Ond he geseah þæt on ðæm clife hangodan on ðæm isigean bearwum manige swearte saula be heora handum gebundne. Ond þa fynd þara on nicra onlicnesse heora gripende wæron, swa swa grædig wulf. Ond þæt wæter wæs sweart under þæm clife neoðan. Ond betuh þæm clife on ðæm wætre wæron swylce twelf mila, ond ðonne ða twigo forburston þonne gewitan þa saula niðer þa þe on ðæm twigum hangodan, ond him onfengon ða nicras. Ðis ðonne wæron ða saula þa ðe her on worlde mid unrihte gefyrenode wæron, ond ðæs noldan geswican ær heora lifes ende. Ac uton nu biddan Sanctus Michael geornlice þæt he ure saula gelæde on gefean, þær hie motan blissian abuton ende on ecnesse. AMEN. (Morris 1967)

But let us now bid the high angel Saint Michael and the nine orders of holy angels that they might be an aid for us against hell-foes. They were the holy ones for the taking of the souls of men. So, Saint Paul was looking in the northern region of this world where all the waters drop down, and he saw there over that water a certain hoar stone, and, north of that stone, very frosty woods had grown. And there were dark mists, and under that stone was the dwelling place of *nicors* and *weargs*. And he saw that on that cliff hung, on the icy trees, many black souls, bound by their hands, and their enemies, in the likeness of *nicors*, were grasping at them, just like the greedy wolf. And that water was black down under the cliff, and between the cliff and the water it was about twelve miles, and when the branches broke, then those souls that had been hanging on those branches fell, and the *nicors* seized them. These, then, were those souls who unjustly had sinned here in the world, and did not wish to stop before their life's end. But let us now bid Saint Michael eagerly that he lead our souls into joy, where they might rejoice always without end in eternity. AMEN.

Though most of the verbal similarities cluster in lines 1357b–64, some, including the *har stan*, also appear in 1408–17a. The connection between the description of the mere in *Beowulf* and Blickling XVI[61] has been noted since Richard Morris edited the *Blickling Homilies* in the late nineteenth century. Morris considers the homily "probably a direct reminiscence" of the passage in *Beowulf*, but the situation is complicated by the fact that the homily's conclusion and, therefore, the corresponding lines in *Beowulf* seem to come in some fashion from the apocryphal *Visio Pauli* (1967, vii). The relationship between the three works has proven difficult to unravel, but a later editor of the *Visio Pauli*, Theodore Silverstein, disagrees with Morris, suggesting that the "main founda-tion of the passage was the account of the unrepentant sinners hanging on fiery trees, which appears in all but three of the abbreviated versions [of the *Visio Pauli*]"; *Beowulf*, he says, "furnished merely a transform-ing suggestion" (1935, 11). Antonette DiPaolo Healey, agreeing with Carleton Brown (1938), suggests that Blickling XVI is a fusion of ele-ments from the *Visio* and *Beowulf* (attributing to *Beowulf* the change from fire to ice), commenting that "we cannot state with any certainty that the *Beowulf*-poet knew the *Visio* and drew upon it" (1978, 52). Rowland L. Collins (1984) shows that the possibility of the Blickling homilist drawing on *Beowulf* is highly unlikely and suggests that Blickling XVI may have influenced "growth" in the poem after 971.[62] While it would be tedious to relate the various arguments in detail, the situation seems to have been resolved relatively recently by Charles D. Wright, who offers convincing evidence that the *Beowulf*-poet and the author of Blickling XVI were borrowing independently from the same lost version of a vernacular *Visio Pauli*.[63]

Blickling Homily XVI (the collection is dated to the second half of the tenth century, sometimes specifically to 971) is a homily on the feast of St. Michael the Archangel, the pericopes for which are verses in Daniel VII.9–10, 13–14 (a vision of heaven in which we see the minis-tering angels about the throne of God, prepared to execute his will) and John I.47–51 (angels ascending and descending, mentioned by Christ to Nathanael). The bulk of the homily, however, concerns the building of St. Michael's church in Campania, in northern Italy, and the con-flict between the Christians and pagans who live in the area. Michael, of course, is the angel who battles the dragon in heaven (Apocalypse XII.7–9), and the tradition behind this particular passage is a develop-ment of the strange detail in II Corinthians XII.2–4 that Paul knows a man who was taken up to paradise. In the apocryphal *Visio*, Michael is Paul's guide. In other words, Blickling Homily XVI has a strange appro-priateness to *Beowulf* in its connection to dragon fighters and dragon fights. Even if the *Beowulf*-poet and the homily author only borrow inde-pendently from the *Visio*, some evidence suggests that the *Beowulf*-poet may have been familiar with traditions of Saint Michael, beyond the sort of role the passage quoted above suggests: the homily invokes Michael's aid (*fultum*) against hell-foes (*helsceaðan*); Beowulf is sent as *frofor ond fultum* (698a) against a range of fiends and *-sceaþa* compounds, including a *feondscaða* in the contest with Breca and the *synscapa* himself, Grendel (707a; 801a).[64]

The textual history of the *Visio Pauli* is extraordinarily complex, evolving from what was probably a third-century Greek original into different versions in Latin, Syriac, Coptic, Armenian, Slavonic, Ethiopic, and Old English (even though Aldhelm and Ælfric both strongly condemn the work).[65] Several Long Latin versions have survived, and the text was redacted often,[66] though most of the redactions, at least in manuscript form, date from the eleventh century and later; however, almost a third of the manuscripts of the various redactions are English (Wright 1993, 106–8; Silverstein 1935, 10). The Old English version of the *Visio* (in a mid-eleventh century manuscript) is unfortunately not useful for our passage, as it comes from a Long Latin version that has not survived and breaks off before Paul's vision of hell. The redactions, of which there are at least eleven, eliminate much of the Long Latin text, including the episode of the going out of souls and the entire vision of heaven, focusing instead on Paul's tour of hell, which is augmented with particularly vivid details. Redactions IV, VI, and XI have insular connections, and Redactions VI and XI "are extant in manuscripts of the ninth century, and both have Irish or Anglo-Saxon connections" (Dwyer 1988, 136; Wright 1993, 111). In short, the *Visio* has extensive insular connections and no doubt circulated in many lost forms, likely in Old English and Latin.

Of the redactions with insular connections, Redactio IV is the most interesting, including close parallel to Blickling XVI:

> Vidit vero Paulus ante portas inferni arbores igneas et peccatores cruciatos et suspensos in eis ... Postea vidit flumen orribile, in quo multe bestie dyabolice erant quasi pisces in medio maris, que animas peccatrices devorant sine ulla misericordia quasi lupi devorant oves. (Brandes 1885, 75–6)

> Paul saw before the gates of hell fiery trees and, in them, sinners, tortured and suspended ... Afterwards, he saw a terrible river in which were many diabolical beasts, just like fish in the heart of the sea, and the beasts devour the sinful souls without any mercy, just as wolves devour sheep.

Redactio VI has no parallel to this passage, and Redactio XI contains only the fiery trees and river full of beasts (without the devouring of souls and thus without the simile that also appears in Blickling XVI).

However, other redactions have details that seem to appear in *Beowulf* and Blickling XVI and details that seem to have influenced *Beowulf*, at least, or perhaps both:

1. The great river Oceanus:
   Redactio II: "[Paul is in heaven, gazing at the foundation of heaven, which is over a great river; Michael describes it as] Occeanus, qui circumierat omne mundum" (Oceanus, which had encircled the whole world; Silverstein 1935, 156)
   Blickling XVI: "þær ealle wætero niðergewitað"
   Beowulf: "ðær fyrgenstream/ under næssa genipu niþer gewiteð,/ flod under foldan" (1359b-61a)
2. The fiery river:
   Redactio II: "Et uidit flumen igneum feruens, et fluctus eius exaltabantur usque ad celum" (And Paul saw a fiery river, seething, and its waves were raised right up to the heavens; Silverstein 1935, 156)
   Beowulf: "fyr on flode" (1366a);[67] "ðygeblond up astigeð/ won to wolcnum" (1373b-74a)[68]
3. The fiery/colossal dragon:
   Redactio III: "Et erat ibi draco ingens, habens mille capita, et mille oculos et mille dentes in unoquoque capite; et erant oculi eius quasi gladii acuti. Semper ore aperto absorbebat animas. Et erat nomen eius Pahtmot. Ab eo procedunt serpentes; et conspuit in terram, et de eo ueniunt rane et omne genus uermium." (And a colossal dragon was there, with 1000 heads and 1000 eyes and 1000 teeth in each head; and its eyes were as sharp as swords. Ever with an open mouth was it swallowing souls. And its name was Pahtmot. Serpents issue out of it; and it spits on the earth, and from it come frogs and each species of worms; Silverstein 1935, 164–6)[69]
   Beowulf: "dracan lege" (2549b); "wyrmcynnes fela" (1425b)

The details here demonstrate that, although the situation in *Beowulf* and Blickling XVI is obviously that of the *Visio*, at the level of individual detail the correspondences between these versions of the *Visio* and *Beowulf* and Blickling XVI are really quite scattered. The *Visio* is not so much concerned with the topography of the place as our vernacular works. Still, the details, as Charles D. Wright concludes, show a strong likelihood that the *Beowulf*-poet and the Blickling homilist had independent access to some version of the *Visio Pauli*: the details that correspond to the *fyr on flode* and *wyrmcynnes fela*, although not sufficient to be conclusive, add evidence for the *Beowulf*-poet's independent knowledge of the *Visio*. The unusual detail of the *twelf mila* from the cliff to the water at the conclusion of the homily must be intended to parallel the distance from *Sepontus* to Saint Michael's church at the top of the mountain at the beginning of the homily,[70] but it is also tempting to see the twelve years of Hrothgar's suffering (147a) as somehow related, at least to a general sense of twelve miles, as in *Christ and Satan*, and the number twelve having some relationship to hellish scenes.[71] Further, the *draco igneus* of the *Visio* has rarely been mentioned in the context of the poem: surely this beast is at least in part behind the sea-beasts of the mere, and, therefore, Grendel and his mother. The connecting detail of the *har stan*—the presence of which in such a setting might stretch back to Circe's instructions to Odysseus for getting to Hades and the πέτρη (rock) where the rivers meet (*Odyssey* 10.515; Homer 1995)—further suggests that the *draco igneus* is connected to Sigemund's dragon and to Beowulf's, meaning that the dragons in the poem are also connected to the *draco magnus* of Apocalypse and that Sigemund and Beowulf have parallels to Michael.

4.4   The Charter Evidence

We have seen that the *har stan* appears four times in *Beowulf* and once in each of *The Ruin*, *Riddle 40*, and *Andreas*, and in Blickling XVI. The *har stan* occurs over twenty more times in the Old English corpus, and each of these occurrences is in an Anglo-Saxon charter, specifically in the bounds portions of these charters. The form of the phrase varies, but *on (þone) haran stan* is most common, with *of (þam) haran stane* appearing several times. Only twice do we see plural stones, *on ða haran stanas*. In the charters, in other words, the significance lies not in the repetition of the feature, but in the prevalence of the *har stan* itself, which is why *se hara stan* in *Riddle 40* seems more likely to be illuminated by the charter evidence than the poetic evidence and Blickling XVI. Though the connection of the *har stan* in *Beowulf* to boundary stones and the charters has been noted before,[72] the full significance of the charter evidence has not been considered. The nineteen charters that contain the *har stan* (some have multiple examples) are as follows:

Sawyer 55: AD 757. Eanberht, Uhtred and Ealdred, under-kings of the Hwicce, to Milred, bishop, and St Peter's, Worcester; grant of 30 hides (*cassati*) at Tredington, Warwicks. (formerly Worcs.), previously held by Tyrdda, *comes*.

Sawyer 179: AD 816. Coenwulf, king of Mercia, to Deneberht, bishop, and his clergy at Worcester; grant of privileges for land at Hallow, Spetchley, Himbleton, Ravenshill in Tibberton, Worcs.; Lapworth, Warwicks.; and at Oddingley and Chaddesley Corbett, Worcs. Bounds of Hallow inserted.

Sawyer 298: AD 847 [= 846] (Dorchester, Dorset, 26 Dec.). Æthelwulf, king of Wessex, to himself; grant of 20 hides (*cassati*) *om Homme* (at South Hams, Devon).

Sawyer 312: AD 854. Æthelwulf, king of Wessex, to the church of SS Peter and Paul, Winchester; grant of 20 hides (*mansae*) at Wanborough (i.e., Little Hinton), Wilts.

Sawyer 414: AD 931. King Athelstan to the *familia* of St Peter's, Bath; grant of 10 hides (*mansae*) at Priston, Somerset, and 5 at Cold Ashton, Gloucs., forfeited by Alfred for conspiracy.

Sawyer 448: AD 939. King Athelstan to Eadwulfu, a nun; grant of 15 hides (*mansae*) at Brightwalton, Berks.

Sawyer 553: AD 950. King Eadred to Glastonbury Abbey; confirmation of the grant by King Edmund of 15 hides (*cassati*) at Pucklechurch, Gloucs.

Sawyer 668: AD 922 (perhaps for 972). King Edgar to Eadric, his faithful *minister;* grant of 10 hides (*mansae*) at *Winterburnan* (Winterbourne Bassett, Wilts.), of which 5 hides lie in the common land.

Sawyer 673: AD 958 for 959. King Edgar to Abingdon Abbey; confirmation of privileges and restoration of 10 hides (*mansae*) at Ginge, 15 at Goosey, 30 at Longworth and 5 at Bessels Leigh, Berks.

Sawyer 757: AD 968. King Edgar to Abingdon Abbey; grant of 30 hides (*cassati*) at Cumnor, Berks.

Sawyer 896: AD 999. King Æthelred to St Mary's, Abingdon; grant of 15 hides (*cassati*) at South Cerney, Gloucs.

Sawyer 969: AD 1033. King Cnut to Bovi, his faithful *minister;* grant of 7 hides (*mansae*) at Horton, Dorset.

Sawyer 1028: AD 1059. King Edward to St Denis; grant of land at Taynton, Oxon.

Sawyer 1034: AD 1061. King Edward to Wulfwold, abbot; grant of land at Ashwick, Somerset.

Sawyer 1335: AD 977 (? for 974). Oswald, archbishop, to Wulfheah, his *fidelis*; lease, for three lives, of 5 hides (*mansae*) at Cutsdean, Gloucs., with reversion to the bishopric of Worcester.

Sawyer 1353: AD 987. Oswald, archbishop, to Æthelmund; lease, for three lives, of 5 hides (*mansae*) at Cutsdean, Gloucs., with reversion to the bishopric.

Sawyer 1380: AD 996 (for 994). Sigeric, archbishop of Canterbury, confirms a grant by Wulfrun for the monastery at Wolverhampton of land at Upper Arley, Worcs.; *Eswich* (? Ashwood), Bilston, Willenhall, Wednesfield, Pelsall, Ogley, Hilton near Wall, Hatherton, Kinvaston, Hilton near Wolverhampton, and Featherstone, all in Staffs.

Sawyer 1549: [Undated] Bounds of Bishops Cleeve, Gloucs.

Sawyer 1572: [Undated] Bounds of Washford in Old Cleeve and Kentsford, near Watchet, Somerset. (Sawyer 1968)[73]

A representative example of one of these boundary clauses is Sawyer 298, which describes the boundaries of 20 hides in Ham that were conceded to King Æthelwulf by his councillors, in Dorchester, on the second day of Christmas, in the presence of witnesses whose names are also on the charter. The boundary clause opens as follows:

Ærest on merce cumb ðonne on grenan pytt ðonne on ðone torr æt mercecumbes æwielme ðonne on dene waldes stan ðonne on ðone dic ðær esne ðone weg fordealf ðonon of dune on ðæs wælles heafod ðonne ðær of dune on broc oð tiddes ford ðonne up on broc oð heottes dic to ðære flodan from ðære flodan of dune ðær fyxan dic to broce gæð ond ðonne of dune on broc oð sæ. Ðonne from ðyrelan stane up on broc oð smalan cumb fram smalan cumbes heafde to græwan stane ðonon wiðufan ðæs wælles heafod on odencolc ðonon on ðone healden weg wið huitan stanes ðonon to ðæm beorge ðe mon hateð æt ðæm holne ðonon an haran stan ðonon on secgwælles heafod ...

First to boundary coomb, then to (the) green pit, then to the tor at boundary coomb's spring or source, then to Denewald's stone, then to the dyke where Esne dug the way, thence down to the source of the spring/streamlet, then down the brook as far as Tiddesford (Tetta's ford), then up the brook as far as Heott's dyke to the flood (?intermittent spring/mass of water), down from the flood where (the) vixen's dyke runs to the brook, then down the brook as far as (the) sea. Then from Thurlestone up the brook as far as narrow (small) coomb, from the head of narrow coomb to (the) grey stone, thence above the head of the spring (stream) to (the) lime-kiln, thence to the old way towards (the) white stone, thence to the barrow which is called "at the holly," thence to the *har stan*, thence to the head of sedge spring/streamlet ... (Hooke 1994, 105–12)

Sawyer 298, dating from 846, has a boundary line that runs from the barrow known as *æt ðæm holne* to a *har stan*, and eighteen other charters mention similar stones. Clearly, the *har stan* was a regular feature of the English landscape,[74] a boundary marker, to be connected with boundary markers and stones through the ages, perhaps ultimately derived from the pile of stones that Jacob and Laban place between their territories in Genesis XXXI.51–2. Anglo-Saxon audiences of the poem would no doubt have been familiar with biblical interdictions about such boundary stones: one of the twelve curses of Moses is "Maledictus qui transfert terminus proximi sui"/ "Si se man awirged þe forhwyrfe his freondes landgemæro" (Cursed be he who moves the boundary of his neighbor), an interdiction that is also mentioned earlier in Deuteronomy and that appears in slightly different terms in Proverbs: "Ne transgrediaris terminos antiquos quos posuerunt patres tui" (Do not cross the old boundaries that your fathers put in place).[75] Casting about for other appearances of great, old stones might turn up the *saxum antiquum* that Turnus hefts in his attempt to defeat Aeneas,[76] references to old boundary stones in Latin poetry such as Prudentius' *Contra Symmachum*, a work apparently well-known in Anglo-Saxon England that connects boundary stones to the god Terminus and superstition,[77] or the highly suggestive passage with which Saxo Grammaticus concludes the introduction to his *Gesta Danorum*:

Danicam uero regionem giganteo quondam cultu exercitam eximie magnitudinis saxa ueterum bustis ac specubus affixa testantur. Quod si quis ui monstruosa patratum ambigat, quorundam montium excelsa suspiciat dicatque, si callet, quis eorum uerticibus cautes tante granditatis inuexerit ... Vtrum uero talium rerum auctores post diluuialis inundationis excursum gigantes extiterint an uiri corporis uiribus ante alios prediti, parum notitie traditum. Talibus, ut nostri autumant, subitam mirandamque nunc propinquitatis, nunc absentie potestatem comparendique ac subterlabendi uicissitudinem uersilis corporum status indulget, qui hodieque scrupeam

inaccessamque solitudinem, cuius supra mentionem fecimus, incolere per-
hibentur. Eiusdem aditus horrendi generis periculis obsitus raro sui exper-
toribus incolumitatem regressumque concessit.

That the Danish area was once cultivated by a civilization of giants is tes-
tified by the immense stones planted upon ancestral barrows and caves. If
anyone is doubtful whether or not this was executed by superhuman force,
let him gaze at the heights of certain mounds and then say, if he has the
wit, who carried such enormous boulders to their summits ... There is too
little evidence to decide whether those who contrived these works were
giants who lived after the irruption of the Flood or men of preternatural
energies. Such creatures, so our countrymen maintain, are today supposed
to inhabit the rugged, inaccessible wastes which I mentioned above and
be endowed with transmutable bodies, so that they have the incredible
power of appearing and disappearing in turn, of being present and suddenly somewhere else. But entry to that land is beset with perils so hor-
rific that a safe homecoming is seldom granted to those who adventure it.
(Saxo 2015, Pr.3.1, 18–19)

In addition to how the *har stan*, outside of its literary context,
evokes boundaries, tradition, giants, Romans, and tombs, its presence
in the charters may offer further evidence about the poem. As the list
above shows, the dates associated with these charters range from 757 to
1061. Of the four that predate the tenth century, three certainly have
issues: Sawyer 55's boundary clause is a later addition; Sawyer 179 is
an eleventh-century fabrication; and Sawyer 312 is spurious.[78] Sawyer
298, quoted above, is "suspected by some authorities but accepted by
most" (Hooke 1994, 105). If we eliminate the three that are almost certainly not pre-tenth century, we are left with fourteen dated charters,
ten of which are tenth century, with a calculated median date of 971.
Overwhelmingly, then, the evidence suggests that the *har stan* is a feature of tenth-century boundary clauses. Further, if we add to this list
Sawyer 416, another land grant, this time of King Æthelstan to Wulfgar,
minister, grant of 9 hides (*cassatae*) at Ham, Wiltshire, that includes the
boundary markers *Beowan hammes hecge* (the hedge [or fence] of Beow's
meadow [or enclosure or dwelling]) and *Grendles mere* (Grendel's mere),
the whole becomes at very least a suggestive body of some particular
tenth-century developments. We have two charters of King Æthelstan
dated to 931, that contain, respectively, the *har stan* (Sawyer 414) and
Beow's meadow and Grendel's mere (Sawyer 416).

To rehearse, even in brief, arguments for the date of *Beowulf* is beyond the scope of this chapter. The poem has otherwise been dated to the tenth century or later, of course, by Kevin Kiernan and John D. Niles,[79] among others, although the most recent collection on the topic points almost exclusively to an early *Beowulf*, though no author there tackles the question of the *Visio Pauli* or Blickling XVI.[80] What is certain, however, given the weight of the evidence we have seen, is that the *har stan* is a particularly English feature of the poem, placed in a particularly English monstrous topography. Because the *har stan* appears also in so many Anglo-Saxon charters, the landscape feature seems to have been chosen in the poem and in the Blickling homily to evoke the natural, local setting of the poem. Whether or not the poem is dated to the tenth-century reign of Æthelstan, suggesting that the feature of the *har stan* is not a tenth-century development of the poem seems difficult indeed. Further, when the repetition of the *har stan* is considered along with the sophisticated structures and parallels we have noted in the digression and Fitt 1, for example, that reach across the poem, how such details could have been added so seamlessly to a pre-existing poem is hard to imagine.

A further feature of the charters is geographical. The group refers to territory from Devon to Warwick, including charters also from Somerset, Dorset, Wiltshire, Berkshire, Gloucester, Oxford, and Worcester. Approximately a third of them, however, have associations with Gloucester, and thus derive not far from the vicinity of Malmesbury, which is, of course, a point of particular importance for students of the poem, as Michael Lapidge (1982) demonstrates when he connects the *Liber monstrorum* to Beowulf, Aldhelm, and Wessex. Though Lapidge is arguing for Aldhelm's Wessex and an eighth-century *Beowulf* here, as he does elsewhere on the basis of scribal error (Lapidge 2000), the combination of date and locale suggested by the appearance of *har stan* in the poem is surely worthy of further consideration.

4.5   Conclusion

Adrien Bonjour concludes that the "very number and variety of the episodes [and digressions] renders the background of the poem extraordinarily alive"; to avoid problems with artistic unity and confusion, the poet "was careful to create a number of various links between the different episodes and some aspect of the main story, or between two

or more convergent episodes so grouped as to achieve an artistic effect
which has a bearing on the main theme" (1950, 71–2). Andy Orchard
further links these connections to the poet's method as a whole: "It is
as if the poet has extended the patterns of repetition and variation that
are his stock-in-trade at the sub-verbal, verbal, and phrasal levels to the
wider levels of theme and scene, and is inviting his audience continually
to compare and contrast different aspects of his text" (2003a, 92). The
Sigemund-Heremod digression is a particularly rich passage, as we have
seen, rich in its internal significance, rich in the way it reflects upon the
prior narrative and anticipates what is to come, and rich in the way it
reaches outside the poem to connect the passage and the characters of
the poem as a whole with other characters and traditions.

At the moment of the Sigemund-Heremod digression, the poet has
already included a prologue about Scyld and the restoration of Danish
fortunes, a brief prolepsis on the fate of Heorot, an analepsis about creation, sung by the scop, an analepsis about Cain and his offspring, a brief
analepsis about Beowulf's youthful exploits from Beowulf himself, and
the two analeptic tellings of the Breca story. We have already seen how
the first four of these are interwoven with the themes and scenes of the
entire poem, but it is worth pointing out how the Sigemund-Heremod
digression participates in the poet's digressive tendencies. The Scyld
episode is echoed in Sigemund's treasure (*on bearm scipes*), but this
parallel is also a contrast because Sigemund is not yet dead. The Scyld
episode also gives the audience some hints about Heremod: even without Hrothgar's sermon, I suspect the audience senses in Heremod's
development *to aldorceare,* and the hope that he would become *to bote,*
and particularly the use of *gepeon* to parallel the gnomic statement about
generosity that his career is very much part of lines 1–52. Heremod,
therefore, parallels Scyld and Beow(ulf) early in his career, but then
stands in stark contrast to their successful reigns. Heorot is built, and
we learn of its destruction by fire in a conflict that will be familial, a conflict that brings to mind the traditions of Sigemund and Fitela. The scop
sings a song of the world's creation, and we expect to hear of the world's
destruction, but instead we hear about Grendel and Cain, and their histories are very much a part of the "monster" fights we hear about in the
next three digressions. The scop sings the song of creation in the hall,
the hall where Beowulf has come *wordum wrixlan* with Hrothgar, and
the hall where Beowulf and Unferth next exchange stories, demonstrating, I believe, the kind of variation and choice with which the scop is

presented when the time comes to think about weaving Beowulf's fight against Grendel into this world of associative story-telling. Beowulf's career is linked in all its successes to the kin of Cain and further back to Sigemund and the dragon, and Beowulf's parallels with Scyld are thus reinforced, though the traditions are different (monster fights versus good kingship). Heremod, on the other hand, seems to pass into the power of giants and to be a poor king, meaning he fails on both fronts, becoming equated in the process more with Grendel and the kin of Cain than perhaps with any other character we have met in the poem, though Unferth's kin-killing admits him into this group, and even Geatish history is tugged in through Herebeald's death. Even at this point in the poem, however, as we have noted, the audience is not precisely sure about the three main characters of the digression, and if nothing else, the audience is certainly left with the sense that Beowulf's career could end in at least two different ways.

As the narrative unfolds and as the audience continues to be nudged to look forward and back,[81] the parallel presentation of Sigemund and Heremod enters into conversation with at least two other pairs in the poem. Robert E. Kaske (1959, 492) has made much of the link to Hama and Hygelac, suggesting that Hama is the positive figure and Hygelac the negative. The two passages, taken together, indicate the role of *fortitudo* in preserving fame (Sigemund does; Heremod does not) and the role of *sapientia* in preserving wealth (Hama does: Hygelac does not).[82] The other possible pair lies in the obscure and brief reference to Hygd and a queen whose career has a trajectory opposite to Heremod's (1925–62). This queen—Modthryth, Thryth, or Fremu[83]—transforms from an evil woman of terrible crimes (*firen' ondrysne*; 1932b) whose punishments involve a *mundgripe* and *mece* (1938) to, after a *sið* across the sea, a queen who is loved and famous for good things.[84] The most important question would seem then to concern where Beowulf fits in, and I believe the digression shows, despite Kaske's assertion that the second half of the poem demonstrates the "endurance" of Beowulf's *fortitudo* and *sapientia*, that Beowulf's career is ultimately called into question, predominantly by Wiglaf's comments on his decision to fight alone and by Beowulf's thoughts about and the final disposition of the dragon's treasure.[85] Further, Beowulf's career seems to be the reverse of Heremod's, moving from a lack of promise (2183b–9) to an *edwenden*, therefore mirroring the taming of the evil woman by Offa, the point being that every contrast has within it parallels, and every parallel has within it contrasts.[86] Indeed, one of the most difficult comparisons of the poem is the Hrothgar/Beowulf comparison, for Hrothgar moves from prosperity to grief, and wallows in misery until delivered by a Scyld-like hero from across the water. Beowulf moves from a lack of promise to being *god cyning*, but as he grows, queenless, to be Hrothgar, facing the same kind of depredations, he makes a choice that leaves his people precisely in the desperate circumstances of the Danes at the beginning of the poem, circumstances that we know are the fault of Heremod.

The Sigemund-Heremod digression also reaches outside the poem. Though the poet has already connected Grendel to the kin of Cain and suggested at least partially a temporal setting for the poem that is not long after the Flood, the introduction of the dragon, particularly as its lair is marked by the *har stan*, picks up the hint in the burning of Heorot of Christian eschatology and Michael's fight with the dragon. The digression helps to suggest a possible allegorical layer to the poem. Though, again, I would not at all suggest that this should be a primary way to read the poem, the parallels with Beowulf's descent into the hellish mere and Christ's harrowing of hell would have been obvious to a Christian audience, making the fight with the dragon even more clearly a kind of battle with the devil. Further, very much further, if critics are correct in seeing in the details of Beowulf's unpromising youth, the taming of the evil woman, and the curse of the treasure elements that have their origin in a folktale tradition, like the first half of the poem as a whole, then the descent to the mere and the fight against the dragon also make sense as elements in a tale that may originally have been told about the attempt to slay death itself.[87]

Overall, I believe the poem's digressions and episodes constitute, among other things, a three-way split optic: the poet composes his digressions with an eye upon the historical or mythical past, an eye upon the subject at hand, and an occasional glance toward the future. As Alvin Lee notes, there is no "mechanistic sense of causal relations ... rather, one event, one character, or one scene is associated with another because of symbolic and thematic appropriateness" (1972, 204n15), an effect we have also seen in Fitt 1. The digression brings Sigemund's fight into Beowulf's fight with Grendel, Grendel's mother, and the dragon, and mixes all four of those fights with Heremod's internal struggle, looking forward to Beowulf's last days. However, the digression also merges the world of the poem and Christian world, bringing the cycle of Christian history in as a parallel and contrast. The Sigemund-Heremod digression, in particular, has the effect of collapsing time, of giving the poem a kind of atemporal quality, a fusing of poetic perspectives into a kind of universal present, what H. Ward Tonsfeldt would call a "compression of time" and a "juxtaposition of past and present" (1977, 448).[88] The effect is a moment that seems like all of history in a spontaneous now, but such a summary neglects the way the digressions and episodes draw the poem into and draw into the poem yet a third world of story, a world of stories long since told, stories currently being told, and stories not yet ready to tell.

NOTES

1. Tolkien's scholarship on the poem is reviewed in more detail in Chapter 6, pp. 195–8.
2. For an overview of the adoption and eventual dismissal of this *Liedertheorie*, see Bjork and Niles (1997, 154–60).
3. From the lists in Klaeber and Bonjour, Diller would thus exclude 1–52, 82b–85, 499–589, 1724b–57, 2183b–89, and 2247–66.
4. See Chapter 3, pp. 91–3 and p. 97n44.
5. "The subtle and consummate art that underlies the use of digressions in *Beowulf* can best be explained by its unity of authorship" (Bonjour 1950, 75–6).
6. For an excellent discussion of this feature of the poem through the lens of narratology, see Lapidge (2001, 70–6).
7. Karkov and Farrell identify 140 lines of gnomic content, roughly 4% of the poem (1990, 295).
8. On *edwenden*, see Lapidge (2001, 63–7).
9. Parks (1989, 32). In Parks' opinion, "the introduction of the Sigemund-Heremod digression provides us with a clear emblem of its interperformativity [in lines 868-72]" (32).
10. Brodeur calls this our "clearest and most detailed account of a Germanic poet in action" (1960, 133).
11. Though ingenious, Talbot's (1983) suggestion that Sigemund and Fitela have their origin in Tacitus' *Historiae* as Civilis and Verax is also difficult to accept.
12. The *Historia* also contains the well-known reference to Chlochilaichus (OE Hygelac), a Danish king who unwisely attacks the Franks (III.3).
13. In an effort to "establish the chronological bounds of [the] heroic legend," Frank traces all the early sources, and this presentation of them partly relies on her account (1981, 130–1).

14. In *Völsunga saga*, Fáfnir is described as a *lyngormr* (heather-snake); see Jónsson (1954b, ch. 13, 142).
15. See also Taranu (2015, 28–30).
16. See also Orchard (2003a, 108 and n55). The right panel of the eighth-century Franks Casket has been suggested to depict the death of Sigurðr, but the scene has not been definitively identified.
17. These events are recounted by Hagen as he looks out to see who has arrived among the Burgundians (strophes 87–100). See Bartsch and de Boor (1996) and Flood (1998).
18. For a summary, including the relationship of the Norse and German material, see Finch (1993).
19. In *Þiðreks saga*, however, King Sifjan is father to Sigmundr, and the account of Sigurðr's youth is also markedly different than in other sources.
20. See Würth (1993, 435–6).
21. Precisely the same remark appears in *Völsunga saga* (ch. 7): the family relationship to poison is a well-known part of the legend.
22. For a discussion of the possible origins of the Völsung name, see Finch (1965, xxxv–vi).
23. The flyting, as it is sometimes called, also has significant connections with *Örvar-Odds saga*, as we shall see in Chapter 5. See Clover (1980).
24. The saga, with Reginn's tripartite attempts to forge a blade appropriate for Sigurðr's strength, seems likely to represent a later development of the story.
25. Compare *Völsunga saga*, ch. 32 (Jónsson 1954b, 194).
26. See Garmonsway et al. (1968, 116–23).
27. The story of Baldr has, in fact, been connected to *Beowulf* through the accidental slaying of Herebeald by Hæthcyn (Orchard 2003a, 116–19).
28. The background to the Danish royal house, including Frotho's dragon fight, is usefully discussed by Chambers (1967, 89–97).
29. On the whole of Hrothgar's speech, see Orchard (2003b, 48–53).
30. See also Orchard (2003a, 111–12) and Fulk et al. (2008, 169–71, notes to lines 901–15).
31. The references, however, are to Grendel (137a; 153a), Sigemund and Fitela (879a), and to the feuds between the Swedes and Geats, as Beowulf himself reports (2480a).
32. I omit the following from consideration, though it could be said that they are evidence that both names remained in use: in the ninth-century Northumbrian (Durham) *Liber uitae*, under the *nomina clericorum*, Sigemund appears twice (166, 250) and Heremod once (190). Incidentally, the same text contains the name Biuuulf among the *nomina monachorum* (342), but see the discussion, for example, in Chambers

(1967, 367n2) and the full analysis of Fulk (2007, 119ff). Sigemund Sigeharding is entered in the *Saxon Genealogies* (18), among a number of Sig- compounds, and both names appear occasionally in Saxon-Kentish and Kentish charters. See Sweet (1885) for the *Liber uitae* (153–66) and the *Saxon Genealogies* (179).

33. For a general consideration of the problem of the identity and form of the Germanic dragon-slayer, see Taranu (2015).

34. Griffith mentions the possibility that the *wiges heard* (886a) and the *æþelinges bearn* (888) of the dragon fight could, in fact, refer to Sigurðr, but such a reading would, as he says, render the passage "incoherent" (1995, 14). Another fanciful explanation would be that the poet's source had some such phrase as *mid sweorde Sigemundes*, given the possible origin of Gram, but that would not solve the problem of the details of the fight itself.

35. However, trace references to a method of killing poisonous beasts suggest links between both methods of killing the dragon. The fullest account is in Aethicus Ister's *Cosmography* (a text that would seem to have been known in Anglo-Saxon England, given the manuscript evidence), an account that seems related to an unnamed beast in the *Liber monstrorum* that is loaded with poison so strong it can melt iron (II.23). In Aethicus Ister, the poison has the same qualities, and the locals deal with these beasts (probably *lacedaemones*, though the text here is a *locus desperatus*) by making caverns with trenches in the rocky terrain, rigging the traps with *falces* (scythes), and waiting for the beasts to pour out their poison: the dissolving and burning *lances* consume the beasts. The original link to Aethicus was made, I believe, by Brown (1980, 442). See Herren (2011, xliv and §37c, p. 45) and Orchard (2003c, 300–1).

36. Orchard has also shown some convincing parallels between Beowulf's fight with Grendel and David's (*manu fortis*; strong in hand) fight with Goliath (2003a, 142–4). On Sigemund's name, the name in the poem, and the conflation of the careers of Sigmundr and Sigurðr, see Abram (2017, 395–406).

37. See above n32. The genealogy is traced by Yorke (1985, chart on p. 17); the tradition is traced further back, dealing with the question of Offa Sighering and Offa Bedcing and *Beowulf's* Offa, in Newton (1993, 69–71).

38. I have translated *har stan* as "hoar stone" to try and convey both color and age. The word is semantically both "grey" and "old," and may lean more to age than greyness (Bragg 1985 for 1982).

39. I have translated as the passage is usually understood, that is, that the poet continues here to talk about Sigemund, but I discuss an alternate reading below. See Robinson (1985, 18–19) and Mitchell (1999) on

the possibility that the poet deliberately introduces different kinds of ambiguity.

40. "The passage ... is extremely artfully arranged, including a number of clusters of assonance, clustered towards the beginning ... and the use of rhyming parallel phrases" (Orchard 2003a, 107). See also Griffith (1995).

41. This structure appears in a rhyming doublet in *Judith* (*hlynede ond dynede* [23b]), suggesting how these structures might have been conceived (as well as suggesting the raucousness of Holofernes' behavior).

42. Howlett would also link the structure of Fitt 13 to Fitt 2. In fact, Howlett, based on the relationship of the parallel and chiastic structures he identifies, other calculations of proportion, and six vertical marks in the manuscript under the word *stan* (887b; f. 149r) finds in the passage the name of the *Beowulf*-poet: Æþelstan. However, eleven similar marks appear above the last line of the same folio, making those under *stan* less significant.

43. The link is again made in the so-called "Lay of the Last Survivor" (2247–66), a scene that resonates in many ways with the Sigemund-Heremod digression.

44. The trial has recently been argued to be the first line of a poem invoking the theme of "The Scop's Repertoire" (a theme that includes the motifs of "copiousness," "orality," and "antiquity") instead of a line with a direct connection to *Beowulf*. If true, and the argument is convincing, the moment in the poem is even more significant. See Battles and Wright (2018).

45. For a similar passage, see 1688b-93. The manuscript would appear to be punctuated after *fyrngewinnes* (1689a; f. 170r), meaning that here the adverb is suggesting that the ornamentation on the hilt depicts events before the Flood; afterward, the Flood slew the race of giants.

46. Blake (1962, 285–7) links these lines to Hrothgar's comments in 1720b–22a, which he says mean exactly the same thing.

47. On the variable meaning of *eotenas*, see Kaske (1967). For an overview of the word in relation to the digression, see Griffith (1995, 29–30).

48. See, for example, Bremmer (1980), and, in general, Garbáty (1977).

49. Bremmer constructs a genealogy whereby Beowulf has an unnamed and unmentioned sister, who married Weohstan/Wihstan, son of Wægmund, thus making Wiglaf Beowulf's sister's son (1980, 36).

50. Augustinian readings of *Beowulf* are hardly current, but a useful way of thinking about the poem's conflicts is provided by *De ciuitate Dei* and the Augustine's two cities. Augustine suggests that the earthly city (the city of men, founded by Cain, the first fratricide) and heavenly city (the city of God, founded by Abel) are constantly at war, which is exemplified

in the struggles between Beowulf and his three otherworldly opponents. As a pagan, Beowulf is also part of the earthly city, and the earthly city is often divided against itself: that struggle is manifest in the conflict between Geats, Frisians, and Swedes and the chaos that is coming for the Geats at the end of the poem. The layering of the different kinds of conflict, particularly in the final third of the poem, is masterful; Beowulf's dual citizenship is the kind of deliberate playing with categories that we see in the blurring of distinctions between Beowulf and his adversaries. At another level, of course, man's wars are figurations of the battle within. Alvin Lee, looking at Hrothgar's speech, suggests that speech makes just that point: "It is possible for the spirit of Cain and the spirit of Abel to exist in one man, making necessary an initial choice and continual alertness against the avaricious, murderous Cain elements in human nature" (1972, 188–90). See Augustine, the two cities (1955, XV.1–5) and the internal war (1955, XXI.15). See further Huppé (1984).

51. Similarily, David Quint's study of chiasmus in the *Aeneid* finds that structural parallels and oppositions produce "conflicting senses": "The conflict asks the reader to *think twice*" (2018, xiii).

52. This is not to argue, however, that Heremod, the "Last Survivor," and the dragon are effectively the same, as Tripp suggests (1983).

53. Even the dragon's ire is aroused by a solitary person: all is well *oð ðæt hyne an abealch* (until one [man] enraged him; 2280b); *mon* appears in the next line.

54. Sisam is suggesting, in fact, that the story might not have been familiar to the audience, so immediately to juxtapose the two dragon fights might be a mistake (1965, 4n2).

55. The difficulty, of course, is whether to look for parallels to Beowulf's death in Sigmundr's death or in Sigurðr's. Sigmundr dies as an old man, but somewhat abruptly when, in battle, his time runs out; Sigurðr dies relatively young. On the appropriateness of Beowulf's end, see Tolkien (1983, 32).

56. The only other occurrence in the poem describes the kind of terrible language (*frecnan spræce*; 1104b) that might renew the hostilities between Danes and Frisians in the Finn episode.

57. Beowulf also assumes God is *bitre gebulge* (2331a) after the burning of the *giftstol*. The sense here seems slightly different, and Fulk, Bjork, and Niles here gloss it as "offend."

58. See, too, how the party, upon arrival at the mere, kills a sea-beast and then inspects the corpse: *weras sceawedon/ gryrelicne gist* (1440b-1a).

59. For a discussion of the geography of this scene in *Andreas*, see Bolintineanu (2009, esp. 155–6).

60. See, most recently, North and Bintley: (2016, 62–81); but also Orchard (2016, 331–70); Powell (2002); and Friesen (2008, 107–241, esp. 175–87, which treats some of the parallels mentioned here).

61. See also Chapter 3, pp. 87–9 on the *Visio Pauli* and waste places.

62. For evidence that the language of the scene is more deeply infused in Blickling XVI, meaning the homilist did not borrow from *Beowulf*, see Collins (1984, 66). For the homily possibly influencing *Beowulf* in the late tenth century, see Collins (1984, 68–9).

63. For Wright's evidence, see below, pp. 133–4 and p. 148n68.

64. On evidence for knowledge of Michael in Anglo-Saxon England generally, see Johnson (2005, 50–63). On Michael as dragon fighter and preservations of his dragon fights in text and iconography, see Rauer (2000, 116–24). As Rauer reports, "the hagiography of St. Michael presents the only known textual parallel of a dead, dismembered dragon which is transported to the sea by a local population," in an account that "was demonstrably circulating in Anglo-Saxon England for an unknown period sometime between the early ninth century and the late tenth century" (123). Further, Orchard has noted that Hrothgar's speech contains a phrase, *sawele hyrde* (1742a), which is rare and usually used in "homiletic prose" to "describe Saint Michael in his role as psychopomp" (Rauer 124; Orchard 2003b, 51). By contrast, kings in the poem are often *folces hyrde* (610a [Hrothgar]; 1832a [Hygelac]; 2644b [Beowulf]; 2981a [Ongentheow]) and the dragon is *hringa hyrde* (2245a).

65. For a brief overview, see Elliott (1993, 616–20). For the Long Latin versions, see Silverstein and Hilhorst (1997).

66. Silverstein assigns the development of the many redactions of the *Visio* to the ninth–eleventh centuries, though it may have begun as early as the eighth (1935, 9). The redactions have unique (and new) characteristics, enumerated by Wright (1993, 107n4).

67. Orchard discusses *fyr on flode* more as a pairing of fire and flood (2003b, 42–4), and Abram, though acknowledging the possibility of the *Visio's* influence, suggests the phrase is a periphrasis for gold (2010, 198–216).

68. Wright both notes that *Beowulf's fyrgenstream* is closer to the *Visio* than the homily's place where all waters go down, and, more significantly, identifies the raising of the rivers' waves (Cogiton) with the odd comment in *Beowulf* 1373–4a that the waters rise up dark to the skies (1993, 134–5).

69. The quote is from variant "a"; all versions of the redaction (and, indeed, of Redactio I and Redactio II, as well) are similar. For the version in Redactio II, see Chapter 3, p. 87.

70. This connection (and others that link the main section of the homily to the concluding passage) has been pointed out by Johnson (2005, 54).

Johnson also points out possible connections between Blickling XVI and Ælfric (55–63).

71. Wright points out the connection to both *Christ and Satan* and the sermon *Be heofonum ond be helwarum* (1993, 130, 219–20). Though the latter mentions only twelve iron walls and twelve dragons in hell, the passage in *Christ and Satan*, when added to the repetition of twelve in Blickling XVI, strongly suggests the twelve years of Hrothgar's suffering is significant: Satan comments that he and the rebels have nothing to hope for but cold and fire, woe and punishment, worms, dragons, and snakes, and the poet then adds that, because of that suffering, anyone within twelve miles of hell could hear the gnashing of teeth (334–9a). That Grendel instead hears the sounds of joy in Heorot (86–90a), even if simply coincidence, is a satisfying inversion. Beowulf receives twelve treasures from Hrothgar (1867b) and advances as one of twelve (the thief would be the thirteenth) to seek the dragon (2401a). Twelve is also the number of parts into which Michael slices his dragon in the account in the *Homiliary of Saint-Père* (Rauer 2000, 158–61).

72. Swisher (1998, 133–6) and Cooke (2003, 297–301).

73. Cross-referenced with The Electronic Sawyer (2010).

74. On, for example, Yorkshire boundary stones, which were often inscribed, see Dobson (1993).

75. Deuteronomy XIX.14 and XXVII.17; Proverbs XXII.28. Latin biblical quotations from Gryson, Weber, and Fischer (1994); Old English quotation from Marsden (2008).

76. Virgil, *Aeneid*, XII.896–8. On the significance of the stone, see Huskey (1999).

77. Prudentius, *Contra Symmachum*, II.1004–1011.

78. Sawyer 1380 may also be spurious, but is likely "modelled on an authentic document of the 990s" (The Electronic Sawyer).

79. Kiernan (1981) and Niles (1983). Kiernan links the Blickling homily manuscript and the *Beowulf*-manuscript, in fact, though Orchard has pointed out some weaknesses in that association (2003a, 21–2).

80. At least, the index includes a reference to neither work. See Neidorf (2014), responding to and updating Chase (1981).

81. See also Abram (2017, 401). The expression comes from Orchard (2003a, 267).

82. On the theme generally, see Kaske (1958).

83. See the (biased toward Fremu) discussion in Fulk et al. (2008, 222–6). As Hieatt points out, Modthryth would be a neat anagram of Heremod (1984, 179).

84. See, in particular, Hieatt (1984, esp. 179–82).

85. Kaske's formulation ought perhaps to be qualified by the triad later mentioned by Hrothgar, *mægenes strang ond on mode frod,/ wis wordcwida* (strong of might and learned in mind, wise in speeches; 1844–45a) or strength, wisdom, and words (as opposed also to the regular combination of words and deeds that we see elsewhere in the poem).

86. Huppé (and others) would suggest that "polarity is at the centre of the poet's narrative technique," but the apparent narrative polarities of the poem are relentlessly subverted. Huppé says that the "true ethical polarity rests in the contrast between heavenly and earthly reward," and that no doubt is true, but the poet does not seem to me to be very much concerned with making that point. See Huppé (1984, 49–50).

87. Shippey applies Vladimir Propp's folktale morphology to *Beowulf* and reaches just such a conclusion (1969, 2–11). See also Barnes (1970).

88. See further Chapter 3, pp. 91–3.

References

Abram, Christopher. 2010. New Light on the Illumination of Grendel's Mere. *Journal of English and Germanic Philology* 109 (2): 198–216.

Abram, Christopher. 2017. Bee-Wolf and the Hand of Victory: Identifying the Heroes of *Beowulf* and *Vǫlsunga saga*. *Journal of English and Germanic Philology* 116 (4): 387–414.

Augustine. 1955. *Sancti Aurelii Augustini: De ciuitate Dei, CCSL 47*, ed. Bernhard Dombart and Alphonse Kalb. Turnhout: Brepols.

Barnes, Daniel R. 1970. Folktale Morphology and the Structure of *Beowulf. Speculum* 45: 416–434.

Bartlett, Adeline Courtney. 1966. *The Larger Rhetorical Patterns in Anglo-Saxon Poetry*. New York: AMS Press.

Bartsch, Karl, and Helmut de Boor. 1996. *Das Nibelungenlied*, 22nd ed., ed. Roswitha Wisniewski. Wiesbaden: Heinrich Albert Verlag.

Battles, Paul, and Charles D. Wright. 2018. *Eall-feala Ealde Sæge*: Poetic Performance and "The Scop's Repertoire" in Old English Verse. *Oral Tradition* 32 (1): 3–26.

Biddle, Martin. 1966. Excavations at Winchester 1965 Fourth Interim Report. *Antiquaries Journal* 46: 308–332.

Bjork, Robert E. 1997. Digressions and Episodes. In *A Beowulf Handbook*, ed. Robert E. Bjork and John D. Niles, 193–212. Lincoln: University of Nebraska Press.

Bjork, Robert E., and John D. Niles (eds.). 1997. *A Beowulf Handbook*. Lincoln: University of Nebraska Press.

Blake, N.F. 1962. The Heremod Digressions in *Beowulf. Journal of English and Germanic Philology* 61: 278–287.

Bolintineanu, Alexandra. 2009. The Land of Mermedonia in the Old English *Andreas*. *Neophilologus* 93 (1): 149–164.

Bonjour, Adrien. 1950. *The Digressions in Beowulf*. Oxford: Basil Blackwell.

Bragg, Lois. 1985. for 1982. Color Words in *Beowulf*. *Proceedings of the Patristic, Mediaeval, and Renaissance Conference* 7: 47–55.

Brandes, Herman (ed.). 1885. *Visio S. Pauli: ein Beitrag zur Visionslitteratur mit einem deutschen und zwei lateinischen Texten*. Halle: Max Niemeyer.

Bremmer Jr., Rolf H. 1980. The Importance of Kinship: Uncle and Nephew in *Beowulf*. *Amsterdamer Beiträge zur älteren Germanistik* 15: 21–38.

Briem, Ólafur. 1985. *Eddukvæði*. Reykjavík: Skáholt.

Brodeur, Arthur. 1960. *The Art of Beowulf*. Berkeley: University of California Press.

Brown, Alan K. 1980. The Firedrake in *Beowulf*. *Neophilologus* 64: 439–460.

Brown, Carleton. 1938. *Beowulf* and the Blickling Homilies and Some Textual Notes. *PMLA* 53: 905–916.

Byock, Jesse L. (trans.). 1990. *The Saga of the Volsungs*. Berkeley: University of California Press.

Chambers, R.W. 1925. *Beowulf* and the Heroic Age. In *Beowulf: Translated into Modern English Rhyming Verse*, trans. Archibald Strong, xii–xxxii. London: Constable and Co.

Chambers, R.W. 1967. *Beowulf: An Introduction to the Study of the Poem*, 3rd ed. Cambridge: Cambridge University Press.

Chase, Colin (ed.). 1981. *The Dating of Beowulf*. Toronto: Toronto University Press.

Clover, Carol J. 1980. The Germanic Context of the Unferþ Episode. *Speculum* 55: 444–468.

Collins, Rowland L. 1984. Blickling Homily XVI and the Dating of *Beowulf*. In *Medieval Studies Conference Aachen 1983*, ed. W.-D. Bald and H. Weinstock, 61–69. Frankfurt: Peter Lang.

Cooke, William. 2003. Two Notes on *Beowulf* (with glances at *Vafþrúnismál*, Blickling Homily 16, and *Andreas*, lines 839–846). *Medium Ævum* 72 (2): 297–301.

Diller, Hans-Jürgen. 1984. Contiguity and Similarity in the *Beowulf* Digressions. In *Medieval Studies Conference, Aachen, 1983*, ed. W.-D. Bald and H. Weinstock, 71–83. Frankfurt: Peter Lang.

Dobson, J.Howard. 1993. Boundary Stones. In *Yorkshire Boundaries*, ed. Hilda Elizabeth Jean Le Patourel, John Le Patourel, Moira H. Long, and May F. Pickles, 53–57. Leeds: Yorkshire Archaeological Society.

Dwyer, M.E. 1988. An Unstudied Redaction [Redactio XI] of the *Visio Pauli*. *Manuscripta* 32: 121–138.

Elliott, J. K. 1993. *The Apocryphal New Testament: A Collection of Apocryphal Christian Literature in an English Translation*. Oxford: Oxford University Press.

Eyvindr Finnsson skáldaspillir. 1912–15. *Hákonarmál*. In *Den norsk-islandske skjaldedigtning*, ed. Finnur Jónsson. 4 vols., BI.59. Copenhagen: Gyldendal.

Faulkes, Anthony (trans.). 1987. *Snorri Sturluson: Edda*. London: J. M. Dent and Sons.

Faulkes, Anthony (ed.). 1998. *Snorri Sturluson: Edda, Skáldskaparmál*, 2 vols. London: Viking Society for Northern Research.

Finch, R. G. (ed. and trans.). 1965. *Vǫlsunga saga/The Saga of the Volsungs*. London: Thomas Nelson and Sons.

Finch, R. G. 1993. Vǫlsung-Niflung Cycle. In *Medieval Scandinavia: An Encyclopedia*, ed. Phillip Pulsiano and Kirsten Wolf, 707–710. New York: Garland.

Flood, John L. 1998. Siegfried's Dragon-Fight in German Literary Tradition. In *A Companion to the Nibelungenlied*, ed. Winder McConnell, 42–65. Columbia, SC: Camden House.

Frank, Roberta. 1981. Skaldic Verse and the Date of *Beowulf*. In *The Dating of Beowulf*, ed. Colin Chase, 123–139. Toronto: University of Toronto Press.

Friesen, Bill. 2008. Visions and Revisions: Sources and Analogues of the Old English *Andreas*. PhD diss., University of Toronto.

Fulk, R.D. 2007. The Etymology and Significance of Beowulf's Name. *Anglo-Saxon* 1: 109–136.

Fulk, R.D., Robert E. Bjork, and John D. Niles (eds.). 2008. *Klaeber's Beowulf*, 4th ed. Toronto: University of Toronto Press.

Garbáty, Thomas J. 1977. The Uncle-Nephew Motif: New Light into Its Origins and Development. *Folklore* 88: 220–235.

Garmonsway, G.N., Jacqueline Simpson, and Hilda Ellis Davidson. 1968. *Beowulf and Its Analogues*. London: J. M. Dent and Sons.

Griffith, Mark S. 1995. Some Difficulties in *Beowulf*, Lines 874–902: Sigemund Reconsidered. *Anglo-Saxon England* 24: 11–41.

Gryson, Roger, Robert Weber, and Bonifatius Fischer. 1994. *Biblia sacra iuxta uulgatam uersionem*, 4th ed. Stuttgart: Deutsche Bibelgesellschaft.

Gwara, Scott. 2008. *Heroic Identity and the World of Beowulf*. Leiden: Brill.

Hart, Thomas E. 1972. Tectonic Design, Formulaic Craft, and Literary Execution: The Episodes of Finn and Ingeld in *Beowulf*. *Amsterdamer Beiträge zur älteren Germanistik* 2: 1–61.

Healey, Antonette DiPaolo. 1978. *The Old English Vision of St. Paul*. Cambridge, MA: Medieval Academy of America.

Herren, Michael (ed. and trans.). 2011. *The Cosmography of Aethicus Ister*. Turnhout: Brepols.

Hieatt, Constance B. 1975. Envelope Patterns and the Structure of *Beowulf*. *English Studies in Canada* 1: 249–265.

Hieatt, Constance B. 1984. Intertwined Threads in the *Beowulf*-Poet's Web of Words. *Journal of English and Germanic Philology* 83 (2): 173–182.

Homer. 1995. *Odyssey*, trans. A. T. Murray, revised by George E. Dimock, Loeb Classical Library, 103–104. Cambridge, MA: Harvard University Press.

Hooke, Della. 1994. *Pre-conquest Charter Bounds of Devon and Cornwall*. Woodbridge: Boydell Press.

Howlett, David R. 1997. *British Books in Biblical Style*. Dublin: Four Courts Press.

Huppé, Bernard F. 1984. *The Hero in the Earthly City: A Reading of Beowulf*. Binghamton: MRTS.

Huskey, S.J. 1999. Turnus and Terminus in *Aeneid* 12. *Mnemosyne* 52 (1): 77–82.

Johnson, Richard F. 2005. *Saint Michael the Archangel in Medieval English Legend*. Woodbridge: The Boydell Press.

Jónsson, Finnur (ed.). 1912–15. *Eiríksmál*. In *Den norsk-islandske skjaldedigtning*, 4 vols. BI.165. Copenhagen: Gyldendal.

Jónsson, Guðni (ed.). 1954a. *Fornaldar sögur Norðurlanda*, 4 vols. Akureyri: Íslendingasagnaútgáfn.

Jónsson, Guðni (ed.). 1954b. *Völsunga saga*. In *Fornaldar sögur Norðurlanda*, vol. 1, 107–218. Akureyri: Íslendingasagnaútgáfn.

Karkov, Catherine, and Robert T. Farrell. 1990. The Gnomic Passages in *Beowulf*. *Neuphilologische Mitteilungen* 91: 295–310.

Kaske, Robert E. 1958. *Sapientia et fortitudo* as the Controlling Theme of *Beowulf*. *Studies in Philology* 55: 423–456.

Kaske, Robert E. 1959. The Sigemund-Heremod and Hama-Hygelac Passages in *Beowulf*. *PMLA* 74: 489–494.

Kaske, Robert E. 1967. The *eotenas* in *Beowulf*. In *Old English Poetry: Fifteen Essays*, ed. R.P. Creed, 285–310. Providence, RI: Brown University Press.

Ker, N.R. 1957. *Catalogue of Manuscripts Containing Anglo-Saxon*. Oxford: Clarendon Press.

Ker, W.P. 1904. *The Dark Ages*. New York: Charles Scribner's Sons.

Kiernan, Kevin. 1981. *Beowulf and the Beowulf Manuscript*. New Brunswick, NJ: Rutgers University Press.

Kisor, Yvette. 2009. Numerical Composition and *Beowulf*: A Reconsideration. *Anglo-Saxon England* 38: 41–76.

Klaeber, Friedrich (ed.). 1950. *Beowulf and the Fight at Finnsburg*, 3rd ed. Lexington, MA: D. C. Heath and Company.

Krusch, Bruno, and William Levison (eds.). 1951. *Gregorii episcopi Turonensis libri historiarum X, MGH, Scriptorum rerum Merovingicarum I.1*, 2nd ed. Hannover: Impensis Biblopolii Hahniani.

Lapidge, Michael. 1982. *Beowulf*, Aldhelm, the *Liber monstrorum*, and Wessex. *Studi Medievali* 23: 151–191.

Lapidge, Michael. 2000. The Archetype of *Beowulf*. *Anglo-Saxon England* 29: 1–41.

Lapidge, Michael. 2001. *Beowulf* and Perception. *Proceedings of the British Academy* 111: 61–97.

Lee, Alvin. 1972. *The Guest-Hall of Eden*. New Haven: Yale University Press.

Leyerle, John. 1967. The Interlace Structure of *Beowulf*. *University of Toronto Quarterly* 36: 1–17.

Marsden, Richard (ed.). 2008. *The Old English Heptateuch and Ælfric's Libellus de ueteri testamento et nouo*, vol. 1, EETS o.s. 330. Oxford: Oxford University Press.

Minchin, Elizabeth. 2001. *Homer and the Resources of Memory: Some Applications of Cognitive Theory to the Iliad and the Odyssey*. Oxford: Oxford University Press.

Mitchell, Bruce. 1999. "Apo koinu" in Old English Poetry? *Neuphilologische Mitteilungen* 100: 477–497.

Morris, Richard. 1967. *The Blickling Homilies of the Tenth Century*. EETS os 58, 63, and 73. 1874–8. Oxford: Oxford University Press. Reprinted as one volume, 1967.

Neidorf, Leonard (ed.). 2014. *The Dating of Beowulf: A Reassessment*. Cambridge: D. S. Brewer.

Newton, Sam. 1993. *The Origins of Beowulf and the Pre-viking Kingdoms of East Anglia*. Cambridge: D. S. Brewer.

Niles, John D. 1983. *Beowulf: The Poem and Its Tradition*. Cambridge: Harvard University Press.

North, Richard, and Michael D.J. Bintley (eds.). 2016. *Andreas: An Edition*. Liverpool: Liverpool University Press.

Orchard, Andy. 2003a. *A Critical Companion to Beowulf*. Cambridge: D. S. Brewer.

Orchard, Andy. 2003b. *Pride and Prodigies: Studies in the Monsters of the Beowulf-Manuscript*, Rev. paperback ed. Toronto: University of Toronto Press.

Orchard, Andy (ed. and trans.). 2003c. *Liber monstrorum*. In *Pride and Prodigies*, 254–320. Toronto: University of Toronto Press.

Orchard, Andy. 2011. *The Elder Edda: A Book of Viking Lore*. London: Penguin.

Orchard, Andy. 2016. The Originality of *Andreas*. In *Old English Philology: Studies in Honour of R. D. Fulk*, ed. Leonard Neidorf, Rafael J. Pascual, and Tom Shippey, 331–370. Cambridge: D. S. Brewer.

Parks, Ward. 1989. Interperformativity and *Beowulf*. *Narodna Umjetnost* 26 (1): 25–34.

Powell, Allison. 2002. Verbal Parallels in *Andreas* and Its Relationship to *Beowulf* and Cynewulf. PhD diss., University of Cambridge.

Pulsiano, Phillip, and Kirsten Wolf (eds.). 1993. *Medieval Scandinavia: An Encyclopedia*. New York: Garland.

Quint, David. 2018. *Virgil's Double Cross: Design and Meaning in the Aeneid*. Princeton: Princeton University Press.

Rauer, Christine. 2000. *Beowulf and the Dragon*. Cambridge: D. S. Brewer.

Robinson, Fred C. 1985. *Beowulf and the Appositive Style*. Knoxville: The University of Tennessee Press.

Sawyer, Peter H. 1968. *Anglo-Saxon Charters: An Annotated List and Bibliography*. London: Royal Historical Society.

Saxo Grammaticus. 2015. *Gesta Danorum*, ed. Karsten Friis-Jensen, trans. Peter Fisher, 2 vols. Oxford: Clarendon Press.

Shippey, Thomas A. 1969. The Fairy-Tale Structure of *Beowulf. Notes and Queries* 16: 2–11.

Silverstein, Theodore. 1935. *Visio Sancti Pauli: The History of the Apocalypse in Latin together with Nine Texts*. London: Christophers.

Silverstein, Theodore, and Anthony Hilhorst (eds.). 1997. *Apocalypse of Paul: A New Critical Edition of Three Long Latin Versions*. Geneva: Patrick Cramer.

Sisam, Kenneth. 1965. *The Structure of Beowulf*. Oxford: Clarendon Press.

Strong, Archibald (trans.). 1925. *Beowulf: Translated into Modern English Rhyming Verse*. London: Constable and Co.

Sweet, Henry (ed.). 1885. *The Oldest English Texts*. EETS Original Series No. 83. London.

Swisher, Michael. 1998. Beyond the Hoar Stone. *Neophilologus* 86 (1): 133–136.

Talbot, Annelise. 1983. Sigemund the Dragon-Slayer. *Folklore* 94: 153–162.

Taranu, Catalin. 2015. Who Was the Original Dragon-Slayer of the Nibelung Cycle? *Viator* 46 (2): 23–40.

The Electronic Sawyer. 2010. Simon Keynes (Project Manager), October 1. http://www.esawyer.org.uk/about/index.html.

Thornbury, Emily V. 2000. *Eald enta geweorc* and the Relics of Empire: Revisiting the Dragon's Lair in *Beowulf. Quaestio insularis* 1: 82–92.

Tolkien, J. R. R. 1982. *Finn and Hengest: The Fragment and Episode*, ed. Alan Bliss. London: Allen & Unwin.

Tolkien, J.R.R. 1983. *Beowulf*: The Monsters and the Critics. In *The Monsters and the Critics and Other Essays*, ed. Christopher Tolkien, 5–48. London: Allen & Unwin.

Tonsfeldt, H.Ward. 1977. Ring Structure in *Beowulf. Neophilologus* 61: 433–452.

Tripp, Raymond P. 1983. *More About the Fight with the Dragon: Beowulf 2208b-3182, Commentary, Edition, and Translation*. Lanham, MD: University Press of America.

West, M.L. 2014. *The Making of the Odyssey*. Oxford: Oxford University Press.

Whaley, Diane (ed.). 2012. *Poetry from the Kings' Sagas 1: From Mythical Times to c. 1035, Skaldic Poetry of the Scandinavian Middle Ages 1*. Turnhout: Brepols.

Wright, Charles D. 1993. *The Irish Tradition in Old English Literature*. CSASE 6. Cambridge: Cambridge University Press.

Würth, Stefanie. 1993. *Nornagests þáttr*. In *Medieval Scandinavia: An Encyclopedia*, ed. Phillip Pulsiano and Kirsten Wolf. New York: Garland.

Yorke, Barbara. 1985. The Kingdom of the East Saxons. *Anglo-Saxon England* 14: 1–36.

CHAPTER 5

The Folktale Formula: *Beowulf* and *Örvar-Odds saga*

As a potentially informative analogue[1] to *Beowulf* and participant in the story-patterns that have been seen to be related to the poem, *Örvar-Odds saga* has not garnered much attention. The first mention of the saga in the context of *Beowulf* and its monsters seems to have been made by R. W. Chambers in his first update to his introduction to the study of *Beowulf*. Chambers very briefly mentions a series of Old Norse-Icelandic analogues to Grendel and his mother, of which *Örvar-Odds saga* is one. He notes that the saga includes a "giantess dwelling under a foss, the mother of a monstrous son" (1959, 460).[2] Nora Chadwick, in her wide-ranging treatment of "The Monsters and *Beowulf*" (1959), names Örvar-Oddr as one of the line of Ketill hængr, progenitor of a "great Hálogaland family" that traditionally fights against just the sort of foes we see in *Beowulf*: the *draugr*, the evil supernatural woman, and the dragon; and Chadwick's remarks on the *draugr* Ögmundr are later repeated with a slightly different emphasis by Michael Lapidge in his study of terror in *Beowulf* (1993). Chadwick also notes some of the interesting genealogical links between Grettir Ásmundarson and the Hrafnistumenn, but does not, perhaps, make enough of the entire genealogical landscape of related (shape-changing?) bear and wolf heroes. More recently, Carol Clover (1980), investigating the background to the Unferth episode, offers the verbal contest in *Örvar-Odds saga* as a particularly full example of a Norse *flyting*, and Andy Orchard, considering the seemingly magical properties of the mail-shirt that Beowulf wears in his swimming match with Breca and in his descent into the mere, offers the magical shirt made for Örvar-Oddr as the "most elaborate example" of such clothing from the *fornaldarsögur* (2003a, 127–8). The only other considerations of *Örvar-Odds saga* of which I am aware that have a bearing on *Beowulf* occur in the context of discussions related to "The Bear's Son Tale." Friedrich Panzer's collection and collation of Bear's Son tale versions (1910) does not include any significant remarks on *Örvar-Odds saga*, but a few relatively recent further studies do. Joaquín Martínez Pizarro examines the tales of the Hrafnistumenn (a set that includes *Örvar-Odds saga*) as examples of "The Bear's Son Tale" and argues for the tale's influence on *Beowulf*, although he allows that "*Örvar-Odds saga* does not use the Bear's Son pattern as a whole, but selects groups of three or four interesting elements which it then applies and transforms with good dramatic sense" (1976–1977, 281). Peter Jorgensen examines the "two-troll" variant in *Hálfdanar saga Brönufóstra* and *Gríms saga loðinkinna*: on the basis of suggestive verbal parallels between these two sagas, Jorgensen posits "conscious, literary borrowing," not between the two sagas, but from an older source that may also have influenced *Ketils saga hœngs* and *Örvar-Odds saga*, both of which also contain two-troll episodes (1975, 42).[3] J. Michael Stitt's *Beowulf and the Bear's Son* includes most of the relevant texts, but really says little about *Örvar-Odds saga* itself, or in relation to *Beowulf*, other than to point out that the two-troll scene in *Örvar-Odds saga* is conflated "with several elements of a Polyphemos tradition" and thus contains quite a few differences from other versions (1992, 64).[4]

5.1   Development and Survival of *Örvar-Odds Saga*

The attempt to deploy much later analogues in the study of *Beowulf* can be in itself somewhat of a vexed question, as we have seen. Magnús Fjalldal, for example, has been a consistent voice of caution, suggesting that most of what has been seen as "evidence" for the relationship between *Grettis saga* and *Beowulf* is at best coincidental, even the evidence of the hapax legomena *hæftmece/heptisax* (1998). Fjalldal has also argued that Chadwick's "The Monsters and *Beowulf*" and her "extremely liberal interpretation of what constituted analogous material" led to a proliferation of misguided analogue studies and that the two-troll analogue is a poor choice of focus, as parallel features are far more common in Old Norse stories about *draugar* and *haugbúar* (2013, 542). In contrast, Christopher Abram recently introduced evidence from

Völsunga saga and Sigmundr's deception of the she-wolf through the trick of honey to "activate further intertextual links" between *Beowulf* and a distant Old Norse analogue (2017, 411). *Örvar-Odds saga*, taken as an analogue, adds an extra degree of difficulty in ways that can at least partly be appreciated by readers of *Beowulf*: three main versions of the saga are extant, and the three versions contain significant differences. Evidence has been produced to demonstrate that stories (or "narrative poems") about Oddr circulated orally, episodes in the saga appear in other sources, and it is often difficult to tell the direction of influence of some clearly shared motifs. Some have suggested, on the basis of an Odd, *regulus Jathriae*, in Saxo's *Gesta Danorum*, that there is an historical basis to the saga, perhaps in a minor southwest Norwegian king of the ninth century who journeyed to Bjarmaland. Oddr certainly appears earlier in Saxo (as Arvaroddus), showing that stories about him predate the manuscript tradition (Saxo, Book VIII, 245; Book V, 153–4).[5] *Örvar-Odds saga* in its first written form is "one of the oldest preserved specimens of the *fornaldarsögur* genre" (Ferrari 2006, 241), but the best-known version of the saga is also the latest version of the saga, and every version of the saga seems to shift the thematic focus.

The evidence for an earlier, perhaps oral, tradition rests on four features or episodes of the story. The inclusion in Saxo of the battle on the island of Samsø/Sámsey against Angantýr and the other sons of Arngrímr and the way Arvaroddus dispatches these famous berserks, swinging a giant piece of wood, suggest a knowledge predating Saxo concerning Oddr's strength and prowess.[6] The fight against the sons of Angrímr also appears in *Hervarar saga ok Heiðreks konungs*, a work from perhaps the middle of the thirteenth century, demonstrating knowledge of Oddr, his magical shirt, and his travels (Oddr is known as *Oddr inn víðfǫrli* as well as *Örvar-Oddr*) outside of *Örvar-Odds saga*, though there are significant differences between the two sagas.[7] Oddr is also among the roster of fighters in the legendary battle at Brávellir, although that episode does not feature in the saga.[8] Arguments specifically for an oral origin involve first the flyting or "drinking contest," in which many of the events of Oddr's career are recited in verse. Lars Lönnroth calls this a "double scene"—"something that occurs in the course of an oral performance whenever the narrative appears to be enacted by the performer or his audience on the very spot where the entertainment takes place"—and connects this doubling to the Unferth episode in *Beowulf* (1979, 95, 97).[9] Secondly, and significantly, Oskar Bandle has suggested that the presence of Proppian functions (and Greimas' actants) in the earliest written version of the saga is evidence of at least a closeness to orality; even if Bandle's notion that folktale structures indicate orality at some stage in a story's development is problematic, his attempt to reconstruct the formation and the development of the saga should be of interest to readers of *Beowulf*, especially as he sees the saga move toward a more literary form in its later versions (1988, 201–5).[10]

The saga in its written form(s) is usually dated to the end of the thirteenth or the beginning of the fourteenth century and is extant in a rather large number of vellum manuscripts and paper copies, suggesting that Örvar-Oddr was not an unpopular hero.[11] However, studies of these manuscripts have demonstrated that there are in fact three quite different versions of the saga. The oldest manuscript is Stock. Perg. 4to no. 7, f. 43v-57r, saec. xiv^in (S), and this manuscript contains what is likely the earliest version of the saga. S lacks the famous episode on the island of Sámsey, although the appearance of the manuscript suggests the omission is an accident.[12] An older version of the saga is also extant in AM 344a 4to, f. 1r-24v, saec. xiv² (M), but this manuscript still has significant differences from S. Two manuscripts of the fifteenth century demonstrate that the relationship between *Ketils saga hœngs*, *Gríms saga loðinkinna*, and *Örvar-Odds saga* was well-known, as both AM 343 4to, saec. xv (A) and AM 471 4to, saec. xv (B) contain the three sagas in order, though the version of *Örvar-Odds saga* preserved therein is quite different from the older versions in S and M. There is also a fifteenth-century fragment, AM 567 4to, saec. xv (C), and quite a few paper manuscripts, including AM 173 fol. (E), most of which are descended from the two fifteenth-century manuscripts that contain the younger version of the story.[13]

The three main versions of the saga are S, M, and AB, though the version in AB is best known because it is the version included in Guðni Jónsson's edition of the *Fornaldar sögur Norðurlanda* (Jónsson 1954f) and translated by Paul Edwards and Herman Pálsson as *Arrow-Odd: A Medieval Novel*.[14] S and M have not been edited since the nineteenth-century editions of R. C. Boer, who gives a synoptic edition of S and M with variants from ABCE in the apparatus (1888) and an edition of S with the missing episode supplied from M (1892a). As Fulvio Ferrari has observed, "the three versions of the saga—four, if we also consider the E redaction as a separate version—have peculiar literary qualities, manifest different literary tastes and ideological concerns, and have thus to be considered apart" (2009b, 91).[15] Such a situation makes analysis difficult, but the differences between the three versions also provide insight into the compositional process and thereby comment, at least, on how *Beowulf* might have developed into the form in which we have it. Briefly, S and M are roughly the same length and contain roughly the same material (setting aside the apparent lacuna in S). S and M are both structured around the prophecy that initiates the action and Oddr's conversion (Tulinius 2002, 159). M, however, has a "certain playfulness," developing, to give an example, a "rather humdrum conversion scene of S into a wonderfully reworked comic episode that emphasizes the self-confidence and pagan qualities of the hero and his followers, as well as their total ignorance of Christian customs" (Ferrari 2009b, 87; Mitchell 1991, 113), a change that likely reflects the changing concerns of the periods in which they were composed. Oskar Bandle notes a developing role for the narrator (1988, 201), and Judy Quinn (1998, 35–6, 46) and Martin Arnold (2010, 90) have pointed out some changed details, such as the length of the prophecy (100 years in S; 300 years in M),[16] the very different reaction to the Irish princess in M (where she is called a troll and an evil being, a detail absent from S), and the change from Oddr's epithet when he arrives in Húnaland (*viðfǫrull* in S; *næframaðr* in M). S and M also contain only one fight between Oddr and Ögmundr, and the episode, therefore, remains puzzling in the first two versions of the saga.[17] Ferrari, in fact, has called it a "blind motif," though it seems more "truncated" than "blind," given that the fight can be argued to have a narrative function (2009a, 372).[18]

The longest version of the saga, the version in AB, adds a second trip to Giantland and four fights with Ögmundr and his family. In other words, all the major additions in AB are what we might call "fantastic" material, and the additions reflect a complete change in focus. Though Ferrari calls the longest version "literary bricolage," suggesting that the text of AB is "less cohesive than that of the short redaction," AB uses the motif of the prophecy as an overarching structure for a saga that explores the hero's repeated fights with Ögmundr and his mother[19]; the conversion episode, which was important in S and important but diminished in seriousness in M, is in AB an episode that feels somewhat out of place in the saga. AB has, I would argue, become a text with close parallels to *Beowulf* (with its three fights) and *Grettis saga* (with its five fights), though the parallels are not restricted to one shared structural feature. Oskar Bandle, in fact, observes that AB has more causal connections (*die*

Kausalzusammenhänge) than S (1989, 435). In the genre of the *fornal-darsögur*, AB also establishes Örvar-Oddr as one of the Hrafnistumenn, as is shown by the manuscript context of the saga and the many episodes the three sagas have in common.[20]

5.2   THE STRUCTURE OF *ÖRVAR-ODDS SAGA*

Because, as Stitt observes, the saga "resists easy summary" (1992, 60), I will discuss the structure of the text in AB rather than its content, and thus give a sense of the story somewhat indirectly. Though it is more difficult in *Örvar-Odds saga* to perceive the kind of structure that, say, Fox and Pálsson (1974, viii–xiii) or Andy Orchard (2003b, 140–68) have proposed for *Grettis saga*, there are a few signposts for the reader. The most obvious, of course, is the way that the saga begins and ends with the prophecy of Heiðr.[21] Her unwanted prognostications about his life force Oddr, having killed and buried Faxi—the prophesied instrument of his death—to leave Berurjóðr, ostensibly never to return, and it is the return, after 300 years of wandering, that signals the end of Oddr's remarkable life, establishing a broad chiastic structure for the saga as a whole.

Oddr's first adventure after visiting his father, Grímr loðinkinni, and receiving the arrows known as *Gusisnautar* (Gusir's Gifts), is to visit Bjarmaland (or Permia, literally translated, "the land of radiance of light," no doubt on account of its northerly location). This adventure becomes the foundation of his fame, as his subsequent adventures are generally introduced by some sort of recognition of Oddr on the basis of that exploit: "Ertu sá Oddr, er fór til Bjarmalands?" (Are you that Oddr who went to Bjarmaland?). The question appears seven times in the saga, more or less in this form, until the final query, after Oddr's transformation from the *næframaðr* (birch bark man) back into Oddr at the court of Herrauðr, where the question is now "Ertu eigi sá Oddr, er fór til Bjarmalands fyrir löngu?" (Are you not that Oddr, who went to Bjarmaland a long time ago?).

In the aftermath of the trip to Bjarmaland, Oddr and his blood-brother Ásmundr are blown ashore among giants. The first giant episode constitutes the saga's "two-troll" fight, for Oddr fights first a giantess (repelling her with his magical arrows), then, in a separate encounter, incites a brawl among the giants by hitting the female of a pair with an arrow, before taking out the male's eye with another arrow. Here, we see a Polyphemos episode (AT 1137) with a new motif incorporated, "Ogres duped into fighting one another" (K1082).[22] A second journey to Risaland, this time alone, is also unintentional: Oddr is plucked off a cliff by a vulture (*gammr*)[23] and has a series of adventures that culminate in fathering a half-giant child, Vignir, and helping a giant outwit his brothers to win the rule of Risaland. The second trip, especially, emphasizes Oddr's intelligence, and the episode tightens the structure of the saga as a whole by giving Oddr another parallel with Ögmundr: a half-giant son.

The exploits in Bjarmaland are not only the foundation of Oddr's fame, but also the source of what is at once the defining conflict of Oddr's life and the driving force behind his wanderings. Though the explanation comes in the second half of the saga, after their first encounter, and is provided by a character who is at least Odinic, we learn that Ögmundr Eyþjófsbani is a being bred by the Bjarmalanders specifically for the purpose of exacting revenge for Oddr's visit. Oddr encounters Ögmundr four times in the saga, losing someone close to him each time, and, after the first skirmish, also seeks and kills Ögmundr's monstrous mother. Thus, there are five encounters between Oddr and the monster-family of Ögmundr (his mother and his son), just as most critics now agree that there are five significant recurrences of a "fight" with related narrative sequences in *Grettis saga*. The broad chiastic structure that begins with Oddr's birth, the prophecy, and departure and ends with his return and death thus becomes an annular structure with the fight in which Oddr loses his son at the center of the saga.

Örvar-Odds saga, therefore, seems to be structured around four main themes that recur or are alluded to in various ways. The prophecy initiates the action (and Oddr's travels) and its fulfillment obviously signals the end of the saga. The expedition to Bjarmaland is the foundation of Oddr's fame, and the question "Are you that Oddr who went to Bjarmaland?" reminds the reader not only of that first exploit throughout the saga, but also of the origins of Oddr's most challenging adversary. Two trips to the land of the giants function in very different ways: the first is a "two-troll" fight that links Oddr to the rest of the Hrafnistumenn, and the second is a much more humorous trip that establishes even more parallels between Oddr and Ögmundr. Interwoven with the repetition of the identifying question and the trips to Risaland, of course, are the five battles with the not-quite-human Ögmundr, his mother, and his son, the last of which is the last battle Oddr fights before traveling home to check on his property in Hrafnista and to die at Berurjóðr.

5.3   Genealogy

In looking at the sagas of the Hrafnistumenn, Joaquín Martínez Pizarro concludes that "genealogical connections have been regular conducts of thematic and structural influence between sagas" (1976–1977, 280), and the extended genealogy of Oddr is, therefore, significant in establishing connections between several heroes whose exploits have been seen to be similar, for Oddr, Grettir, and Ormr Stórólfsson are all related. The "family tree" (Fig. 5.1) also helps to demonstrate the generational relationships of many prominent names, such as, for example, showing that Oddr would have been of the same generation as Egill Skallagrímsson. To begin with Grettir, though, he is the son of Ásdis and Ásmundr. Ásmundr's ancestry is traced back only a few generations in the saga, to Ivarr Prick, and is not of interest here. Ásdis, on the other hand, has quite a suggestive set of ancestors: most prominently, if we supplement *Grettis saga* with information from *Landnámabók* or *Vatnsdæla saga*, we can trace her line back nine generations to a character suggestively named Jötunbjörn (Giant-Bear).[24] In between, we also find Raumr, and Ketill raumr, which may refer to the region in Norway where they live (present day Romsdal on the Rauma river), but may also mean "giant," or at least "large" or "ugly." To press further back, one needs to consult the *fornaldarsögur* and *Hversu Noregr byggðist*, where we discover that Jötunbjörn is the son of Bergdís (the daughter of Þrymr the giant of Vermá) and Raumr, and the grandson of Nórr, and there are giant ancestors on this side of the family as well, as Nórr married the daughter of Svaði-jötunn, and in fact is said to rule the mainland "norðan frá Jötunheimum ok suðr til Álfheima, þat heitir nú Nóregr" (from the north from Giant-home and south to Elf-home, that land that is now called Norway).[25] This is fairly distant evidence, and it could be argued that absolutely nothing is made of this connection in *Grettis saga* itself: as Marlene Ciklamini, who has made these connections before, observes: "Grettir's kinship to giants is underplayed" and "is evident only to *cognoscenti* of *fornaldarsögur* lore" (1966, 137).[26] One might compare making much of this link to giants with trying to make the fact that the genealogy of King Æthelwulf of Wessex can be traced back to Óðinn, or even Sceaf and Noah, significant—which of course it very much is, though not in the way I am suggesting here[27]—and I would more or less agree on the basis of this evidence alone, but the other branches of genealogy make this one link to a character named Jötunbjörn all the more

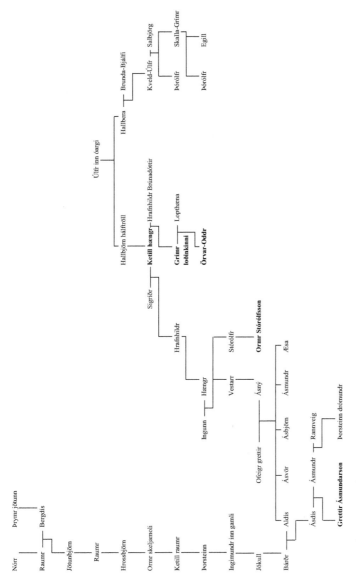

Fig. 5.1 Genealogy

interesting. Grettir's sword, *Jökulsnautr*, obviously belonged to Jökull, Grettir's great-grandfather, but Ásdís makes it clear when she gives it to him that it also belonged to earlier generations on that side of the family (Jónsson 1936, ch. 17, 49–50). In fact, in *Vatnsdæla saga*, Þorsteinn wins a *sax* from Jökull's namesake, a man much larger than Ketill raumr, the biggest of men (*manna mestr*), who had been robbing everyone in the vicinity.[28]

What Ciklamini does not do, though this is perhaps hardly more convincing evidence in the case of Grettir than the Jötunbjörn link, is trace the line back through Ásdis's mother, Áldis: now we are starting to get into territory that is also significant to *Örvar-Odds saga*. Here we again need to consult *Landnámabók*, but the chapter on Ketill hængr allows us to see that the wife of Ofeig Grettir, Ásný, is descended from Vestarr, from Hængr, from Hrafnhild, who is the daughter of the famous Ketill hængr of Hrafnista. Ketill hængr's father is Hallbjorn hálftröll, himself the son of the great and somewhat mysterious Úlfr inn óargi (Wolf the Fearless), who is said in *Landnámabók* to be of Hrafnista.[29] For Grettir, this means that in his mother, with whom he had such a close relationship, there converged two great lines of giant/bear/troll/wolf families. Grettir's blurring of the boundaries between human and monster or troll has often been noted, though his name, curiously, has been connected to "snake," meaning perhaps "one who snarls (hisses),"[30] potentially connecting him onomastically to Ormr Stórólfsson. Grettir's strength seems to be his defining characteristic, as Oláfr Haraldsson greets him with the question "Ertu Grettir inn sterki?," and strength specifically connects Grettir and Ormr in *Grettis saga*.[31]

On the side of Úlfr's daughter Hallbera, we find Egill Skallagrimsson, whose ancestry is of course front and center in *Egils saga*, where his descent ultimately from Úlfr inn óargi is explicit. We might also recall that Egil's grandfather, Úlfr Bjalfason, was a *berserkr* and becomes known as Kveld-Úlfr (Evening-Wolf), on the basis of his strange nocturnal habits. The saga author (Snorri?) comments that Kveld-Úlfr would become *styggr* toward evening, a word that has quite an interesting semantic range, from *dag-styggr*, or "day-shy," "shunning light," which can be used of a dwarf, or simply "bad-tempered," "peevish." In any case, something happens: "Var hann kveldsvæfr. Þat var mál manna, at hann væri mjǫk hamrammr" (He was fond of sleep in the evening. That was the talk of men, that he was a great shape-changer; Nordal 1933, ch. 1, 4).

Being a great shape-changer ought to put us in mind of another celebrated hero, and this moves us more or less laterally on the genealogy to Stórólfr Haengsson, whose connection to Egill and Grettir's family is made clear also in *Egils saga*.[32] In *Orms þáttr*, Stórólfr is said to be the greatest of the sons of Hængr: "Stórólfr var allra manna sterkastr, ok þat var allra manna mál, at hann væri eigi einhamr" (Stórólfr was the strongest of men, and that was the talk of all men, that he was not single-shaped; Vilmundarson and Vilhjálmsson 1991, ch. 1, 398). In *Landnámabók*, Stórólfr fights Dufþakr (both are said to be *hamrammr mjǫk*) in the form of a bear (Benediktsson 1986, S350/H309/M14, 355–6).[33] Ormr, of course, is the son of Stórólfr, and he has many adventures that might bear fruitful comparison with *Beowulf*. Ormr defeats the cannibalistic giant Brúsi and his black she-cat of a mother, becoming so known for his strength that he is identified by Eiríkr Hákonarson with a question: "Ertu Ormr sterki?" (Vilmundarson and Vilhjálmsson 1991, ch. 10, 419). Panzer (1910, 401) has analyzed the career of Ormr Stórólfsson in detail, even though some critics, like R. C. Boer, dismiss the *þáttr* in rather harsh terms, suggesting it has nothing to do with *Beowulf*, and is "a dreadful, sorry effort, without either literary or mythological value; the action ·is partly simply invented by its author, and partly manufactured by the plundering of *Grettis saga* and *Örvar-Odds saga*."[34] Nevertheless, *Orms þáttr* has been of primary interest as an example of a "two-troll" fight.

Of particular interest here are the careers of the so-called Hrafnistumenn, Ketill hængr, Grímr loðinkinni, and Örvar-Oddr, each of whom has a two-troll encounter. Ketill hængr consistently fights giants and trolls and, in fact, even seems to marry one, as his father Hallbjörn, even though himself called "half-troll," consistently laments: "Er þat illt, at þú vilt elska tröll þat" (it is evil that you should love that troll; Jónsson 1954e, ch. 4, 165), and Grímr's resistance to iron weapons is attributed to a circumstance of the conjugal act, though not, it would seem, to his mother herself, an addition perhaps attributable, suggests Pizarro, to the detail being an addition "necessary at a time when the saga writer was no longer conscious of the narrative logic of Grímr's descent" (1976–1977, 272). Ketill slays a dragon that flies out of the hills in the north, though in a characteristic litotes he reports that it was a fish (and hence the nickname) and has an encounter with a giant whom he wounds and who flees to a giant dwelling. Interestingly, Ketill, though of course not a Christian, was neither a follower of Óðinn: "Þá reiddist Ketill, er hann [Böðmóðr] nefndi Óðin, því at hann trúði ekki á Óðin" (Then Ketill grew angry, when he named Óðinn, because Ketill did not believe in Óðinn; Jónsson 1954e, ch. 5, 177).

Grímr loðinkinni has an immunity to iron, though his saga and Ketill's seem to disagree on whether the imperviousness applies just to his hairy cheek, or to his entire body. Grímr is a great foe of giants and trolls, and one such reports: "Eru þeir feðgar meir lagðir til þess er aðrir menn at drepa niðr tröll ok bergbúa" (He [Grímr] and his father are more to blame than other men for the slaying of trolls and berg-dwellers [giants]; Jónsson 1954b, ch. 1, 189). One particular fight, against the male and female trolls in the cave, echoes *Beowulf* in many respects, and, as Jorgensen noted, also *Hálfdanar saga Brönufóstra*[35]: Grímr fights the sisters Kleima and Feima, pursues the mortally wounded Feima back to the family cave, and there decapitates the male giant (Hrímnir, a *jötunn*) before wrestling the female (Hyrja, a *tröll*) into submission and chopping off her head. Grímr's wife, Lofthæna, spends quite some time as a hideous troll before he manages to free her from the spell (he technically sleeps with a troll as his father did), and the end of his saga reports enigmatically: "Hann var rammr at afli ok fullhugi inn mesti ok bjó þó mjök einn um sitt" (He was strong in deeds of force and the most fearless hero, and yet he often spent time alone; Jónsson 1954b, ch. 4, 198).

5.4   *ÖRVAR-ODDS SAGA* AND *BEOWULF*

All of which brings us to Oddr. First of all, it must be said that critics are generally agreed that Oddr, of whom there is no historical record, is an addition to the Hrafnistumenn, as he appears in the genealogies nowhere but in his own saga, *Ketils saga hœngs*, and *Grims saga loðinkinna*, and in the latter two sagas, the mention of Oddr comes at their conclusion, suggesting that he has been added as the three sagas came to be connected, much as Beowulf appears to be inserted into Geatish (and Danish) history. Where the genealogy appears in *Gísla saga Súrssonar*, Oddr is the brother of Grímr loðinkinni, suggesting some fluidity in his ancestry (Þórólfsson and Jónsson 1943, ch. 4, 16). Still, as we have seen, that such a character should have been felt to belong among the men of Hrafnista is perhaps relationship enough, and there are some particular parallels between *Örvar-Odds saga* and *Beowulf* that bear mention.

1. Oddr lives for three hundred years. This may not be an independent feature of the saga (and recall that the number changes between

versions S and M), for *Nornagests þáttr* has a three-hundred-year-old pagan turn up at the court of Óláfr Tryggvason, a character named Gestr, who has been prophesied to live only so long as a candle shall burn.[36] Gestr's arrival at court has many parallels to Oddr's arrival at Herrauðr's court, and Gestr knows and tells all about Sigurðr and the Völsungs. In *Orms þáttr Stórólfssonar*, Ásbjörn is told by a *völva* that he will only live so long as he does not head too far north in Norway ("á Norðmæri í Nóregi eðr norðr þaðan í þat land"), and he dies at Brúsi's hands when he can no longer avoid testing the prophecy. In *Beowulf*, the dragon has occupied its mound of apparently cursed treasure for three hundred years—"Swa se ðeodsceaða þreohund wintra/ heold on hrusan hordærna sum/ eacencræftig" (And so the ravager of the people, huge and cunning, for three hundred winters held a treasure-house in the earth; 2278–80a)[37]—a number of perhaps further significance in the poem, and the same number of winters assigned to Noah in *Genesis A* (although Noah gets a bonus fifty years).[38]

2. Örvar-Oddr is not born at home and seems to have, as his mother observes, no great affection for his family, which is just a hint of the common Bear's Son motif of the one who lies about in the kitchen and does not get along with one or more members of his family. Örvar-Oddr has only slightly strained relations with his foster-father, but those problems are seen quite clearly in the cases of Ketill hængr, Grettir, and Ormr and are hinted at in *Beowulf* by what we can infer about Beowulf's childhood, the unhappiness and insecurity of which has been creatively reconstructed by Richard North (2018, 229–34), including the slightly awkward passage, somewhat peculiarly placed, that suggests that people once thought Beowulf would never amount to much.[39]

3. Oddr's character is assessed very early on, and, like his grandfather, we are told that "ekki vandist Oddr blótum, því at hann trúði á mátt sinn ok megin" (Oddr did not take care about sacrifices, because he believed in his own might and strength; Jónsson 1954f, 205). In fact, there is a peculiar confusion in the saga about Oddr's religion: he is certainly not a follower of Óðinn, but, though he is baptized in Aquitaine, he is certainly not a Christian, either, preferring rather to follow his old, personal habits, even though he thoroughly abuses the priestess, wife of Álfr, toward the end of the saga and professes that he believes in one god (*trúik guði einum*). In other words, as does *Beowulf*, the saga exhibits some slippage in the faith and knowledge of the characters. Oddr has been suggested to be an example of the "noble heathen," a concept

introduced by Lars Lönnroth (1969) in the context of the sagas, but an idea that will be familiar to readers of *Beowulf* from Charles Donahue's arguments (1949–1951) about the *naturale bonum* and the characters of the poem.[40]

4. The association of Beowulf and the protagonists of *Beowulf's* analogues with bears is a vexed problem. Scholarship has all but demolished the idea that Beowulf means "bee-wolf" and is thus a kenning for bear, meaning that, outside of some possible shared motifs with much later tales, motifs such as youthful indolence, nothing at all connects *Beowulf* to bears.[41] The analogue of Bóðvarr bjarki (*bjarki* has been equated with "little bear"),[42] from *Hrólfs saga kraka* and the *Bjarkarímur*, would be suggestive if the earlier versions of the story, at least as preserved in what we know of *Bjarkamál* and *Skjǫldunga saga* and in Saxo, did not completely fail to mention bears, except once as a foe (Biarco kills a bear in Saxo, and Hialto drinks the blood).[43] In fact, the total number of heroes with direct bear descent in Old English and Norse-Icelandic sources is only perhaps two: Bóðvarr bjarki, directly descended from bears and with the ability to fight as a bear (but only in late fourteenth- or very early fifteenth-century versions of his story), and Úlfr, Cnut's brother-in-law, whose life story is told by Saxo and is worth relating in an abridged form:

Vluo/Vlfo, a man known more for trickery than strength, was recruited from Sweden by Cnut to help solidify his hold on his English territories. Vluo's great-grandfather was a bear who kidnapped a young woman and fell in love with her. To feed her and himself, the bear raided nearby herds of cattle, and the owner of the cattle soon organized a watch and tracked the bear to its remote inaccessible den (*inuiis paludibus clausum*) where men surrounded it and killed it with spears. The offspring of this union created a son with "untamed blood" yet a normal body, and he was named after the one who sired him (the name is not given in Saxo). He was the father of Thrugillus, known as Spracaleg, who was in turn the father of Vluo/Vlfo.[44]

This story appears at nearly the same time in the *Vita et passio Waldeui comitis* and its discussion of Siward (d. 1055), who is descended from the same family: Ursus begets Spratlingus, who begets Ulsius, who begets Beorn, who had the nickname "Bear's Son," who begets Siward.[45] Siward is also a dragon fighter, and thus, as Christine Rauer has demonstrated, provides a tremendously interesting analogue to *Beowulf*.[46]

Further, Andy Orchard has connected the *Vita Waldeui* to several other Latin texts, including the *Gesta Herwardi*, and demonstrated particularly close connections between Hereward's career and Grettir's. Curiously, the career of Örvar-Oddr contains many of the same details, clustered as the Grettir parallels are in the early chapters of the *Gesta Herwardi* (Orchard 2015, esp. 19–21). However, the only prominent bear of the *Gesta Herwardi* is again a foe of Hereward, a creature with a human head and feet, the son of a bear who raped a woman: killing a bear connects Bóðvarr bjarki, Grettir, Hereward, and Örvar-Oddr. What is surely striking here, and what becomes clear especially when *Örvar-Odds saga* is incorporated in Orchard's discussions of *Grettis saga* and the *Gesta Herwardi*,[47] is that there are plausible connections between all of these "bear" stories. Indeed, Axel Olrik (1919, esp. 370–3) and Oscar Ludvig Olson (1916, esp. 59–60) have demonstrated that *Hrólfs saga kraka* is a product of the interweaving of the early stories of Biarco and the accounts of Siward.[48]

In *Örvar-Odds saga*, then, we have a hero who is clearly not directly descended from bears, but whose genealogy suggests all kinds of non-human influence. Oddr's *fylgja* is a rather menacing polar bear[49] that appears only in a dream when two of his relatives are reluctant to allow him on their journey to Bjarmaland. Further, Oddr's behavior in his encounter with the male and female giants contains the quite puzzling episode in which he kills a giant bear and mounts it on a stake. He places glowing embers in its mouth and shoots arrows through it at an approaching female giant: Oddr, in a sense, becomes the fighting bear. The leader of the giants calls him a creature (*dýr*) that blows arrows and burning fire, and one might be attempted again to point out the degree to which seemingly distant texts exhibit relationship, for Sigurðr's response to Fáfnir's initial query about his name is "ek heiti göfugt dýr" (I am called the noble beast; Jónsson 1954g, ch. 18, 151), and Sigurðr is the Norse form of the name Siward (Old English Sigeweard; Orchard 2015, 15). *Dýr* here has been connected to "wolf,"[50] and it is in this context tempting to see Beowulf as at least open to being read as *beo wulf* (I am wolf),[51] which would further connect Beowulf even more closely to the Wulf of *Solomon and Saturn II*[52] and, in turn, to the Úlfr of bear descent from Saxo and the *Vita Waldeui*.[53]

5. Oddr's expedition to Bjarmaland is the foundation of his fame. Structurally, as we have seen, the question that identifies him punctuates the whole of the saga: "Ertu sá Oddr, er fór til Bjarmalands?"

(Are you that Oddr who went to Bjarmaland?), and the median use of
the question comes from Ögmundr himself when the two of them first
meet. The question is reminiscent of Unferth's query to Beowulf: "Eart
þu se Beowulf, se þe wið Brecan wunne/ on sidne sæ, ymb sund flite?"
(Are you the Beowulf who contested with Breca, competed at swimming on the broad sea?; 506–7). Even the setting is similar, for Beowulf,
stranger to Heorot, is challenged by Unferth and engages in a sophisticated bit of verbal jousting with Hrothgar's *pyle* on the topic of the
apparent swimming (or rowing?) contest. In *Örvar-Odds saga*, the flyting that Carol Clover has compared to *Beowulf*[54] is the third stage of
a three-part series of contests in which Oddr represents the two lowly
men with whom he has been sitting in the hall. The first contest involves
shooting arrows, the second is a swimming contest,[55] and the third is
a drinking contest/flyting. Counting Beowulf's accusation of drunken-
ness, it would seem that we have three of four elements from the saga
in the poem, as well as that curious question: "Ertu sá/Eart þu se."
Admittedly, the question in the saga comes only after the contests, but
that is because Oddr has arrived at Herrauðr's court in disguise, not
openly as Beowulf has.

In the corpus of *fornaldarsögur*, such queries of identity are quite
uncommon. In *Hjálmþés saga ok Ölvis*, which is probably quite a late
saga, Tóki asks: "Ertu sá Hjálmþér, sem drapst bróður minn, Koll, í
fyrra sumar?" (Are you that Hjálmþér who killed my brother, Koll, last
summer?; Jónsson 1954c, ch. 5, 187). Obviously, this single question
is not really the same sort of thing as we find in *Örvar-Odds saga* and
Beowulf, as the identification by strength ("Ertu Grettir inn sterki?") is
also not the same. There is, however, a classical precedent for the remark
in Virgil, though the situation is again somewhat different. After Aeneas
has announced himself to Dido, using his name and giving some slight
details about who he is ("Coram, quem quaeritis, adsum,/ Troius
Aeneas, Libycis ereptus ab undis" [I, the one you seek, am here, Aeneas
of Troy, rescued from Libyan waves]), Dido seeks to confirm his identity
with a question that is grammatically almost identical to those in *Beowulf*
and *Örvar-Odds saga*: "Tune ille Aeneas, quem Dardanio Anchisae/
alma Venus Phrygii genuit Simoentis ad undam?" (Are you that Aeneas
whom gracious Venus bore to Dardanian Anchises by the wave of the
Phrygian Simois?; Virgil 1986, I.595–6, I.617–18). The connection
between *Beowulf* and *Örvar-Odds saga* with the flyting and the identifying question would seem to be highly unusual, and both scenes are central to their respective narratives.

5.5   THE FIVE FIGHTS

By far the most thorough analysis of a *Beowulf* analogue to date is Andy Orchard's comparison of *Beowulf* and *Grettis saga*. Orchard devises a "narrative paradigm" for the first two fights of *Beowulf* and then compares that paradigm with five remarkably similar fights in *Grettis saga*. The *Beowulf* paradigm consists of thirty(!) "elements," and some of the elements repeat as Beowulf, for example, first hears of the depredations of Grendel, and then of the attack of Grendel's mother (that is, the paradigm already has within it some parallel sequences). Each of the five fights in *Grettis saga* is then examined for elements shared with *Beowulf*:

> Fight 1: against Kárr the *draugr* (ch. 18); fourteen elements in common
> Fight 2: against the bear (ch. 21); eleven elements in common
> Fight 3: against Glámr (ch. 31–5); ten elements in common[56]
> Fight 4: against the trolls/giants at Sandhaugar (ch. 64–6); sixteen elements in common
> Fight 5: Þorbjǫrn's fight against Grettir (ch. 81–2); ten elements in common

Overall, the paradigms overlap only in roughly a third to a half of their elements. Two of the elements from *Beowulf* do not appear in any of the five fights (though one of these is the second time Beowulf hears of a monster's depredations), and ten of the elements from *Beowulf* appear in only one of the five fights in *Grettis saga*. No element from *Beowulf* appears in all five fights, and the five elements that appear in four of the fights reduce to a narrative paradigm that is not terribly distinctive:

> 4. The "hero" hears of the monster's depredations.
> 6. The "hero" undertakes a voyage.
> 12. The "hero" fights his opponent; the place is wrecked.
> 19. The "hero" arrives at the opponent's lair in the evening.
> 27. The "hero" leaves the opponent's lair with booty.[57]

In other words, this analysis does not show identical or even closely parallel sequences recurring time after time, even if there are many similarities between paradigms. Instead, to look only for the moment at *Grettis saga*, the evidence demonstrates an author choosing very carefully where and when and how to deploy different elements, sometimes for practical and sometimes for thematic reasons. Two examples should suffice:

first, the resolve against advice to act is an important element that goes a long way to establish the character of the hero. The element appears in the fights against Kárr, Glámr, and the troll-wife/giant at Sandhaugar. The element is omitted in the fight against the bear because the fight is a reaction already against Bjǫrn, who has an antagonistic relationship with Grettir from the beginning; and, for obvious reasons, the element is omitted in the episode of Grettir's death. Second, amputation of a limb (a paw, an arm, or a hand) appears three times. This tripled element serves to link Grettir with his more monstrous foes (the bear and the *trollkona*), while the fact that decapitation is only for Kárr, Glámr, and Grettir links those three in a different way. In the final fight, the saga author is taking no chances: Grettir has doubly become the things he fights, taking the place of both a *draugr* and a monster (bear/troll/giant).

The point is that the *Beowulf*-poet and the author of *Grettis saga* have at once attempted to link and to differentiate the fights of their respective works for dramatic and thematic effect. Orchard has noted that the dragon fight in the poem contains nine of the elements of his narrative paradigm (2003b, 143),[58] and other homogenizing features are often remarked upon. The *har stan*, to give the most clear linking example, that appears at the mere and at the dragon's lair (1415a and 2553b) even serves to connect the poem's monsters with Sigemund's dragon (887b).[59] However, the fights are also differentiated in many ways: Beowulf's age, Beowulf's preparations, Beowulf's companions (or lack thereof), and the outcomes, to give just a few examples, lead the audience to wonder by the end of the poem if Beowulf is quite the same hero as he was in his youth. The same is true of *Grettis saga*, where the five fights are connected by similarity, but serve finally to signal Grettir's transformation into both a *draugr* and a troll/giant. Like *Grettis saga*, *Örvar-Odds saga*, in its most recent versions, at least, contains five fights. If *Örvar-Odds saga* is to be a useful analogue to *Beowulf*, and analyzed usefully for its similarities to *Grettis saga*, the five fights need to be examined in detail.

Fight 1 (ch. 13)
The first fight is present in all versions of the saga, and the major details are the same. Oddr and his companion Hjálmarr limp away from a tough fight and sail to the Tronu Creeks in the Elfar Skerries. They see two ships draped in black. Hjálmarr advises Oddr not to act, but Oddr heads over to ask who is in charge. He does not recognize the

name Ögmundr ("Hvat Ögmundr ertu?"), and Ögmundr is surprised that Oddr has not heard of Ögmundr Eyþjófsbani, though he has never seen a more ill-looking man. Ögmundr has black hair that hangs over his face such that only his eyes and teeth can be seen. With him, he has eight men whom iron will not bite and who look more like *jötnar* than men. They fight for a time, until Ögmundr pauses the proceedings to ask Oddr what he thinks. Oddr feels that something is not right, as if he might be fighting *fjándr* instead of men. Ögmundr remarks that both of them might say the same of the other, that he seems more like a troll than a man ("Þat mun mæla mega hvárr okkar við annan, at hér sé eigi síðr átt við tröll en menn"; Jónsson 1954f, 248), and tells Oddr that if they keep fighting, everyone will die until only the two of them remain and Oddr kills Ögmundr. Oddr chooses to fight further. Ögmundr pauses the fight a second time, when he has eight men left and Oddr has just Hjálmarr and Þórðr. Oddr agrees to call a truce, so long as he is not accused of cowardice (*bleyðiorð*). Ögmundr sneakily kills one of Oddr's two remaining companions as they make camp (Þórðr), but disappears into the wilderness before Oddr and Hjálmarr can take revenge.

The significant features of the fight include the elements of the sea-voyage and the resolve against advice to fight, but the narrative elements from *Beowulf* and *Grettis saga* are not otherwise in evidence. This first fight already does much to associate Oddr and Ögmundr: both are immune to weapons, both appear to each other as trolls, and even the name Ögmundr is suggestive.[60] Because this is the only fight that is present in versions S and M, it is important also to consider how the scene changes in the three main versions of the saga. First of all, in the earliest version, in S, Hjálmarr does not ask Oddr not to investigate the two ships draped in black. This exchange is introduced in M, remains in AB, and becomes a key feature of the rest of the fights, as it was in Orchard's analysis of *Beowulf* and *Grettis saga*.[61] In S, too, though Oddr still asks "Hvat Ögmundr ertu?," Ögmundr's full name elicits a response that Oddr has likely heard of him, and Oddr adds cuttingly that what he has heard definitely fits, for an uglier man he has never seen ("Ek hefi þín víst heyrt getit, ok eptir því sem þú ert sjálfr at sjá, þvíat ek sá þér aldri illmannligra mann"; Boer 1888, 89). In M and AB, the description of Ögmundr follows, but the description is postponed in S until after Ögmundr has determined just who Oddr is (though not in the "formulaic" way we see repeated in M and AB: "Fórtu til Bjarmalands fyrir nokkuru?") and that they should fight on board their ships instead of on land. In S, Ögmundr has been looking for Oddr for a while (not for all of his life, as in M, or most of it, as in AB). Further, the vocabulary changes quite a bit: in S, Ögmundr's companions are trolls, not giants; Oddr feels as if he is fighting a troll, not a demon, and Ögmundr simply agrees that they could each say the same about the other; and Oddr finally parts from Ögmundr not on the condition that he avoids an accusation of cowardice, but because he now feels he has been fighting *fjándr* and not men.

In effect, what we see in the development from S to M is an author setting the stage for the expansion of the role of Ögmundr in AB.[62] M introduces Hjálmarr's advice to avoid the confrontation, Oddr's complete lack of knowledge of Ögmundr, the formulaic "Ertu sá Oddr?" question, and Ögmundr's long search for Oddr. M also reorders Ögmundr's prognostications about how the fight will go so that Oddr chooses to fight on only after he hears that everyone will die (in S, Oddr makes his choice, and then Ögmundr tells him what will happen), a minor change, but one that has implications for our understanding of Oddr's character. In S and M, Ögmundr now disappears from the saga. In S, this could make sense, as the episode would demonstrate Oddr's prowess against everything except *fjándr*, perhaps also how Oddr appears in the eyes of his enemies, and Oddr's concern for his close companions. In M, the same arguments could be made, but the fact that Ögmundr has been searching for Oddr his whole life becomes quite puzzling, and Oddr is clearly less concerned about his companions and perhaps more concerned about being reported to be a coward.

Fight 2 (ch. 19–20)

AB introduces the character of Rauðgrani, an Odinic figure, who advises Oddr to forget all about Ögmundr and explains the origins of Ögmundr (as Hrothgar after the first fight explains a little about Grendel and his mother),[63] who now is also known as Flóki, when Oddr insists that he wants to find him. The author of AB connects Ögmundr to Oddr's famous early expedition to Bjarmaland, for Ögmundr is a being specifically bred for revenge: his mother is a *gýgr*, found under a great waterfall (*undan forsi stórum*), full of sorcery and witchcraft, and his father was one for sacrifice (*blótmaðr*)[64] and king of the Bjarmalanders, King Harek. He is further trained in magic, made invulnerable to iron, and "því næst blótuðu þeir hann ok trylldu hann svá, at hann var engum mennskum manni líkr" (After that, they carried out rites over him and made a proper troll of him so that he wasn't like any human being on earth; Jónsson 1954f, 281; Edwards and Pálsson 1970, 63). Ögmundr is big, black and blue, and has a lot of black hair. Rauðgrani explains that after the encounter with Oddr, Ögmundr went to see his mother, who seems to have undergone some kind of change as she prepares to attack Oddr:

> En þá var hún orðin at finngálkni. Er hún maðr at sjá upp til höfuðsins, en dýr niðr ok hefir furðuliga stórar klær ok geysiligan hala, svá at þar með drepr hún bæði menn ok fénað, dýr ok dreka. Ögmundr herti þá á hana, at hún skyldi fyrirkoma þér, ok nú hefir hún lagzt á skóga með dýrum ok er komin norðan á England ok leitar at þér.

> But by then she'd turned into a fantastic monster. She looks human as far as the head goes, but further down she's an animal with enormous big talons and a tremendous tail, and she's a killer, men or cattle, deer or dragons. Ogmundr tried to get her to finish you off and now she's living out in the woods with the wild beasts. She's come from the north over to England and she's looking for you. (Jónsson 1954f, 282–83; Edwards and Pálsson 1970, 64)

Where Ögmundr's mother (also known as Grímhildr[65]) had been described as a *gýgr* (an ogress or a witch), this passage and the whole of the fight sequence in the next chapter refer to her as a *finngálkn*. Edwards and Pálsson translate it as "fantastic monster" (1970, 64), but Cleasby and Vigfusson note that the word particularly refers to a "half man, half beast" creature, and the word elsewhere is used for "centaur" (1957, 154). Her appearance accords to a certain extent with Grendel's mother, who is described in the fight sequence as a *brimwylf* (she-wolf of the sea), a *grundwyrgen* (accursed creature of the deep), and a *merewif* (mere-woman or sea-witch). It is worth noting that all of these words appear in Old English only in *Beowulf*,[66] and that the final term has a masculine form, *meremen*, which glosses Latin *sirenae*.[67] The description of Grímhildr is immediately reminiscent also of some of the creatures of the *Liber monstrorum* and its half-man/half-beast catalogue.[68] While Grendel's mother is not described in much detail, she does seem to mix human and monstrous attributes (like the *trollkona* of *Grettis saga*), though she does not clearly have "claws" like Ögmundr's mother.[69]

The fight with Ögmundr's mother is the closest of the fights in *Örvar-Odds saga* in terms of the narrative paradigm: the fight with Ögmundr comes before and motivates his mother (basically 1–14 of Orchard's paradigm), who is especially noted as a ravager of everything;

Oddr hears all about the pair from Rauðgrani (9); Oddr resolves against advice to seek the fight (5); sea-voyage to England (6; 15); Ögmundr's mother kills sixty men, and Oddr hears about her killings (16); Oddr resolves against advice to fight the mother (5); Oddr goes alone (17); Oddr grapples with the monster (21), and she tries to penetrate him with her claws, but his magical shirt protects him; Oddr slices off her tail (13), and she flees only to be felled by an arrow; and then Oddr's companions reappear (26) and hack at the corpse.[70]

Fight 3 (ch. 21–22)

If the first two fights can roughly be seen as the progression in *Beowulf*, from Ögmundr to Ögmundr's mother, with the latter seeking revenge before Oddr finds her, the third fight is the point at which the saga diverges from both the poem and *Grettis saga*. The preliminaries to the third fight are similar to the first two, for Oddr is encouraged not to seek Ögmundr, who seems to be in a remote, water-bound hiding place, hears more about him from his half-giant son, Vignir,[71] and undertakes a sea-voyage to find his foe. On the trip, Oddr and Vignir encounter lesser water-monsters before they arrive at Ögmundr's inaccessible strong-hold. Ögmundr offers a truce, but Oddr declines, and they fight on the condition that Oddr and Vignir alone fight Ögmundr and all his men. Because Oddr questioned Vignir's courage when he advised Oddr not to go, Vignir insists on fighting Ögmundr himself. Though Oddr kills all of Ögmundr's men, Ögmundr kills Vignir by ripping out his throat with his teeth. Ögmundr, injured, flees by disappearing into the sea.

Fight 4 (ch. 23)

The third fight in succession begins again with Oddr resolving against advice to pursue Ögmundr. A sea-voyage to Geirröðr and Geirríðr ensues, and Ögmundr is found at sea, wearing a cloak of beards.[72] Oddr and Ögmundr have a kind of rowing contest before they fight onshore. Oddr kills Ögmundr's father-in-law and wife (Geirröðr and Geirríðr), but Ögmundr has killed thirty men(!) before Oddr's companion, Sirnir, engages him. Ögmundr flees, discards the cloak of beards in order to run faster, but Oddr still catches him. Oddr and Sirnir engage him together, and Sirnir slices off a chunk of Ögmundr's buttocks while Oddr grap-ples with him.[73] To escape, Ögmundr plunges into the ground, but not before Oddr seizes his beard, causing Ögmundr to lose most of his face. In this episode, Rauðgrani seems to take the place of the disappearing companions, and we learn that Ögmundr has a son named Svartr with Geirríðr, setting up a loss to parallel Oddr's loss of Vignir.[74]

Fight 5 (ch. 30)

As the saga is drawing to a close (that is, Fights 1 and 5 are quite separate from the central three fights), Oddr and Ögmundr, now calling himself Kvillánus and wearing a mask, have been ruling distant kingdoms. Oddr hears from afar about Kvillánus, undertakes a sea-voyage, and engages in a tournament. There is no advice not to fight when Oddr finds out that he is facing Ögmundr, and Oddr refuses terms. Svartr, also immune to iron weapons, kills Oddr's companion, Sirnir, and Oddr feels as if he's heard this story before ("ok þótti mjök ór einum brunni bera"; Jónsson 1954f, 335–6.). Oddr takes on Svartr with a club and kills him, thus closing the Vignir incident. When darkness falls, Kvillánus departs with his sixty remaining men, and Oddr wanders off alone into the wilds, has a brief adventure, then arrives home to find he has been rewarded by Kvillánus with treasure. Almost immediately after this, Oddr decides to visit his old home, and the prophecy is fulfilled when he stops at Ingjaldr's old farm and gets bitten by the snake that crawls out of the skull of his old horse, Faxi. Oddr orders himself to be burned in a stone coffin.

5.6   Conclusion

Anatoly Liberman, in assessing with characteristic insight and thoroughness the relationship between *Beowulf* and *Grettis saga*, comments on just how difficult the study of sources and analogues is: "Every part of *Beowulf* has too many close analogues. The Grendel episode resembles 'The Bear's Son Tale' and 'The Hand and the Child,' and scenes from the *Aeneid*. Icelandic, Irish, Latin, and Greek (Homeric) parallels are suggestive in almost equal measure" (1986, 364–5). *Örvar-Odds saga* has not often been a part of this difficult conversation, but there are two main ways that it has been connected in general to *Beowulf*: as an example of the two-troll fight through Oddr's first trip to Risaland, though this episode also has clearly been influenced by Odysseus' experiences, and, quite separately, as an example of the tripartite fights against monsters, as Chadwick (1959, 192) identifies Ögmundr as the *draugr*, as Grendel, Ögmundr's mother as Grendel's mother, and Ögmundr's father, Hárekr, *hinn mesti blótmaðr*, as the dragon (because Hárekr is known from other sagas, such as *Bósa saga ok Herrauðs*, where he changes himself into a dragon). The two-troll fight has been seen as a regular element of "The Bear's Son Tale," and this has connected *Örvar-Odds saga* also to "The Bear's Son Tale" in a pattern of shared motifs. Finally, there are also some individual motifs (such as the "magic" shirt or the flyting) and details (such as the number three hundred and the number thirty) that appear to connect the saga to the poem. This summary would, *mutatis mutandis*, be precisely true for *Grettis saga* as well, although *Grettis saga* is a much closer two-troll analogue (and thus a better example of "The Bear's Son Tale"), but a similarly weak three-fight analogue (Chadwick adds Glámr to the Sandhaugar episode to make the three fights), and contains some more persuasive individual details (such as the *heptisax*). *Grettis saga* and *Beowulf,* as Orchard has shown, also share a much closer correspondence in their narrative paradigms, a correspondence that can be extended suggestively to other episodes and works such as David's fight with Goliath or the *Gesta Herwardi*.

Critics of *Örvar-Odds saga* have suggested that the saga, especially in its longest versions, "exploits the uncanny in order to give its audience an enlarged sense of the spiritual isolation and unquiet mind of its hero" (Tulinius 2007, 457). Ögmundr is a "shadow" or "extension" of Oddr himself (Edwards and Pálsson 1970, xvii–xviii), "a constant reminder of Oddr's fate, a disquieting *memento mori* that will not in itself be Oddr's nemesis but against which struggle is equally futile and which is, in this sense, a personification of the *völva*'s curse" (Arnold 2010, 96–7). Further, Ögmundr may be the devil and the victor in the saga (Ferrari 2009a, 376); Ögmundr is seen as a symbol of death, and "victory over this force is what Oddr wants at all costs, if indeed it is not a death wish that Oddr exhibits by his zealous pursuit" (Tulinius 2002, 163). In general thematic terms, these conclusions fall in line with Orchard's observations about *Grettis saga* and *Beowulf.* Once we get past unprovable considerations of influence either way or an "independent oral source" common to both, we are left with a straightforward observation: "Perhaps the real value of the recognition of the common narrative paradigm which performs such an important structural function in both *Beowulf* and *Grettis saga* is that it concentrates attention on the overlapping of the worlds of monsters and men which is found in each" (Orchard 2003b, 168).

Even if *Örvar-Odds saga* simply participates in a narrative tradition that draws together human and monstrous worlds, the saga deserves more attention as a *Beowulf* analogue. However, I would argue that *Örvar-Odds saga* is in some ways a more valuable analogue to *Beowulf* than *Grettis saga*. The value of the analogue, surprisingly, lies in the very difficulty of its deployment, for being able through the developing versions of S, M, and AB to see how the saga author altered and added is at the very least useful for understanding the possible compositional processes and layers of the poem, precisely the processes that West (2014) has identified in the development of the *Odyssey*.[75] Because of the prophecy and Oddr's need to return home to fulfill it, *Örvar-Odds saga* has a ring structure that parallels the funerals of Scyld and Beowulf. Out of a somewhat disconnected encounter with an insurmountable, inhuman foe, the author of AB has created a balanced five-fight story that is, like *Beowulf*, and like *Grettis saga*, not without its seams. Where critics have often felt that the dragon fight in *Beowulf*, the final third of the poem, is not perfectly integrated in the poem as a whole, and where the poem has truncated or blind motifs (such as the rapid building of Heorot, the evil queen, or the curse on the treasure), and where the final episode of *Grettis saga* has a feel that is entirely inconsistent with the rest of the saga, *Örvar-Odds saga* at times suffers from an erratic narrative pace (like *Beowulf*), a lack of causal explanations, and a curious mixing of motifs. *Örvar-Odds saga* also serves as a warning about how this kind of analysis can go very wrong, for the ripping off of Ögmundr's beard, which has been linked to the loss of the demon's arm, seems likely to have a very different origin, even if the similarity in motifs were noticed and exploited by the author of AB. Overall, *Örvar-Odds saga*, in terms of its correspondence to narrative paradigms and shared motifs and vocabulary, is a poor two-troll analogue and a very poor example of "The Bear's Son Tale." The saga is, though, an excellent third example, with early drafts, of the way a traditional, folktale conflict with a monster can be developed into a narrative that participates fully in considerations of the relative positions of the worlds of monsters and humans. The development of the saga out of the same tradition that generates *Beowulf* and *Grettis saga* itself becomes an analogue, though achieved from a different vantage point, for Tolkien's retelling in *The Hobbit*.

Notes

1. For a discussion of the difficulties of terminology (the terms "parallel," "analogue," and "source"), see Rauer (2000, 9–11). Rauer defines an analogue as a text that "presents parallels with the target text's phraseology and/or imagery," "cannot be shown to predate the target text; is

characterized by a late or undetermined date of composition," and "cannot be shown to have circulated in the same historical and literary context as the target text; is characterized by a different or undetermined historical and literary background" (10).

2. The comment comes in the chapter—entitled "Recent work on *Beowulf* to 1930"—that was new to the second edition (1932).

3. Jorgensen's main argument, however, is that *Hálfdanar saga Brönufóstra* should be considered a *Beowulf* analogue.

4. Specifically, Stitt sees the two-troll sequence in *Örvar-Odds saga* as a "conflation of AT 1137 ['The Ogre Blinded'] and the Two-Troll tradition," and he disputes Jorgensen's ideas about the manuscript transmission of these related tales (1992, 64, 201). The connections with the *Odyssey* are explored by Boer (1892c, 247–52).

5. On the development of the story from a possible ninth-century historical figure through versions AB, see Bandle (1989, 437–9).

6. The episode is in Saxo's *Gesta Danorum* (Book 5). See Tulinius (2007, 456).

7. See Pritsak (1993) and Tolkien (1960, xi–xiv).

8. Arnold observes that Oddr "is listed as a participant in the *Brávallapula* and in the *Sögubrot af fornkonungum*, as well as in Saxo's account of the battle, where he is referred to as Prince Oddi of Jaeren, the location of Oddr's upbringing in the saga (Book 8)" (2010, 86); see also Ferrari (2006, 241).

9. Lönnroth argues for the centrality of the drinking contest to the saga, suggesting that the verses recited might have been a kind of mnemonic for the saga tellers (1979, 105).

10. On the development of the saga, see also Bandle (1990), Ferrari (2006), and Tulinius (2002, 159–64).

11. Although much has been written about the saga, the best account of the manuscripts and their relationships is still to be found in Boer's late nineteenth-century work on the saga. See Boer (1888, 1892a). The relationship between these two works is discussed below.

12. There is a gap of seven scratched-out lines where the episode should be, and the heading prior is *Haugsgörð eptir Hjálmar*; Boer suggests that there was likely a leaf missing in the exemplar of S (1888, i).

13. See Boer (1888, i–vii) and Ferrari (2009b). For a stemma, see Boer (1888, xxxiv) and Arnold (2010, 102), though Arnold and Ferrari (cited above) differ slightly from Boer in terms of the chronological placement of C.

14. The Pálsson and Edwards translation is reprinted in their *Seven Viking Romances* (1985, 25–137).

15. Mitchell says: "In essence, there is no single *Örvar-Odds saga*, but rather several, each reworked by succeeding generations apparently building on the foundations left by earlier editors, or in any event by different writers with differing tastes" (1991, 113). The fact of the saga's survival in multiple forms enables comparison with the slow accretion of features in the *Odyssey* (West 2014) and with the probable development of *Beowulf* into the form in which we now have it.

16. This may be part of what seems to have been a magnification of fantastic elements in the saga. For example, as Bandle points out, Oddr grows from seven ells in S to twelve in AB (Bandle 1989, 436).

17. Bandle says this is true of S in general, that sections of the saga only seem superficially connected. Of Ögmundr, he says: "Steht die Episode des Kampfs mit Ögmundr Eyþjófsbani recht isoliert" (1989, 431–2).

18. As Max Lüthi puts it, a "blind motif" is "an element that is completely functionless," and a "truncated motif" is an element that, "while not entirely lacking a function, remains unconnected in one or another essential respect"; in folktale, at least, blind motifs are very rare (1982, 61).

19. Ferrari comments that "the new *sagnamaðr* [in AB] is no longer concerned with the religious orthodoxy of his audience and does not seem directly interested in the social and political reality of his days, [but instead] takes over and fully develops a motif which was already present in the old redaction: the motif of Oddr's vincibility or imperfect invincibility" (2006, 245).

20. See Boer (1892b, 99–100).

21. On the place of the prophecy in the tradition of such pronouncements, see Quinn (1998, 29–50) and Mitchell (1997, 81–100).

22. This episode is in the earliest version of the saga and remains in M and AB. West's reconstruction of how the Polyphemos episode, a folktale from a prior and separate tradition, becomes part of Odysseus' career is instructive for how the saga blends material from different sources (2014, 12–14, 198–204).

23. The *gammr* transforms into a *flugdreki* ("flying dragon") in E (Ferrari 2009b, 87).

24. "Ketill raumr hét hersir ágætr í Raumsdal í Nóregi; hann var son Orms skeljamola, Hross-Bjarnarsonar, Raumssonar, Jǫtun-Bjarnarsonar norðan ór Nóregi" (Benediktsson 1986, S179/H145, 216–17). *Vatnsdæla saga* has almost the same genealogy, but Raumr (son of Jötun-Björn) is omitted at the opening of the saga (ch. 1). For a fuller family tree, see Sveinnson (1939, 334).

25. *Frá Fornjóti ok hans ættmönnum*, the first part of which is *Hversu Noregr byggðist* (Jónsson 1954d, ch. 1, 75–9).

26. The family tree of Ásdís' side of the family does, however, appear in the edition of *Grettis saga*. See Jónsson (1936, 378).

27. See Garmonsway (1994, 66–7); *Anglo-Saxon Chronicle* 855 CE, esp. MSS B and C; and Chapter 3, pp. 84–5.

28. That is, Þorsteinn, whose grandson is Jökull, kills a giant named Jökull and takes the giant's marvellous *sax* (Sveinsson 1939, ch. 3, 6–11). The phrase *ealdsweord eotenisc* appears three times in *Beowulf*, most significantly in the description of the sword Beowulf finds in Grendel's mother's lair (1558a; 2616a; and 2979a).

29. Orchard has also demonstrated that Grettir and Egill Skallagrímsson share descent from Úlfr inn óargi, whose son and daughter both have bear names; Orchard points out the parallels between Grettir and Egill and Grettir and Ketill hængr (2003b, 160). Chadwick also traces Grettir's descent back to Hallbjörn Hálftröll (1959, 188–9).

30. Chadwick (1959, 189n5). Chadwick is quoting Jónsson (1936, 7n2).

31. "En þat er flestra manna ætlan, at Grettir hafi strekastr verit á landinu, síðan þeir Ormr Stórólfsson ok Þórálfr Skólmsson lǫgðu af aflraunir" (Jónsson 1936, ch. 39, 132; ch. 58, 187). Of *Orms þáttr* and *Grettis saga*, Chadwick comments: "There can be no possible doubt of a connexion between the two stories [that is, *Orms þáttr* likely borrows from *Grettis saga*]" (1959, 188).

32. Ketill hængr (the second) was a close friend of Þórólfr Kveldúlfsson. See the genealogical information in Nordal, *Egils saga*, ch. 23, 57–60.

33. The forms of Stórólfr and Dufþakr suggest Odinic forms of fighting (as does dog or wolf form). See Orchard (2015, 15).

34. Panzer discusses the *þáttr* at length (1910, 344–63).

35. See above, p. 158. *Hálfdanar saga Brönufóstra* has been called the closest analogue to *Beowulf*. Hálfdanr picks his way along a narrow path, finds a lit cave with two cannibalistic trolls in it, first kills Járnnefr by decapitation, then fights Sleggja, who has a short sword, but chooses to wrestle when she has no success with it. As Sleggja falls into a chasm, Hálfdanr miraculously finds another short sword and beheads her with it. Later, he discovers he was helped in that fight by Brana, another ogress. For a summary, see Stitt (1992, 50–7). Hálfdanr's found sword is a *sax gulli búit*, as the blade Beowulf finds is *gylden hilt* (1677a); the sword Höttr gets from the king in *Hrólfs saga kraka* is called *Gullinhjalti*.

36. The prophecy resembles the story of Meleager, who is fated to live only so long as a certain brand should burn (see, among other sources, Ovid's *Metamorphoses*, Book VIII. 260–546, esp. 451–525). The prophecy in *Örvar-Odds saga* is likely influenced by the impossible prophecy of Oleg in the Russian Chronicle of Nestor: see Taylor (1921) and Chadwick (1946, 23–4). A distant folktale influence also cannot be ruled out: West

has pointed out another link to Odysseus and the legend that poisonous droppings from a heron caused his eventual death. As West puts the folktale situation: "Someone enjoys a set of immunities that appear to protect him from every eventuality, until a particular combination of circumstances is brought about that circumvents their seemingly comprehensive provisions" (2014, 14).

37. All citations from *Beowulf* are from Fulk et al. (2008).
38. See Doane (2013), lines 1598–1601c: "þa nyttade Noe siððan/ mid sunum sinum sidan rices/ þreohund wintra þisses lifes/ freomen æfter flode, and fiftig eac,/ þa he forðgewat" (Then Noah enjoyed after that with his sons the broad kingdom for three hundred winters of this life, free men after the flood, and fifty more besides, before he went forth). See also Chapter 3, pp. 84–5.
39. "Hean was lange/ swa hyne Geata bearn godne ne tealdon,/ ne hyne on medobence micles wyrðne/ (dry)hten Wedera [MS wereda] gedon wolde" (Despised was he long, so that the men of the Geats considered him no good, and neither did the lord of the Wederas wish to do him much honor on the mead-bench [lit. "make him worthy of much"]; 2183b-6).
40. Tulinius (2007, 456) suggests that Oddr is an example of the "noble heathen," though Lönnroth does not mention Oddr in his original study. Tulinius further remarks that the function of the three-hundred-year lifespan of Oddr is necessary to have him live fully in both legendary and Christian times and that the conversion links the saga to *Nornagests þáttr*. See Lönnroth (1969) and Donahue (1949–1951).
41. See Benson (1970, 22–5), in which Benson completely dismisses the name as a kenning for bear, and Fulk (2007, 136), in which Fulk concludes that the first element of the name is far more likely simply to be "Bēow [as] found in the West-Saxon king-list."
42. As we have seen, "Björn" appears frequently as a name and name element in dithematic names. Orchard has pointed out the significance of some Björn characters in other sagas (2003b, 147–8), and I would add the Björn who mocks Ketill in *Ketils saga hængs* and dies for it.
43. There is one odd passage in Saxo. As Biarco and Hialto exchange verses and Biarco seems slow to enter the fight, Biarco orders his fire stoked, then Hialto, still exhorting him to join the fray, says: "Igne ursos arcere licet: penetralia flammis/ Spargamus, primosque petant incendia postes" (Bears may be warded off with fire; let us strew the interior with flames, starting at the outer doorposts; 2015, II.7.12; Vol. 1, 128–9). Otherwise, all the relevant passages pertaining to Biarco/Böðvarr bjarki from all the sources can be found in translation in Garmonsway et al. (1968).
44. The summary is mine, adapted from Saxo (2015, X.15.1–4; Vol. 1, 734–7). Adam of Bremen calls him simply *Wolf, dux Angliae*, and this story of his family does not appear (Schmeidler 1917, II.liv [52]).

45. There are two Latin versions of the story. In the other, Siward is the grandson of the bear. See Olson (1916, 13–14).
46. The passage from the *Vita Waldeui* about Siward is printed and translated by Rauer, and her discussion of the passage is most useful (2000, 125–33 [discussion], 162–5 [passage]; for the sources of Siward's life, see particularly 125n1). The *Vita Waldeui* may predate Saxo's *Gesta Danorum*, which was likely completed between 1208 and 1219 (Friis-Jensen and Fisher 2015, xxxiv).
47. One cannot do justice to Orchard's detailed comparisons and discussion, but the connections are strong and suggestive, and *Beowulf* contains the same kind of hero (Orchard 2015, 31–2 et passim).
48. Benson sums up the findings of Olrik and Olson thus: "First, there is the history of Bjarki, who has a reputation for killing bears. To this is joined the tradition of Siward, who is descended from bears and has a reputation for killing monsters and who is noted as a successful exile. Separately, neither of the stories bears any significant relation to the story in *Beowulf*" (1970, 18). There are dissenting voices: see, for example, the lucid assessment of Niles (2011, 54–6).
49. In the *Bjarkarímur*, Böðvarr bjarki also takes the form specifically of a polar bear, while he is simply a bear in *Hrólfs saga kraka*.
50. Breen suggests that Sigurðr's remark refers to the wolf (1999, 35). See also Guðmundsdóttir (2007).
51. It might then also be tempting in the Old English formulation with *beon* to see a nod toward God's response to Moses in Exodus III.14 (*ego sum qui sum*; I am who I am). For problems with "I am wolf," see Fulk's (2007, 119–36) discussion of the Durham *Liber uitae* and the name "Biuulf" (the *Liber uitae* also contains "Boduwar Berki"). See also Orchard (2015, 32).
52. See Chapter 3, pp. 85–6.
53. Though the romances are from the first half of the fourteenth century at the earliest, the ease with which heroes could move from "bear" to "wolf" is perhaps illustrated by *Valentin und Namelos* and *Valentin et Orson*. Namelos in the earliest versions of the story is (obviously nameless and) carried off and raised for a time by a wolf; Orson takes the name of the bear who carries him off. See Dickson (1929, 170–2).
54. Of the nearly forty examples of the flyting that Clover (1980) considers, eight are from the legendary sagas and six of these are from the Sagas of the Hrafnistumenn (three from *Ketils saga Hængs*, one from *Gríms saga loðinkinna*, and two from *Örvar-Odds saga*), a concentration that is statistically significant, although potentially explicable by the borrowing of motifs among members of the same family.
55. Orchard notes many similarities, also, between the swimming contest in *Egils saga einhenda* and *Beowulf* and the fact that a "shirt that no

weapon could bite" also appears later in the saga, as it does in *Beowulf* and *Örvar-Odds saga* (2003a, 126–7). Anlezark notes that Beowulf performs three feats of swimming/rowing (against Breca; dive into the mere; swimming back from Frisia with thirty suits of armor). Oddr's contest is more akin to the dive into the mere (a breath-holding challenge). See Anlezark (2011, 233).

56. Orchard omits Grettir's decapitation of Glámr, which I would argue is important; he includes an eleventh element ("H. Grettir wins but is cursed by the dying Glámr") even though it has no parallel element in the *Beowulf* paradigm. The curse, however, is "central to the structure" of the saga (2003b, 156), as the prophecy is central to *Örvar-Odds saga*, especially in S and M.

57. I have made the elements generic, adapting Orchard's words, and I have left them in numerical order, even though the elements appear in different sequences.

58. Elsewhere, Orchard has demonstrated that the paradigm can be found much farther afield, as, for example, in David's fight with Goliath in I Samuel XVI–XVII (2003a, 144).

59. The *har stan* may also link the poem to Blickling Homily XVI and the *Visio Pauli*, but the direction of influence in that case is a whole different matter. See Chapter 4, pp. 123–39.

60. Chadwick has noted that *draugar* often have *Ag-* and *Ög-* names (1959, 182), and the possibility that the first element is ON *agi*, OE *oga*, related to OE *aglæca*, would make the name have further resonance with *Beowulf*.

61. In *Hervarar saga ok Heiðreks konungs*, Oddr suggests to Hjálmarr that they flee into the woods and avoid the fight with the sons of Arngrímr, but Hjálmarr refuses his advice, also suggesting that this motif is a later addition, transposed to Oddr in a saga in which he is the hero (Tolkien 1960, 6). The warning in *Beowulf* is Hygelac's reminder after the fact (1994b-7a), contradicted by the narrator's (202–4) and Beowulf's own remarks (415–18). Overlooked in this warning are Unferth's accusation that Beowulf and Breca contested against advice (510b-12) and Wiglaf's reminder after the fact that Beowulf could not be dissuaded from fighting the dragon (3077-84a): in effect, there is advice not to undertake the task before each of Beowulf's major solo exploits.

62. The episode changes very little between M and AB.

63. See *Beowulf* 1321–82.

64. Edwards and Pálsson translate *blótmaðr* as "sorcerer" (1970, 63), but it seems likely that the sense of heathen rites here (and below) is intended to contrast Oddr's avowed dislike for heathen practice. The sorcery and witchcraft come from Ögmundr's mother and his instruction with the Lapps (the phrase *galdra ok gerninga* appears in each instance).

65. The name is important in the sagas of the Hrafnistumenn. See p. 188n72, below.

66. *Brimwylf* probably appears twice in the poem (1506a, MS *brim wyl* emended to *brimwylf*; 1599a), and the other two terms are hapax legomena.

67. *Meremenna* (or *meremennena*) glosses *sirenarum* in Aldhelm's prose *De uirginitate* and the Cleopatra glosses.

68. Orchard points out the parallels between the structure of the *Liber monstrorum* and *Beowulf* (three parts; three monster fights) and how that structure is described in the prologue as a *marina puella* or *sirena* with a human head and shaggy and scaly other parts (2003b, 94). For other specific creatures with a human head (or heads), see the *Liber monstrorum* entries for fauns, I.5; sirens, I.6; onocentaurs, I.10; Scylla, I.14; monsters with three human heads, I.34; harpies, I.44; satyrs and incubi, I.46; dracontopodes, I.49; and Triton I.52 (edition and translation in Orchard 2003b, 254–320). Orchard also discusses the possible connections of the *Liber monstrorum* to *Beowulf* (2003b, 86–115). See, in addition, Lapidge (1982).

69. Grendel's mother attempts to pierce Beowulf's armor *laþan fingrum* (1505b), a phrase that is often translated "hostile claws" (see, for example, Liuzza 2013, 145). Grendel does have steel-like tips to his "fingers" (984b-7a), however, so it seems safe to assume his mother does as well.

70. This scene echoes the episode in *Hrólfs saga kraka* in which Höttr/Hjalti attacks the flying beast that Bóðvarr bjarki has already killed (ch. 35–36).

71. Ögmundr is here described as the greatest *tröll* and *óvættr* (Jónsson 1954f, 288) and later calls himself an *andi*, a spirit or ghost (Jónsson 1954f, 291).

72. In this sequence (and others), the author of AB can be seen blending very different material. Geirröðr and Geirríðr are, of course, well-known giant names: the adventures of Þórr at Geirröðargarðr are told in *Skáldskaparmál* 18, and Þórr's adventures can be transferred to other heroes. See, for example, *Þorsteins þáttr bæjarmagns* and the account in McKinnell (2005, 118–22). Geirríðr appears also in *Gríms saga loðink-inna* as the hag who rescues Grímr after the fight over the beached whale, but turns out to be his beloved Lofthæna (ch. 2; Jónsson 1954b, 190–4), who has been under a spell (actually wearing a *trollkona-hamr*) effected by the evil Grímhildr, thus doubling the connection to *Örvar-Odds saga*. The cloak of beards is familiar from Arthurian material, as it appears at least as early as Geoffrey of Monmouth's *Historia regum Britanniae* (ca. 1136), recurs in the two main versions of the *Breta sögur*, and may have a Celtic source (though see Morris 1982, 76–7). The account in Geoffrey, when juxtaposed with the saga, demonstrates well how borrowed incidents can be incorporated in new contexts. In Geoffrey, Arthur speaks of Ritho as his sternest test before he, resolving

to go alone, fights the club-swinging giant on the isolated Mount St Michael and has him beheaded (*Historia* X.3). Ritho wanted Arthur's beard for his cloak, but agreed in lieu of the beard to a duel in which the victor would get the cloak of beards and the loser's beard. Overall, we see in this one contest how Oddr is connected both to Þórr and to Arthur, and we see in the killing of Geirröðr and Geirríðr how the author of AB creates parallel narrative paradigms of his own, looking back from this fight to the Polyphemos-inspired incident that has been identified as the two-troll episode of the saga (ch. 5–6). We also see how motifs that might appear to be connected to one context (the loss of an arm in "The Bear's Son Tale") may in fact at least have another parallel explanation (that is, Ögmundr loses his beard because that was the pact in the Arthurian source of the episode). See also Nickel (1985).

73. This is the only fight in which Oddr fights along with a companion, suggesting a parallel to Beowulf/Wiglaf and even to Grettir/Illugi at the conclusion of *Grettis saga*.

74. Ögmundr's escapes in the third and fourth encounters with Oddr bring to mind Beowulf's promise to Hrothgar before diving into the mere: "Ic hit þe gehate, no he on helm losaþ,/ no on foldan fæþm ne on fyrgen-holt/ ne on gyfenes grund, ga þær he wille!" (I promise you this: he will not escape to cover, not in the embrace of the earth, not in the mountain woods, and not in the depths of the sea, go where he will!; 1392–4). Indeed, Oddr upholds the boast, pursuing Ögmundr despite his disappearances into the wilderness (Fight 1), the sea (Fight 3, Fight 2 against Ögmundr), and into the embrace of the earth (Fight 4, Fight 3 against Ögmundr). Orchard has connected Beowulf's "formulaic boast" to the *Liber monstrorum* and its account of monsters "in abditis mundi partibus" (2003b, 111).

75. See Chapter 1, pp. 37–8.

REFERENCES

Abram, Christopher. 2017. Bee-Wolf and the Hand of Victory: Identifying the Heroes of *Beowulf* and *Vǫlsunga saga*. *Journal of English and Germanic Philology* 116 (4): 387–414.

Anlezark, Daniel. 2011. All at Sea: Beowulf's Marvellous Swimming. In *Myths, Legends, and Heroes: Essays on Old Notes and Old English Literature in Honour of John McKinnell*, ed. Anlezark, 225–241. Toronto: University of Toronto Press.

Arnold, Martin. 2010. *Við þik sættumsk ek aldri. Örvar-Odds saga* and the Meanings of Ögmundr Eyþjófsbani. In *Making History: Essays on the Fornaldarsögur*, ed. Martin Arnold and Alison Finlay, 85–104. London: Viking Society for Northern Research, University College London.

Bandle, Oskar. 1988. Die Fornaldarsaga zwischen Mundlichkeit und Schriftlichkeit zur Entstehung und Entwicklung der Örvar-Odds saga. In Zwischen Festtag und Alltag: zehn Beiträge zum Thema "Mundlichkeit und Schriftlichkeit", ed. Wolfgang Raible, 191–214. Tübingen: Gunter Narr.

Bandle, Oskar. 1989. Die Entwicklung der Örvar-Odds saga als Beitrag zur Gattungstypologie. In Arbeiten zur Skandinavistik: 8. Arbeitstagung der Skandinavisten des deutschen Sprachgebiets, 27.9.-3.10.1987 in Freiburg i. Br., ed. Otmar Werner, 426–443, Frankfurt: Peter Lang.

Bandle, Oskar. 1990. Um Þróun Örvar-Odds sögu. Gripla 7: 51–71.

Bekker-Nielsen, Hans, Preben M. Sørensen, Andreas Faarder, and Peter Foote (eds.). 1979. Medieval Narrative: A Symposium. Odense: Odense University Press.

Benediktsson, Jakob (ed). 1986. Landnamábók. In Íslenzk fornrit, vol. I. Reykjavík: Híð íslenzka fornritafélag.

Benson, Larry D. 1970. The Originality of Beowulf. In The Interpretation of Narrative: Theory and Practice, ed. Morton W. Bloomfield, 1–43. Cambridge, MA: Harvard University Press.

Boer, R.C. (ed.). 1888. Ǫrvar-Odds saga. Leiden: E.J. Brill.

Boer, R.C. (ed.). 1892a. Ǫrvar-Odds saga. Halle: Max Niemeyer.

Boer, R.C. 1892b. Über die Ǫrvar-Odds saga. Arkiv für nordisk filologi 8: 97–139.

Boer, R.C. 1892c. Weiteres zur Ǫrvar-Odds saga. Arkiv für nordisk filologi 8: 246–255.

Breen, Gerard. 1999. "The Wolf Is at the Door": Outlaws, Avengers and Assassins Who Cry "Wolf!". Arkiv för nordisk filologi 114: 31–43.

Chadwick, Nora K. 1946. The Beginnings of Russian History. Cambridge: Cambridge University Press.

Chadwick, Nora K. 1959. The Monsters and Beowulf. In The Anglo-Saxons: Studies in Some Aspects of Their History and Culture presented to Bruce Dickins, ed. Peter Clemoes, 171–203. London: Bowes and Bowes.

Chambers, R.W. 1959. Beowulf: An Introduction to the Study of the Poem with a Discussion of the Stories of Offa and Finn, 3rd ed. Cambridge: Cambridge University Press.

Ciklamini, Marlene. 1966. Grettir and Ketill Hæng, the Giant-Killers. Arv 22: 136–155.

Cleasby, Richard, and Gudbrand Vigfusson, with Sir William A. Craigie. 1957. An Icelandic-English Dictionary, 2nd ed. Oxford: Clarendon Press.

Clover, Carol J. 1980. The Germanic Context of the Unferþ Episode. Speculum 55: 444–468.

Dickson, Arthur. 1929. Valentine and Orson: A Study in Late Medieval Romance. New York: Columbia University Press.

Doane, A. N. 2013. Genesis A: A New Edition, Revised. Tempe: Arizona Center for Medieval and Renaissance Studies.

Donahue, Charles J. 1949–1951. Beowulf, Ireland, and the Natural Good. *Traditio* 7: 263–277.

Edwards, Paul, and Hermann Pálsson (eds.). 1970. *Arrow-Odd: A Medieval Novel*. New York: New York University Press.

Ferrari, Fulvio. 2006. Gods, Warlocks, and Monsters in the *Örvar-Odds saga*. In *The Fantastic in Old Norse/Icelandic Literature: Preprint Papers of the 13th International Saga Conference, Durham and York 6th–12th August 2006*, vol. I–II, ed. John McKinnell, David Ashurst, and Donata Kick, 241–247. Durham: Centre for Medieval and Renaissance Studies.

Ferrari, Fulvio. 2009a. Ögmundr: The Elusive Monster and Medieval "Fantastic" Literature. In *He hafað sundorgecynd: Studi anglo-norreni in onore di John S. McKinnell*, ed. Maria Elena Ruggerini, 365–377. Cagliari: CUEC.

Ferrari, Fulvio. 2009b. Proposals for a New Edition of *Örvar-Odds saga*: How Many Sagas, and How Many Languages? In *On Editing Old Scandinavian Texts: Problems and Perspectives*, ed. Fulvio Ferrari and Massimiliano Bampi, 85–95. Trento: Università degli Studi di Trento.

Fjalldal, Magnús. 1998. *The Long Arm of Coincidence: The Frustrated Connection Between Beowulf and Grettis saga*. Toronto: University of Toronto Press.

Fjalldal, Magnús. 2013. *Beowulf* and the Old Norse Two-Troll Analogues. *Neophilologus* 97: 541–553.

Fox, Denton, and Hermann Pálsson (trans.). 1974. *Grettir's saga*. Toronto: University of Toronto Press.

Friis-Jensen, Karsten (ed.), and Peter Fisher (trans.). 2015. *Gesta Danorum*, By Saxo Grammaticus, 2 vols. Oxford: Clarendon Press.

Fulk, R.D. 2007. The Etymology of Beowulf's Name. *Anglo-Saxon* 1: 109–136.

Fulk, R.D., Robert E. Bjork, and John D. Niles (eds.). 2008. *Klaeber's Beowulf*, 4th ed. Toronto: University of Toronto Press.

Garmonsway, G.N., Jacqueline Simpson, and Hilda Ellis Davidson. 1968. *Beowulf and Its Analogues*. London: J. M. Dent and Sons.

Garmonsway, G. N. (trans. and ed.). 1994. *The Anglo-Saxon Chronicle*. London: J. M. Dent.

Guðmundsdóttir, Aðalheiður. 2007. The Werewolf in Medieval Icelandic Literature. *Journal of English and Germanic Philology* 106 (3): 277–303.

Jónsson, Guðni (ed.). 1936. Grettis saga Ásmundarsonar. In *Íslenzk fornrit*, vol. VII. Reykjavík: Hið íslenzka fornritafélag.

Jónsson, Guðni (ed.). 1954a. *Fornaldar sögur Norðurlanda*, 4 vols. Akureyri: Íslendingasagnaútgáfn.

Jónsson, Guðni (ed.). 1954b. Gríms saga loðinkinna. In *Fornaldar sögur Norðurlanda*, vol. 2, 183–198. Akureyri: Íslendingasagnaútgáfn.

Jónsson, Guðni (ed.). 1954c. Hjálmþés saga ok Ölvis. In *Fornaldar sögur Norðurlanda*, vol. 4, 177–187. Akureyri: Íslendingasagnaútgáfn.

Jónsson, Guðni (ed.). 1954d. Hversu Noregr byggðist. In *Fornaldar sögur Norðurlanda*, vol. 2, 75–87. Akureyri: Íslendingasagnaútgáfn.

Jónsson, Guðni (ed.). 1954e. Ketils saga hængs. In *Fornaldar sögur Norðurlanda*, vol. 2, 149–181. Akureyri: Íslendingasagnaútgáfn.

Jónsson, Guðni (ed.). 1954f. Örvar-Odds saga. In *Fornaldar sögur Norðurlanda*, vol. 2, 199–363. Akureyri: Íslendingasagnaútgáfn.

Jónsson, Guðni (ed.). 1954g. Völsunga saga. In *Fornaldar sögur Norðurlanda*, vol. 1, 107–218. Akureyri: Íslendingasagnaútgáfn.

Jorgensen, Peter A. 1975. The Two-Troll Variant of the Bear's Son Folktale in *Hálfdanar saga Brönufóstra* and *Gríms saga loðinkinna*. *Arv* 31: 35–43.

Lapidge, Michael. 1982. *Beowulf*, Aldhelm, the *Liber Monstrorum*, and Wessex. *Studi Medievali* 23: 151–192.

Lapidge, Michael. 1993. *Beowulf* and the Psychology of Terror. In *Heroic Poetry in the Anglo-Saxon Period: Studies in Honor of Jess B. Bessinger, Jr.*, ed. Helen Damico and John Leyerle, 373–402. Kalamazoo, MI: Medieval Institute Publications.

Liberman, Anatoly. 1986. Beowulf-Grettir. In *Germanic Dialects: Linguistic and Philological Investigations*, ed. Bela Brogyanyi and Thomas Krömmelbein, 353–391. Amsterdam: John Benjamins.

Liuzza, Roy (ed. and trans.). 2013. *Beowulf*, 2nd ed. Peterborough, ON: Broadview.

Lönnroth, Lars. 1969. The Noble Heathen: A Theme in the Sagas. *Scandinavian Studies* 41 (1): 1–29.

Lönnroth, Lars. 1979. The Double Scene of Arrow-Odd's Drinking Contest. In *Medieval Narrative: A Symposium*, ed. Hans Bekker-Nielsen et al., 94–119. Odense: Odense University Press.

Lüthi, Max. 1982. *The European Folktale: Form and Nature*, trans. John D. Niles. Bloomington: Indiana University Press.

McKinnell, John. 2005. *Meeting the Other in Norse Myth and Legend*. Cambridge: D. S. Brewer.

Mitchell, Stephen A. 1991. *Heroic Sagas and Ballads*. Ithaca: Cornell University Press.

Mitchell, Stephen A. 1997. *Blåkulla* and Its Antecendents: Transvection and Conventicles in Nordic Witchcraft. *Alvíssmál* 7: 81–100.

Morris, Rosemary. 1982. *The Character of King Arthur in Medieval Literature*. Woodbridge: D. S. Brewer.

Nickel, Helmut. 1985. The Fight About King Arthur's Beard and for the Cloak of Kings' Beards. *Arthurian Interpretations* 16 (1): 1–7.

Niles, John D. 2011. On the Danish Origins of the Beowulf Story. In *Anglo-Saxon England and the Continent*, ed. Hans Sauer and Joanna Story, 41–62. Tempe, AZ: ACMRS.

Nordal, Sigurðr (ed.). 1933. Egils saga Skalla-Grímssonar. In *Íslenzk fornrit*, vol. II. Reykjavík: Hið íslenzka fornritafélag.

North, Richard. 2018. Hrothulf's Childhood and Beowulf's: A Comparison. In *Childhood and Adolescence in Anglo-Saxon Literary Culture*, ed. Susan Irvine and Winfried Rudolf, 222–243. Toronto: University of Toronto Press.

Olrik, Axel. 1919. *The Heroic Legends of Denmark*, trans. Lee M. Hollander. New York: The American-Scandinavian Foundation.

Olson, Oscar Ludvig. 1916. *The Relation of the Hrólfs saga kraka and the Bjarkarímur to Beowulf.* Urbana, IL: Publications of the Society for the Advancement of Scandinavian Study.

Orchard, Andy. 2003a. *A Critical Companion to Beowulf.* Cambridge: D. S. Brewer.

Orchard, Andy. 2003b. *Pride and Prodigies: Studies in the Monsters of the Beowulf-Manuscript*, rev. paperback ed. Toronto: University of Toronto Press.

Orchard, Andy. 2015. Hereward and Grettir: Brothers from Another Mother? In *New Norse Studies: Essays on the Literature and Culture of Medieval Scandinavia*, ed. Jeffrey Turco, 7–59. Ithaca, NY: Cornell University Library.

Pálsson, Hermann, and Paul Edwards (eds.). 1985. *Seven Viking Romances.* London: Penguin.

Panzer, Friedrich. 1910. *Studien zur germanischen Sagengeschichte I. Beowulf.* Munich: Oskar Beck.

Pizarro, Joaquín Martínez. 1976–1977. Transformations of the Bear's Son Tale in the Sagas of the Hrafnistumenn. *Arv* 32–33: 263–281.

Pritsak, Omeljan. 1993. Hervarar saga ok Heiðreks konungs. In *Medieval Scandinavia: An Encyclopedia*, ed. Philip Pulsiano and Kirsten Wolf, 283. New York: Garland.

Quinn, Judy. 1998. "Ok verðr henni ljóð á munni"—Eddic Prophecy in the *fornaldarsögur. Alvíssmál* 8: 29–50.

Rauer, Christine. 2000. *Beowulf and the Dragon.* Cambridge: D. S. Brewer.

Saxo Grammaticus. 2015. *Gesta Danorum*, ed. Karsten Friis-Jensen, trans. Peter Fisher, 2 vols. Oxford: Clarendon Press.

Schmeidler, Bernhard (ed.). 1917. *Gesta Hammaburgensis ecclesiae pontificum.* Hannover: Handsche Buchhandlung.

Stitt, J. Michael. 1992. *Beowulf and the Bear's Son: Epic, Saga, and Fairytale in Northern Germanic Tradition.* New York: Garland Publishing.

Sveinnson, Einar Ól. (ed.). 1939. Vatnsdæla saga. In *Íslenzk fornrit*, vol. VIII. Reykjavík: Hið íslenzka fornritafélag.

Taylor, Archer. 1921. The Death of Ǫrvar Oddr. *Modern Philology* 19: 93–106.

Þórólfsson, Björn K., and Guðni Jónsson (eds.). 1943. Gísla saga Súrssonar. In *Íslenzk fornrit*, vol. VI, 1–118. Reykjavík: Hið íslenzka fornritafélag.

Tolkien, Christopher (ed. and trans.). 1960. *Saga Heiðreks konungs ins vitra/The Saga of King Heidrek the Wise.* London: Thomas Nelson and Sons.

Tulinius, Torfi H. 2002. *The Matter of the North: The Rise of Literary Fiction in Thirteenth-Century Iceland*, trans. Randi C. Eldevik. Odense: Odense University Press.

Tulinius, Torfi H. ' 2007. Sagas of Icelandic Prehistory (*fornaldarsögur*). In *A Companion to Old Norse-Icelandic Literature and Culture*, ed. Rory McTurk, 447–461. Malden: Blackwell Publishing.

Virgil. 1986. *Aeneid*, ed. G.P. Goold, trans. H. Rushton Fairclough, Loeb Classical Library, 63–64. Cambridge, MA: Harvard University Press.

Vilmundarson, Þórhallur, and Bjarni Vilhjálmsson (eds.). 1991. *Orms þáttr Stórólfssonar*, *Íslenzk fornrit*, vol. XIII. Reykjavík: Híð íslenzka fornritafélag.

West, M.L. 2014. *The Making of the Odyssey*. Oxford: Oxford University Press.

CHAPTER 6

The Formula Reformulated: *Sellic Spell* and *The Hobbit*

Though not a prolific scholar of *Beowulf* by today's standards, J. R. R. Tolkien has been associated with the poem perhaps more than any other critic.[1] His 1936 Gollancz lecture, "*Beowulf*: The Monsters and the Critics," has been credited with changing the course of *Beowulf* scholarship, and his 1939 Andrew Lang lecture, "On Fairy Stories," complements his more famous address in useful ways. Tolkien also contributed a preface to John R. Clark Hall's revised translation of the poem, a commentary on the difficulty of rendering Old English verse into Modern English prose. What has less often been realized is just how much *The Hobbit* has to say about (at least Tolkien's view of) *Beowulf* and its composition, and the recent publication of *Sellic Spell* as an addendum to Tolkien's translation of and commentary on the poem is a similarly rich work, standing somewhere between fiction and scholarship, even if closer to the former. This chapter will demonstrate through an analysis of Tolkien's traditional scholarship and two of his creative works how Tolkien's view of the poem corresponds to the analysis in the preceding chapters and how *Sellic Spell* and *The Hobbit* in effect bookend this entire study of formulaic composition: *Sellic Spell* takes its place beside the earliest folktale versions of the poem, tales best represented by *Dat Erdmänneken* and the tale-type AT 301, and *The Hobbit* stands as a contemporary reformulation, displaying precisely the same kinds of emulation and difference as *Beowulf* and *Örvar-Odds saga*.

Perhaps because Tolkien writes on *Beowulf* before the advent of oral-formulaic theory, he has nothing to say specifically about formulas

© The Author(s) 2020
M. Fox, *Following the Formula in Beowulf, Örvar-Odds saga, and Tolkien*, https://doi.org/10.1007/978-3-030-48134-6_6

and formulaic systems. Tolkien does, however, comment on diction and the structure of the Old English line. Tolkien pays particular attention to the language of the poem, pointing out through the examples of *beorn* (as a "bear" word) and *freca* (as a "wolf" word) that the diction was already archaic when the poem was composed (1940, xv). This point would scarcely be worth making except for the fact that Tolkien elsewhere claims strongly the relationship between language and mythology—"the making of language and mythology are related functions" (2016, 24)[2]—making the case for Tolkien's awareness, along the lines of Watkins' reduction of the dragon-slayer formula to one sentence and the attention paid to the *hæftmece*, for Tolkien's awareness of the depth of Old English vocabulary: as he puts it, "many Old English poetical words … come down to us bearing echoes of ancient days beyond the shadowy borders of Northern history" (1940, ix). When words are then repeated, the recurrence is usually important, but Tolkien's focus for that comment is the difficulty of signaling that repetition via a single modern word (1940, viii). Though Tolkien never connects them explicitly, repetition and balance seem to be similar aspects of the poem's structure: "[The Old English poetic line is] founded on a balance; an opposition between two halves of roughly equivalent phonetic weight, and significant content, which are more often rhythmically contrasted than similar" (1983, 30). Tolkien elsewhere calls this "parallelism," effectively apposition across the poetic line, and suggests that parallelism is "characteristic of the style and structure of *Beowulf*" (1940, xl).

Tolkien is similarly too early to have much to say about type-scenes, themes, and motifs, though he certainly recognizes and then develops Old English themes in his creative work, as we shall see, but Tolkien extends his comments on the structure of the poetic line: "[Parallelism] is seen not only in these lesser verbal details, but in the arrangement of minor passages or periods (of narrative, description, or speech), and in the shape of the poem as a whole. Things, actions, or processes are often depicted by separate strokes, juxtaposed, and frequently neither joined by an expressed link nor subordinated" (Tolkien 1940, xl). Tolkien finds these "separate strokes" at the smallest possible scale, words apposed without conjunctions, at the level of larger syntactic units, sentences apposed within sentences, and even at a larger narrative scale in the non-linear interweaving of passages describing the conflict between the Swedes and the Geats in the second half of the poem. The whole of the poem, in fact, "is like a line of its own verse written large, a balance of two great blocks, A + B; or like two of its parallel sentences with a single subject but no expressed conjunction. Youth + Age; he rose–fell" (1940, xl–xli). In response to Klaeber's famous comment about the lack of steady advance, Tolkien affirms that the poem was not meant to advance at all. Instead, it is "a simple and *static* structure," "a balance, an opposition of ends and beginnings," "a contrasted description of two moments in a great life, rising and setting" (1983, 28). Tolkien not only finds a balance and a parallelism at every level of the poem, working his way out from the line to the thematic balance of youth and age, but his adaptation of W. P. Ker's and of R. W. Chambers' language of important and unimportant, of center and outer edges, of folktale and episodes and digressions, would seem to suggest that he also sees a kind of parallelism with contrast in the content of the poem inside its balanced two parts.

Tolkien's main concern in 1936 is that very little criticism of *Beowulf* assesses the poem as a complete and unified poem; instead, critics are inclined to isolate features of the poem for study, a process Tolkien compares to a stone tower with a view of the sea, built from a mix of old stone and new, pushed over by visitors that they might examine the building materials and the site before they even climb up to appreciate the view.[3] Tolkien's "allegory" of *Beowulf* scholarship captures well his view of the poem, which he sees as a fresh use of traditional material (1983, 7–9). Tolkien's aim is to ignore the origins of the material and focus on what the poet did with it, a point he makes twice in his lecture "On Fairy-Stories": "It is precisely the colouring, the atmosphere, the unclassifiable individual details of a story ['the effect produced *now* by these old things in the stories as they are' (2014a, 48)], and above all the general purport that informs with life the undissected bones of the plot, that really count" (2014a, 39). Tolkien would certainly agree that one of the building blocks of the poem is folktale, but he disagrees that the core folktale plot of the poem has "usurp[ed] the place of honour."[4] We must at once be careful of the term folktale, recognize how closely it is related to myth, and remember to consider the undissected whole:

> The term "folk-tale" is misleading; its very tone of depreciation begs the question. Folk-tales in being, as told—for the "typical folk-tale," of course, is merely an abstract conception of research nowhere existing—do often contain elements that are thin and cheap, with little even potential virtue; but they also contain much that is far more powerful, and that cannot be sharply separated from myth, being derived from it, or capable in poetic hands of turning into it: that is of becoming largely significant—as a whole, accepted unanalysed. (1983, 15)

As Tolkien points out, the bare plot (which he interestingly calls a "recipe") also of something like the story of Ingeld is "as 'simple' and as 'typical' as that of folktales," even while, in any case, much of the work of narrative paradigm hunters is not something to be endorsed (1983, 17).[5]

For Tolkien, the "special virtue" of *Beowulf* "resides … in the theme, and the spirit this has infused in the whole," and that fact that the poet has felt "rather than [made] explicit what his theme portends" (1983, 14–15). That theme is presented variously, as "man at war with the hostile world, and his inevitable overthrow in Time"; "each man and all men, and all their works shall die"; and "the wages of heroism is death" (1983, 18, 23, 26). Tolkien in a way agrees with Watkins' assertion that the serpent represents chaos and dissolution—the winner in the battle of the northern gods—noting that *Beowulf*'s dragon is more *draconitas* than *draco*, an effect of symbolism *The Hobbit* does its best to suppress. To the theme(s) the things at the edges add depth, what Tolkien calls a sense "of antiquity with a greater and yet darker antiquity behind," an effect achieved mostly through episodes and allusions to other (older) stories, even while meaning may be difficult to isolate (1983, 21, 17, 27, 31). Tolkien sees the same kind of effect in fairy-story, where the whole has an effect that cannot be predicted from the parts, a sense of something beyond analysis that is important for thinking about *Sellic Spell* and *The Hobbit*. The fairy-story should satisfy certain "primordial desires," including to "survey the depths of space and time" and "to hold communion with other living things" (2014a, 34–5). More concretely, fairy-story offers fantasy ("arresting strangeness") and, as components of that fantasy, recovery (the "regaining of a clear view"), escape, and consolation, his "eucatastrophe" or "sudden joyous turn" (Tolkien 2014a, 59–76).

6.1   SELLIC SPELL

With his knowledge of R. W. Chambers' introduction to *Beowulf* and no doubt also of Panzer's study of "The Bear's Son Tale," Tolkien's focus on the presence of a "wild folktale" as the "main story" of the poem is not surprising. Tolkien would also have been familiar with the *Kinder- und Hausmärchen* of Jacob and Wilhelm Grimm and even Antti Aarne's first edition of the types of the folktale (1910) or Stith Thompson's translated and revised edition (1928), meaning that Tolkien's *Sellic Spell*, which he was probably working on in the early 1940s (2014b,

359), cannot be considered to have been composed free of the influence of a thorough understanding of folktale in general and of AT 301 and "The Bear's Son Tale" in particular.[6] In fact, Tolkien remarks in "On Fairy-Stories" that some have said "*Beowulf* 'is only a version of *Dat Erdmänneken*'" (2014a, 38), and the most recent editors of the lecture have discovered a note of Tolkien's (perhaps from 1943) suggesting that "[*Beowulf*] should be retold as a fairy-story" (2014a, 100).[7] Paul Acker has also pointed out that *Sellic Spell* has the same opening ("Once upon a time there was a King in the North") as Andrew Lang's "The Story of Sigurd."[8] Even the title *Sellic Spell*, which comes from *Beowulf*, could be an Old English term for "fairy-story."[9] The words appear in an important passage in which Beowulf is retelling the events of the first part of the poem, a touch Tolkien thinks begins to repair a flaw in the poem, that all the action does not take place in one setting:

> Þær wæs gidd ond gleo; gomela Scilding,
> felafricgende feorran rehte;
> hwilum hildedeor hearpan wynne,
> gome(n)wudu grette, hwilum gyd awræc
> soð ond sarlic, hwilum syllic spell
> rehte after rihte rumheort cyning;
> hwilum eft ongan eldo gebunden,
> gomel guðwiga gioguðe cwiðan,
> hildestrengo; hreðer (in)ne weoll
> þonne he wintrum frod worn gemunde. (2105–14)

There was song and entertainment; the old Scylding, being wise, told of ancient things; sometimes, the one brave in battle touched the music-wood, joy of the harp; sometimes, he recited a song, true and sad; sometimes, the big-hearted king rightly told a marvelous tale; sometimes, in turn, bound up in age, the old battle-warrior began to mourn his youth and battle-strength; his heart surged as he, wise in winters, remembered many things.

The passage is important for many reasons, including the connection through *hwilum* to the Sigemund-Heremod digression, as we have seen, but the key feature of the title must surely be the word *syllic*, which only appears only four times in the poem. The word otherwise appears describing the *sædracan* in the mere (1426a), as part of the description of Grendel's *glof* just a few lines before this passage, *sid ond syllic* and made *dracan fellum* (2085b–88), and as a descriptor of the dragon, *syllicran wiht/ wyrm on wonge* (3038b–39a), the comparative referring to the prior discovery of Beowulf's body in the sand, our hero who *wundordeaðe swealt* (3037b) as Sigemund's *draca morðre swealt* (892b). The poet is here saying, I believe, that Hrothgar could tell stories about dragons,[10] and that is precisely the kind of tale Tolkien wants to tell—his commentary notes the contrast of the *soð* and the *syllic* and everything the latter might entail (2014b, 348–9)—the marvellous tale that lies at the heart of the poem.

Though Tolkien's description of his *spell* is limited to a few words, his aims tell us a great deal about his views on the relationship between the poem and folktale. First of all, he states absolutely that "the folk-tale element in *Beowulf*" comes from a full folktale; second, Tolkien suggests that the folktale would have explained away some of the difficulties of the poem, or at least that his story is designed to link most easily with the "Historial Legend"; and, third, Tolkien also believes that "more than one tale (or motive of tales) was associated with the Danish and Geatish royal houses" (2014b, 355–6). Tolkien's story, however, is "*a* story, not *the* story," principally designed to "exhibit the difference of style, tone, and atmosphere if the particular heroic or *historical* is cut out … by making it timeless [he says] I have followed a common habit of folk-tales as received" (2014b, 355). The tale itself (which Tolkien also offers in Old English) tells the story of Beewolf, who grows from an inauspicious beginning to become a king. Tolkien's story is purely and recognizably folktale, and it would not be out of place among the *Kinder- und Hausmärchen* of Jacob and Wilhelm Grimm. In fact, a comparison of *Sellic Spell* with *Dat Erdmänneken* (Grimm 91) demonstrates much in common, but also the unique engineering required to align the folktale with the poem.

Dat Erdmänneken begins with the disappearance of the king's three daughters, the youngest of whom disobeys an interdiction against picking the apples of one particular tree. Three huntsmen quest to find them, taking turns staying alone at a castle they find in their journeys while the others keep searching. The eldest two are abused by a gnome while alone, but the least promising of them, and the youngest (whom they called stupid Hans, because he is not quite sure about the world) overcomes the gnome and learns where the king's daughters are being held under the earth. The huntsmen again take turns being lowered through the well entrance to the lower world, but the elder two ring a bell to be pulled back up before reaching the bottom. Stupid Hans kills three multi-headed dragons, each with an attendant princess. The elder two huntsmen pull up the princesses one by one, but the youngest, having been warned of treachery by the gnome, puts a stone in the basket when his turn comes to be raised to the surface. The rope is cut. Abandoned, but finding a magic flute on the wall, Stupid Hans plays, and with each note a gnome appears until there are sufficient gnomes to fly him to the surface. He returns just as one of the princesses is to be married, he is recognized, the elder two huntsmen are executed, and he marries the youngest daughter.

Dat Erdmänneken is technically a sub-type of AT 301, AT 301A ("Quest for a Vanished Princess"), a type that omits the first movement, the hero of supernatural origin and strength,[11] though Stupid Hans is very much an unpromising hero, just as the hero of AT 301 usually is. In fact, the tale demonstrates quite a bit of deviation from AT 301 and its subtypes, including the interdiction and interdiction violated, two of Propp's preparatory folktale functions, and quite a few examples of trebling in parallel positions, just to give two examples. In Pizarro's rendering of Panzer's study, *Dat Erdmänneken* is a tale with a C introduction (the disappearing daughter[s] of a king), that joins introduction A at the point where the hero and his companions come to a deserted dwelling in the woods (1976–1977, 265–9).[12] Introduction C is very rare in early Germanic sources—Pizarro finds a trace only in the disappearance of Lofthæna in *Gríms saga loðinkinna*—but the rescued maiden also plays a key role in *Der starke Hans* (Grimm 166), which has a different introduction (AT 650A; "Strong John") and in which the hero meets two extraordinary companions (itself an AT 513 tale-type; "The Helpers" or "The Extraordinary Companions"). AT 650A is preserved more purely in *Der junge Riese* (Grimm 90), though *Der junge Riese* in turn has a Tom Thumb introduction (AT 700). What we see here, as Pizarro's three separate introductions also illustrate, is just how much tale-types tend to blend together.

Sellic Spell invokes the bear-hero somewhat ambiguously (unlike, for example, Böðvarr bjarki of *Hrólfs saga kraka*), for the hero is found at the age of three in the lair of a great bear. An unpromising and lazy youth (L114), the hero earns the name Beewolf due to a fondness for honey and perhaps due to the circumstances of his early years (B635.1). He grows strong (F610) and has a "bear-glow" that keeps him warm in the water. While still a boy, Beewolf has a swimming contest with Breaker, and the contest goes much as it does in the poem. Swimming prowess and a contest like this are not normally part of AT 301 in any form; already Tolkien is deploying a new motif to accord with *Beowulf* (F696: marvellous swimmer), a motif that is most common in Old Norse-Icelandic sources.[13] By incorporating the swimming contest in the linear events of the tale, Tolkien is inventing a new introduction to the traditional core of the narrative. The boy with incredible strength and a bear-hug grip grows into an even stronger man, having the strength of thirty. Beewolf hears about an ogre who by night is terrorizing a Golden Hall (G475; H1471) and resolves to help, even though people think the idea foolish. On his quest to the King of the Golden Hall, Beewolf encounters Handshoe and Ashwood, gathering extraordinary companions (F601) with what seem to be magical items, gloves (D1066) and a spear (D1084). Handshoe's gloves of hide allow him to move and tear rock, very much like the gloves Ormr receives from Menglöð, Brúsi's sister; Ashwood's spear, which can put a host of men to flight (D1400.1.4.4), is reminiscent of Gungnir and Óðinn (just as any magic gloves recall Þórr). When they present themselves to the king, Beewolf is thought least likely to succeed, and Unfriend (whom Tolkien also calls Unpeace in some versions) challenges Beewolf, having heard of the contest with Breaker. The companions await the monster, Grinder, in turn, from the one thought most likely to succeed to the least. Beewolf, reassuring the king that the "third time may pay for all," awaits the monster and grapples with him. When Grinder cannot move Beewolf from the hall, he loses his arm at the door. The next day, Beewolf and Unfriend track Grinder (N773.1) to a lake of black water with a waterfall (F531.6.2.2.3). Beewolf lowers a rope and descends (F92), while Unfriend waits. Beewolf beheads Grinder's mother with a "great sword" that he finds in her cave and that no one else could lift (F833.1.1), and he uses Handshoe's gloves to get to Grinder's "chamber" and decapitate him as well (E431.7.2, E446.3). Unfriend sees blood, loosens the knots on the rope (K677), and leaves pleased (K1931.2). Beewolf makes his way back alone, his swimming prowess once again serving him well, surprising the king and his people (N681.0.1) with Grinder's head. He returns home with treasure, is a loyal subject, and finally marries his king's only daughter (L161) and rules himself, always loving honey and serving the best mead.

Tolkien's "folktale" is, like *Beowulf*, full of folktale motifs, although it introduces many new ones, and runs close to the movements of

AT 301 and its more specific sub-types, "The Bear's Son Tale" and the two-troll variant. The gathering of extraordinary companions who are named for their abilities is precisely what happens in *Der starke Hans*, where the heroes are then known as *der Tannendreher* (Tree-twister) and *der Felsenklipperer* (Rock-splitter). The sequential attempts to overcome Grinder explain in some ways the odd death of Hondscio in the poem. Indeed, Michael Drout would say that "Tolkien has shaped his story so that it seems to explain some of the more confusing aspects of *Beowulf* by suggesting that a more elaborate folktale plot has been compressed into the form found in the poem" (2015, 168), and Paul Acker suggests that this impulse goes all the way back to R. W. Chambers' sense of how the poem develops out of folktale (2016, 35–6). In some ways, too, *Sellic Spell* seems to have been influenced by *Grettis saga* and the expedition of Grettir and the priest Steinn to the lair of the *trollkona*. Tolkien includes the happy ending and marriage, even though the king's daughter was never in danger (he says on this point: "The only daughter comes in as a typical folk-tale element" [2014b, 356]), and we can see as well glimmers of *The Hobbit* past in the character of Beewolf and *The Two Towers* to come in the suffering king in the Golden Hall. The most important thing to recognize when considering both the tale-types and what folktales stand as specific examples of those types is the extent to which the tellers and authors have blended movements, borrowed and invented motifs, and shaped their tales through parallelism and repetition. Though the situation with *Sellic Spell* is somewhat artificial, the development from the basic tale-type models to specific tales demonstrates what tends to remain stable in related narratives, things like the descent to the other- or underworld, and what elements change freely. With *Beowulf* and the Old Norse-Icelandic analogues that we have considered via *Örvar-Odds saga*, we have seen how a main story that comes from folktale can be developed and augmented as it is transformed in new genres. Interestingly, C. W. Sullivan III also proposes that Tolkien's work, and particularly *The Hobbit*, should be approached with the idea that Tolkien is a "traditional storyteller," meaning that critics should use "the critical approaches that have proved profitable when applied to ancient, originally oral, narratives" (2013, 62). The argument of the final part of this chapter, though, is that *The Hobbit* stands with *Beowulf* and its analogues, not oral, but definitely traditional, as yet another product of the formula.

6.2   *THE HOBBIT*: INTRODUCTION

The Hobbit seems at least partially to have had its genesis in oral stories Tolkien told to his children, but his motivation might also have been his reading, for Tolkien has been reported to have said that, whether reading fairy-stories or medieval works, his primary response was not analysis, but a desire to compose a creative work of his own (Anderson 2002, 1).[14] The best direct evidence for this kind of response, though published well after *The Hobbit*, is Tolkien's short dramatization of the aftermath of the Battle of Maldon, constructed around two lines of the Old English poem, and his subsequent musings on "defect of character" (1953). Though the precise dates when Tolkien was working on *The Hobbit* are not clear, Douglas A. Anderson calculates the writing of the famous first sentence to have happened between 1928 and 1930 (2002, 11). By 1933, Tolkien definitely had some kind of type-script of the story, and *The Hobbit* was published in England on September 21, 1937.[15] In terms of relative chronology, therefore, Tolkien seems to have been thinking about *The Hobbit*, his *Beowulf* lecture, and *Sellic Spell* over roughly the same ten-year period and likely in roughly that order. On February 20, 1938, *The Observer* printed a letter that Tolkien had intended only as a personal response to a writer with questions about hobbits and the cup-stealing incident. In the letter, Tolkien says a fair bit about his sources, though in a typically playful fashion (he later calls his letter "an ill-considered joke"; Carpenter 1981, Letter 26, 35). After considering where hobbits come from—and commenting in that context about his perhaps generative reading of "books of fairy-tales of the genuine kind"—Tolkien discusses his sources for the novel:

> As for the rest of the tale it is ... derived from (previously digested) epic, mythology, and fairy-story—not, however, Victorian in authorship, as a rule to which George Macdonald is the chief exception. *Beowulf* is among my most valued sources; though it was not consciously present to the mind in the process of writing, in which the episode of the theft arose naturally (and almost inevitably) from the circumstances. It is difficult to think of any other way of conducting the story at that point. I fancy the author of *Beowulf* would say much the same ... My tale is not consciously based on any other book—save one, and that is unpublished: the "Silmarillion," a history of the Elves, to which frequent allusion is made. (Carpenter 1981, Letter 25, 30–1)

Tolkien further remarks that work could be done on the sources and analogues of the riddles and invites researchers to ponder where his writing of the tale paused at two points. Curiously, and tellingly, I think, Tolkien is encouraging (however jokingly) analysis of *The Hobbit* to parallel analysis of *Beowulf* (Carpenter 1981, Letter 25, 32).

Tolkien need not have been concerned, for critical studies of *The Hobbit* have appeared almost unabated since the late 1960s, when the dissertations of Bonniejean Christensen (1969) and William Green (1969) signaled that the novel was an appropriate topic for academic study. Several book-length studies devoted exclusively to *The Hobbit* have appeared in the last few years, including assessments of the influence of Tolkien's life and surroundings on the book and of its place in Tolkien's overall mythology (Atherton 2012; Eden 2014). Studies of the sources of *The Hobbit* are many, and it would seem that most of Tolkien's sources have been identified. Tom Shippey calls the novel "a sort of 'asterisk-world' for the Norse *Elder Edda*," and comments that things like the names of Gandalf and the dwarves (the *Dvergatal* in *Völuspá*), the Misty Mountains, and Mirkwood come right out of Old Norse-Icelandic sources (2003, 70). The trolls turning to stone has an analogue, if not a source, in *Alvíssmál* and Þórr's deception of Alvíss, and the connections of the Smaug episode to Sigurðr's slaying of Fáfnir (mainly as related in *Völsunga saga*) are also well-known. Even the ring and the curse on the gold make appearances in the story of the origin of Fáfnir's treasure in the theft from the dwarf Andvari.[16] *Hrólfs saga kraka* and the bear-hero Böðvarr bjarki have been offered as models for the character of Beorn, and *Hervarar saga ok Heiðreks konungs* and *Vafþrúnismál* have further been suggested as sources for the riddling contest, though riddles are prominent in Anglo-Latin and Old English traditions also, including in a kind of contest of wisdom between Solomon and Saturn.[17] Shippey, again, argues that the "master-text" for Tolkien's portrayal of the dwarves (so, for characterization, now, rather than specific details) is the account of the *Hjaðningavíg* in Snorri's *Prose Edda*; for the elves, the hunting king in *Sir Orfeo*, a text Tolkien himself translated (2003, 62–5).[18] The point is that, even though, as David Day puts it, "a great deal of the Anglo-Saxon epic *Beowulf* found its way into *The Hobbit*" (2011, 124),[19] the poem is far from Tolkien's only source and is, in fact, in terms of the details of *The Hobbit*, not the primary source at all. Instead, *Beowulf* is the model for *The Hobbit*, an execution of a formula from which Tolkien was able to work out *a* formula (if not *the* formula, to paraphrase Tolkien on *Sellic Spell*) and then, plugging in new material and innovations, to produce a story of his own to parallel a narrative like *Örvar-Odds saga*.

In addition to executing the formula, as he points out in his letter about sources, Tolkien locates *The Hobbit* among a set of intertexts, his "mythology," a story influenced by and influencing Tolkien's other works. As Paul Bibire puts it, "*The Hobbit* is shaped internally as a network of repeated and echoing elements, but these are not independent of the wider span of Tolkien's work. This wider interdependence of motif and structuring principle, as well as of narrative, gives meaning to the text beyond its own confines as a distinct work" (1993, 215).[20] To give just one example of motif and episode, the beguiling of Túrin by the dragon Glaurung in the *Silmarillion*—"he fell under the binding spell of the lidless eyes of the dragon"—the killing of Glaurung and Túrin's suicide after the slaying, and the conflict over the unattended treasure in which Húrin slays the dwarf Mîm are very much a part of understanding Tolkien's conception of heroism, dragons, and treasure (1977, 213, 225, 230–1).

6.3   *THE HOBBIT*: FORMULA AND STRUCTURE

Beowulf and *Grettis saga* have long shared the *hæftmece/heptisax* connection, an apparent repetition so limited in distribution that some have found a direct link between the two works difficult to dismiss. In *The Hobbit*, the one repeated word that connects the novel to *Beowulf* is *eorclanstan/Arkenstone*, as has been noted many times, with the Old English appropriately altered to show the difference between the traditions. The appropriateness of the term in its immediate context is obvious: the Arkenstone is emblematic of Thorin's susceptibility to the "bewilderment" of the treasure, and the *eorclanstanas* (1208a) are part of the necklace Hygelac carries with him on his ill-fated Frisian raid, undertaken *for wlenco* ("on account of pride"; 1206a), a disaster from which Beowulf returns wretched and alone (2359b–68). Douglas A. Anderson notes that the word has the Old Norse-Icelandic cognate *jarknasteinn* (which may, however, come from Old English, perhaps as the borrowing of one poet!; Cleasby and Vigfusson 1957, 323) for "gem," used in *Völundarkviða* for the eyeballs Völundr turns into precious stones as part of his revenge (Anderson 2002, 293–4). What has not often been mentioned about this shared term is that *eorclanstan* is not, like *hæftmece*, a hapax legomenon in Old English, but rather, in various forms, a fairly common word for a precious stone or for Latin *margarita* (pearl). The term is also used figuratively (in its rarer spelling *eorclanstan*) when, in Blickling Homily XIII, the Lord says to Mary's body in the process of her assumption: "Ne forlæte ic þe næfre min meregrot, ne ic þe næfre ne forlæte, min eorclanstan, forþon þe þu eart soþlice Godes templ" (Morris 1880, 149; I will never leave you, my pearl; never will I leave you, my *eorclanstan*, because you are truly the temple of God). The connection, which Tolkien would certainly have known, is again deeply appropriate for the preciousness of the stone and the degree to which Thorin covets it, but the connection to Mary, especially when the chapter in which Bilbo delivers the stone to Bard is called "A Thief in the Night" (from I Thessalonians V.2: "For you know very well that the day of the Lord shall come just like a thief in the night"), makes the incident with the stone draw much more than just *Beowulf* into the text's associations.

Tolkien also draws the *har stan* into *The Hobbit*, making "the grey stone" the key to finding the way through the secret door into the mountain as the party looks at the "moon-letters" on the map (2006, 63), though the first time Bilbo stares at the stone (242) he does not recall the map's directions, and it is only the coal-black thrush, smacking a snail against the grey stone, that reminds Bilbo of its significance (243–4). Curiously, the grey stone is mentioned precisely four times, just as in *Beowulf*. The connection, much as with the Arkenstone, draws the two narratives very much together, linking the dragons of Sigemund and Beowulf with Smaug, especially, but also suggesting the danger of Smaug, uniquely among the journey's adventures, matches the perils of the monsters in *Beowulf*. Though it is impossible to know for certain if Tolkien knew of the prominence of the *har stan* in Old English boundary clauses, it seems likely that he would have, making the feature (as it seems to be in *Beowulf*) a way of connecting the story specifically to England.

At the level of phrases and sentences, the structure of *The Hobbit* also has a surprising number of parallels with *Beowulf*. Tolkien is fond of parallelism, or apposition, particularly in formal instances of speech, such as Bilbo's riddling description of himself: "I am the clue-finder, the web-cutter, the stinging fly" (2006, 258). As Beorn crashes into the final battle, the narrator uses three doublets, two in the form of similes forming a tiny ring structure, to describe his arrival: "The roar of his voice was like drums and guns; and he tossed wolves and goblins from his path like straws and feathers" (334). Tolkien also uses chiastic structures for particular effect, such as in the narrator's assessment of the relationship between elves and dwarves: "Dwarves don't get on well with them. Even decent enough dwarves like Thorin and his friends think them foolish (which is a very foolish thing to think), or get annoyed with them" (58), where the pattern is "don't get on well with them ... think ... foolish ... foolish ... think ... get annoyed with them." The structures can be more sophisticated, too, as near the opening of the story when the narrator explains attitudes toward the Bagginses:

> This hobbit was a very well-to-do hobbit, and his name was Baggins. The Bagginses had lived in the neighbourhood of The Hill for time out of mind, and people considered them very respectable, not only because most of them were rich, but also because they never had any adventures or did anything unexpected: you could tell what a Baggins would say on any question without the bother of asking him. This is a story of how a Baggins had an adventure, and found himself doing and saying things altogether unexpected. He may have lost the neighbours' respect, but he gained—well, you will see whether he gained anything in the end. (4)

Here, the paragraph is broadly framed with an envelope pattern "Baggins ... neighbourhood ... respectable" and "he ... neighbour's ... respect," but inside that envelope is a parallel structure interlocked with a chiastic structure in "adventures ... did ... unexpected ... say" and "adventure ... doing ... saying ... unexpected" (although the structure could be complicated further).[21]

Other instances of repetition serve to bind the narrative together. Mark Atherton identifies two main recurring motifs in *The Hobbit*, "the perils and discomforts of the journey that the respectable protagonist is forced to endure" and "adventure" (2012, 25), and both motifs are signaled with repetition and variation and become structural markers for the narrative as a whole. As the journey begins to grow difficult and the rain dampens Bilbo's spirit, he thinks to himself: "'I wish I was at home in my nice hole by the fire, with the kettle just beginning to sing.' It was not the last time he wished that" (2006, 38). The sentiment is repeated in some form at least nine more times in the book, though the penultimate occurrence is split over several pages.[22] Each instance before the last includes reference to "home" or his "hole" or "hobbit-hole";

"eggs and bacon," the "kettle," and a "fire" appear frequently; and the tag "not for the last time" appears three times.[23] The wish for home is distributed evenly throughout the novel, sometimes appearing at the beginning of chapters (55, 81, and 131), and the last full occurrence (with "hobbit-hole," "bacon and eggs," and "not for the last time") is as he finds himself alone in Mirkwood (180). After his time alone in the halls of the Elvenking (203), the remaining expressions of the wish for home are spoken aloud. The first is to the dwarves as he is deciding to head down the tunnel the second time (256), and the second to the Elvenking and Bard as he is about to hand over the Arkenstone (313). By this time, Bilbo has become a very different hobbit, at his most business-like, meaning the wish seems largely rhetorical. After he hands over the stone and returns to the dwarves, he falls asleep and, for the first time, *dreams* of eggs and bacon (316), having done all he can do. The last occurrence is linked to the "adventure" motif, which is repeated often, but is significantly used to signal transitions in the narrative:[24] "So ended the adventures of the Misty Mountains" (129); "that [finding out what happened to the rest of the dwarves in the halls of the Elvenking] belongs to the next chapter and the beginning of another adventure in which the hobbit proved his usefulness" (197); "we are drawing near the end of the eastward journey [having escaped in the barrels] and coming to the last and greatest adventure" (217); and "[Bilbo] turned his back on his adventure" (340). The last wish for home, then, is tied to the end of the adventure, effectively closing both structural patterns at the same point: "I wish now only to be in my own arm-chair!" (340). With the transition between sections of the text, Tolkien seems to break the narrative into three main "adventures": the Misty Mountains, the spiders and the Elvenking, and Smaug, a structure that obviously fits well with those who argue that *Beowulf*'s main structural feature is the three mon-ster fights.

In *Beowulf*, however, the most prominent occurrence of trebling contains several minor occurrences. John A. Nist has called the effect "a brilliant triad of variation": the fights have progressively more rounds as they become more difficult (ending in the three-round fight with the dragon); Beowulf's moral imperative seems to decrease in each fight; each fight sees a more important person die; and Beowulf gives three death speeches after the dragon is killed (Nist 1959, 21; Keller 1981, 222; Niles 1983, 156). The *Beowulf*-poet is also fond of tripled iterations, as in the famous *com* passage with three instances of *mynte* interwoven (702b–66; Orchard 2003, 190–1) or the *weard* formula in the Sigemund-Heremod digression (902b–15). Propp notes that trebling is extremely common in folktale and functions in different ways:

> Trebling may occur among individual details of an attributive nature (the three heads of a dragon), as well as among individual functions, pairs of functions (pursuit-rescue), groups of functions, and entire moves. Repetition may appear as a uniform distribution (three tasks, three years' service), as an accumulation (the third task is the most difficult, the third battle the worst), or may twice produce negative results before the third, successful, outcome. (1968, 74)

Tolkien's *Sellic Spell* gives Beewolf two companions and two negative results before a third successful outcome,[25] and *The Hobbit* contains many different kinds of trebling. If the novel is appropriately divided into three main adventures, then those adventures, each of which includes a kind of "descent" into an otherworld in which the stakes are higher every time, also has a trebling within it. The Misty Mountains (an adventure of three days duration) include episodes with the goblins, Gollum, and the wolves; the trip through Mirkwood features three attempts to join the feast of the Elvenking; and Bilbo descends three times to the dragon's lair. There are isolated treblings, as well, such as the three-fold repetition of the interdiction not to leave the path, a feature of the text that combines Proppian functions (γ, interdiction; and later δ, interdiction violated, also a fairly common motif, J652) with trebling. Finally, the significance of the threes is acknowledged by Bilbo, who agrees to go down the tunnel to see what he can discover about Smaug, a task he considers his third intervention on behalf of the dwarves (having gotten them out of "messes" with the spiders and the wood elves), a slightly different triple action in the narrative, and Bilbo repeats his father's wisdom that "third time pays for all" as he prepares to descend a third time to discover what has become of Smaug (2006, 246, 272). Of course, Beewolf says much the same thing in *Sellic Spell*, and I believe the repetition is deliberate, intended to link the traditional folktale hero with a most untraditional hero in Bilbo, while also connecting the texts in a "world" in which such gnomic wisdom is stable.[26] In slightly different terms, the repetition connects Beewolf and Bilbo across a gulf of tradition, genre, and time; as we have seen with other kinds of repetition, the effect is a collapsing of time and distance, and Beowulf, too, stands nearby, just as the *bar stan* allows Beowulf and Sigemund to stand side-by-side, recognizing the similarity of their deeds.

Like Beowulf's fitts, *The Hobbit* has chapters as a potential structural guide. Jane Chance (2001, 56–8) would see a two-part structure in the novel to mirror the poem and thus divide the book in two also in its chapters, with 1–8 being the Grendel section and 9–19 being the dragon section. She suggests that Gollum enters near the middle of the first part and Smaug near the middle of the second: the whole may be an allegorical scheme in which the trolls, goblins, Gollum, wargs, and spiders are portrayals of bodily sin (gluttony and sloth, lechery omitted, plus anger) and Smaug, the Elvenking, the Master of Dale, and Thorin are portrayals of spiritual sin (pride, envy, covetousness, and again anger). I have not seen any other attempt to analyze the chapters of the novel, but I believe the structure is at least slightly more complicated than Chance suggests. First of all, if we simply consider the structure annular, then chapter 10, the "warm welcome" at Laketown, sits alone at the center of the novel, giving a pivot for a ring structure that appears to have parallel elements within it:

1)	An Unexpected Party	(A): Introduction
2)	Roast Mutton	(B): Initial conflict
3)	A Short Rest	(C): Rest into journey
4)	Over Hill and Under Hill	(D): Stuck in the mountain
5)	Riddles in the Dark	(E): Bilbo acts alone
6)	Out of the Frying Pan into the Fire	(F): Fire/resolution
7)	Queer Lodgings	(G): Rest in the beast's hall
8)	Flies and Spiders	(H): Bilbo acts alone
9)	Barrels out of Bond	(I): Bilbo leads
10)	A Warm Welcome	(J): Balance
11)	On the Doorstep	(I'): Bilbo leads
12)	Inside Information	(G'): Bilbo acts alone
13)	Not at Home	(H'): Rest in the beast's hall
14)	Fire and Water	(F'): Fire/resolution
15)	The Gathering of the Clouds	(D'): Stuck in the mountain
16)	A Thief in the Night	(E'): Bilbo acts alone
17)	The Clouds Burst	(B'): Final conflict
18)	The Return Journey	(C'): Rest into journey
19)	The Last Stage	(A'): Conclusion

In addition, chapters 18 and 19 trace in reverse chapters 9–4 and 3–1, suggesting that chapters 11–17 might be conceived with their own annular structure, putting chapter 14 and the death of Smaug in the center, but such arguments perhaps become overly complex. In any case, some kind of overarching annular structure (as the subtitle "there and back again" would suggest) seems clear.

Ignoring the chapter divisions, other readers have, as for *Beowulf*, found other structures in the novel. William Howard Green sees a four-part structure—departure; Misty Mountains; Mirkwood; Lonely Mountain—based on the following formula: "Each begins with a well-equipped journey into the dark wilderness and moves through want, danger, captivity, and unlikely escape to a hospitable house where the expedition rests and resupplies" (1969, 22). Bonniejean Christensen (1989) would agree, but she finds a four-part structure that parallels *Beowulf*, which she divides into the monsters (everything in the first part of the novel except Gollum, though the elves have been removed to the good), the descendant of Cain (Gollum), episodes and digressions (Beorn, the spiders, and the Elvenking), and the dragon (Smaug). Jane Chance (2014) prefers the bipartite structure to mirror Tolkien's view of *Beowulf* as a "rising" and "setting," as is demonstrated by her view of the chapter divisions, and Jonathan Glenn (n.d.) would agree that the story is primarily concerned with "balance," that is, the structure is also a theme. Glenn devises an eight-point plot structure (trolls; Elrond; goblins/Gollum; Beorn; spiders; Elvenking; Laketown; Smaug), but strikes episodes in which Bilbo does not act and the troll-episode, which he calls a "negative lesson." Glenn, therefore, again finds a story of four significant actions (Gollum; spiders; escape from the Elvenking; Smaug) that reflect a thematic change in the ratio of luck and self-reliance Bilbo requires to act (n.d.). Structurally, however, what is certain is that Tolkien is not slavishly adapting *Beowulf*'s tripartite structure of the monster fights. The chapter divisions might suggest a bipartite structure, with the significant events of the Misty Mountain and Mirkwood in the first part and the dragon in the second, perhaps with the trolls as a kind of youthful trial, but events within each part have their own complications and patterns, just as *Grettis saga* and *Örvar-Odds saga* cannot be made to fit neatly with the poem into one narrative paradigm.

6.4   *The Hobbit*: Theme

Of the themes identified in Old English scholarship to date, Tolkien cannot be said definitively to have used many, partly because identifications such as Diamond's (1961) war theme and De Lavan's (1981) feast theme are based primarily on what they see as formulaic language within those scenes rather than the aspects of something like Greenfield's (1955) exile theme, of which a hint is certainly in evidence in Gollum, but which is not fully developed until *The Lord of the Rings*.[27] Still, Tolkien is clearly working with at least three identified Old English themes in the poem, and he also invokes a third that to date has really only been known as a passage or motif. For example, Donald Fry's "cliff of death" theme has four main elements and two occasional additional elements: "cliffs, serpents, darkness, and deprivation, and occasionally wolves and wind" (1987, 215). The scene is clearly that of the mere in *Beowulf* (and thus also in Blickling Homily XVI) and Fry's elements correspond closely to other Old English descriptions of hell. The setting in the Misty Mountains, though spread somewhat over the sequence of events, contains all of Fry's elements except for the serpents; Smaug's lair in The Lonely Mountain again has many elements of Fry's theme, though not enumerated in one scene. That Tolkien had the "cliff of death" theme in mind during the composition of *The Hobbit* seems certain (especially because of the *har stan*), but the theme is adapted to suit the narrative, just as the closely corresponding fight in *Grettis saga* at the falls at Sandhaugar must be the same kind of place, but has no infestation of serpents or wolves or wind.

The "beasts of battle" motif is a better example of innovation within a theme, for already the theme has been shown in Old English to have many variants (Mark Griffith lists fourteen passages).[28] *The Battle of Brunanburh*, to begin with, has a straightforward scene in which corpses are left behind for the raven, the eagle, and the wolf (60–5b). In *Beowulf*, the scene is far more artful, for the poet, having established a context for both the raven and its color,[29] now notes that warriors shall awaken now not to the sound of the harp, but rather:

> "Se wonna hrefn
> fus ofer fægum fela reordian,
> earne secgan hu him æt æte speow,
> þenden he wið wulf wæl reafode." (3024b–7)

The dark raven, eager above the doomed, shall cry much, tell the eagle how he enjoyed himself at feast, while he plundered the slain with the wolf.

A further innovation may be seen in *The Battle of Maldon*, where the Vikings, as they are there called, are known by the epithet "slaughter-wolves"[30] before the introduction of the ravens and an eagle:

> Wodon þa wæl-wulfas –for wætere ne murnon–
> wicinga weorod, west ofer Pantan ...
> Þær wearþ hream ahafen, hræfnas wundon,
> earn æses georn. Wæs on eorþan cierm. (Pope 2001, 96–107)

> The slaughter-wolves then advanced, for water they did not delay, the host of Vikings, west over the river Pante ... A cry was raised there. Ravens circled, the eagle yearning for food. There was an uproar upon the earth.

Tolkien, for his part, distributes the wolf, the raven, and the eagle within the narrative and assigns them to a new set of roles. The wolf or Warg, a creature familiar from the description of hell in Blickling Homily XVI ("under þæm stane wæs niccra eardung ond wearga"; under that [grey] stone was the dwelling place of nicors and weargs)[31] is, as in *The Battle of Maldon*, the enemy, both after the escape from the Misty Mountains and in the Battle of the Five Armies; the raven appears as Roäc, son of Carc, one of the last of the ravens who were friends of the dwarves and acted and act as their eyes and messengers; and the eagle appears as a friend, rescuing the party from wolves on the other side of the Misty Mountains and playing a vital role in the final battle.[32] In this theme, we see Tolkien's selection and innovation, the freedom of the poet/author, most clearly, for the Old English theme of the beasts of battle is reproduced, but varied, as we have seen happened already in Old English; the eagles rescue the party, and rescue by eagles is also a common motif in AT 301 (B542.1.1 "Eagle carries man to safety" or F101.3 "Return from lower world on eagle"), a motif that appears slightly differently in *Örvar-Odds saga* when our hero is transported by vulture; the wolves are connected via the word "Warg" to hellscapes and a traditional past; the ravens (and apparently the old thrush as well) are linked to the talking birds who help Sigurðr circumvent Reginn's treachery and perhaps to Óðinn's ravens (and we learn retroactively that Bilbo would probably never have found the secret door without the help of the old thrush), and helpful birds (B450) are common in folktale, especially ravens (B451.5) and eagles (B455.3).

Tolkien also selects and develops the theme of flyting, working within and adapting a traditional set of motifs while importing innovative features in the "conflicts" of Bilbo and Gollum and Bilbo and Smaug, where the riddle contest is at once a logical extension of the kind of metaphorical insult we see in the flyting (for example, in the crushing rebukes Sinfjötli delivers to Granmarr in *Völsunga saga*) and a redeployment of contests of wisdom and the extensive early medieval riddle tradition.[33] Here, to understand how various authors might deploy themes in related but also substantially different ways, one might juxtapose Beowulf's exchange with Unferth, Grettir and Sveinn's composition of the *Sǫðulkolluvísur*, Örvar-Oddr's dismantling of Sigurðr and Sjólfr, and Tolkien's two verbal contests in *The Hobbit*. Mark Griffith's warnings about single motifs not being themes is well-taken (1993, 181), but each of these duels overlaps in multiple ways with at least one other scene.

Finally, to understand also how *The Hobbit* might be seen as just one text in Tolkien's developing mythology, Smaug's boasting reply to Bilbo is evidence for Tolkien's desire also to use single motifs, in this case, the well-known *ubi sunt* motif:

> "Revenge!" he snorted, and the light of his eyes lit the hall from floor to ceiling like scarlet lightning. "Revenge! The King under the Mountain is dead and where are his kin that dare seek revenge? Girion Lord of Dale is dead, and I have eaten his people like a wolf among sheep, and where are his sons' sons that dare approach me? I kill where I wish and none dare resist. I laid low the warriors of old and their like is not in the world today." (2006, 262)

The *ubi sunt* motif is very common in Old English, most prominently in verse in *The Wanderer* and in prose in various homiletic texts, particularly Vercelli X, but it probably derives from the Bible, perhaps I Corinthians I.19–20 or Baruch III.16–19, and was made popular by a moving elaboration in Isidore's *Synonyma*.[34] Most often, the motif expresses the transitory value of power and wealth, but here Tolkien has Smaug, though expressing a common element of the motif in referring to powerful men turned to dust, in fact show himself to be wrong: the kin of the King under the Mountain are at the other end of the tunnel, and Bard of the line of Girion will loose the black arrow that sends Smaug from the sky. Further, Smaug's reference to "the warriors of old" echoes Gandalf's assertion that an assault on the front gate would be useless "without a mighty Warrior" (26) and appears just before Thorin's observation that dragons cannot "even mend a little loose scale of their armour" (28), just as Smaug's boast comes just before Bilbo sees the missing patch on Smaug's left breast (263). Significantly, too, as with the Arkenstone and the "thief in the night," Smaug's words echo Christian language in obvious ways in *quasi lupi deuorant oues*, a phrase from, for example, the *Visio Pauli*, and in the warriors of old laid low, the mighty fighters of the past, best exemplified in Genesis VI.4 and Ezekiel XXXII.21 and 27. Claudia Di Sciacca establishes the Old English "tendency towards expansion and variation" in the *ubi sunt* motif (2008, 148), just as we have seen in Tolkien's treatment of the traditional "beasts of battle" theme and just as we see when Tolkien develops the motif more fully (and traditionally) in *The Two Towers*, the song of the Rohirrim that Aragorn sings as they approach Théoden's hall (1991, 136–7). Because his sense of tradition can be reconstructed from his writings and because we can be relatively certain that Tolkien was attempting to emulate the compositional processes of Old English and Old Norse-Icelandic, Tolkien's reworking of themes and motifs also helps in the identification of reworked themes and motifs in those early texts: if it looks like a theme or motif, it probably is, and for the audience familiar with the tradition, it certainly would be.

6.5   *The Hobbit*: Digressions and Episodes

Unlike *Beowulf*, *The Hobbit* is not at all characterized by digressions and episodes. The narrative, in fact, proceeds at a steady pace in an almost perfectly linear fashion, with only the splitting of the role of the dragon-slayer between Bilbo and Bard and Bilbo's bump on the head requiring the narrator's analeptic accounts of the death of Smaug (2006, 285–96) and of the final part of the battle (334–5). The narrator also intervenes on occasion, usually to remove suspense through a proleptic remark, as, for example, when the return of the eagles for the Battle of the Five Armies is announced (132). Narrative events are seldom recounted twice, but when reunited with Gandalf and the dwarves, Bilbo relates the story of what happened to him in the mountain, thus giving us an account that differs slightly from that of the narrator (109–10). When coupled with Gandalf's account of what he did when the goblins surprised the band, we get, as in *Beowulf*, a fairly full recapitulation of events in the first major movement of the text, a version that, instead of adding details one might have expected to know before (Hondscio; the dragon-skin *glof*), removes the detail of the ring.

The only part of *The Hobbit* that breaks sufficiently from the main narrative to be considered a digression is Thorin's account of Smaug's arrival at the Lonely Mountain (2006, 27–30), a story that is marked with the same "long ago" as Tolkien's preface and beginning of the main narrative (2006, 1, 5, 27) and that establishes, as in *Beowulf*, the sequence of events leading up to Thorin's exile from his own hall. However, Tolkien's continued references to the conflict between the goblins and the dwarves is similar to the way the *Beowulf*-poet unfolds the details of the Swedish-Geatish conflict in the second half of the poem. The audience learns early on that Thorin's grandfather Thror was killed in the mines of Moria by Azog the Goblin (30), and Thorin suggests the goblins have had some reward for that deed (31). Elrond mentions the war again, noting that the mines are abandoned (62), and the narrator shares Gandalf's knowledge of the spread of the goblins after the battle in the mines (66). The special grudge of the goblins comes up again in their history, a history that has echoes of Tubal-cain (73–4). The dwarves marching with Dain to support Thorin have "experience in the dreadful dwarf and goblin wars" (313–14), but not until the Battle of the Five Armies is about to be joined do we learn that Dain killed Azog in Moria and that Azog's son, Bolg, is coming for revenge (324), thus connecting the current conflict to a long cycle of feud between dwarves and goblins, rekindled by the killing of the Great Goblin. In the more distant past lies a history of other goblin conflicts, the battle that took the hobbit Bullroarer to the field (22) and the battles of elves and goblins for which Orcrist and Glamdring were forged, those blades that stir up past enmity as in *Beowulf* (1141–5) and (we expect) after the end of the poem, given that Wiglaf bears the sword of Eanmund, whose brother Eadgils would seem to sit on the Swedish throne.

Tolkien also makes frequent allusion to figures, places, and deeds with little or no explicit connection to the events of the main narrative. The Necromancer, connected somewhat to the story through his imprisonment of Thrain the younger, is mentioned several times, and Gandalf seems to have been involved in driving him out of the south of Mirkwood (2006, 31, 161, 343). Great dragons are bred on the Withered Heath (24), which is obviously a poisoned place; Durin was "the father of the fathers of the eldest race of Dwarves" (63); a Master rules such rings as Bilbo's (95); Gandalf has a cousin named Radagast (139); and we sense a stretching history in the stories of Beorn (135) and the place of the Wood-elves among the elves generally (194). Indeed, the world of *The Hobbit* is a world of tales, many of them generated by its most renowned inhabitants, such as Elrond, who "comes into many tales" (61), and Gandalf: "Tales and adventures sprouted up all over the place wherever he went, in the most extraordinary fashion" (6). Characters themselves are constantly singing songs and telling stories, and the richness of the tradition is summed up in Bilbo's return stop at the Last Homely House: "When the tale of their journeyings was told, there were other tales, and yet more tales, tales of long ago, and tales of new things, and tales of no time at all, till Bilbo's head fell forward on his chest, and he snored comfortably in a corner" (343).

To Tolkien, these tales, as he might call them all, those told and those only hinted at, are a vital part of world-building: "Part of the attraction of [*The Lord of the Rings*] is, I think, due to the glimpses of a large history in the background: an attraction like that of viewing far off an unvisited island, or seeing the towers of a distant city gleaming in a sunlit mist" (Carpenter 1981, Letter 247, 333).[35] In *Beowulf*, we have seen that the effect of the digressions and episodes is to give depth to the poem by means of comparison and contrast (Orchard 2003, 92), to lend to the poem a sense of history (and myth) collapsed into an associative world of story. Tolkien assesses the achievement of the *Beowulf*-poet in these terms:

> The whole [of *Beowulf*] must have succeeded admirably in creating in the minds of the poet's contemporaries the illusion of surveying a past, pagan but noble and fraught with deep significance—a past that itself had depth and reached backward into a dark antiquity of sorrow. This impression of depth is an effect and a justification of the use of episodes and allusions to old tales, mostly darker, more pagan, and desperate than the foreground. (1983, 27)

Roberta Frank has argued that the poet presents a world so sophisticated and "internally consistent" that "his illusion of historical truth has been taken for reality" (1987, 51). I would suggest further, as we have seen for example in Fitt 1 and the Sigemund-Heremod digression, that the layering of what we as a modern audience might divide as historical (Scyld/Heremod), biblical (Cain), and mythological (Sigemund) is so complete and apparently effortless that we sense and accept a diachronic dimension in the text. Though John Miles Foley is arguing for the fundamental difference of oral traditional artistry, his sense of how tradition works seems to me to apply also to the *effect* Tolkien achieves in *The Hobbit*: "For tradition is nothing if not diachronic: it has roots which reach back into its pre-textual history and which inform the present avatar of its identity" (1990, 3). To put it another way, Tom Shippey suggests that traditional fairy-tales "are detached from each other," as we saw in *Sellic Spell*, and seem "already to be in a sense in ruins," that is, something imperfectly preserved is unsettlingly in evidence in the tales as we have them (2000, 12–13). In Tolkien's world, every narrative has a connection to another: *The Hobbit*—and *Beowulf* and *Örvar-Odds saga*— are made via episode, digression, reference, and allusion to feel nested in a world of story that reaches from the distant past to our present. The nexus of connections in turn repairs, at least superficially, through connection and causation, the "ruin" of the traditional tale. As Shippey further says about *The Hobbit*, "the book's *distinguishing* characteristic ... is its sense that all these things come from somewhere outside and beyond the author, forming a *Zusammenhang* as solid as every day's and on occasion no more irrational" (2003, 76).

6.6   *THE HOBBIT*: STORY-PATTERN

The fundamental affinity of *The Hobbit* with the traditional story-pattern of AT 301, early examples of which are *Sellic Spell* and *Dat Erdmänneken*, is clear from our analysis of structure. Within that pattern, however, Tolkien's innovations need still to be highlighted. The most effective way to present Tolkien's contributions to the tradition is through an assessment of his protagonist, Bilbo Baggins, and how Bilbo represents Tolkien's reimagining of heroes such as Beewolf, Beowulf, Grettir, and Örvar-Oddr. Bilbo, first of all, is without doubt a hero of unpromising habits (L114), though in different ways from the other heroes we have discussed, where their lack of promise has to do with laziness or a general bad attitude instead of a lack of physical prowess. Tolkien hints at something unusual in Bilbo's ancestry, a mixing, perhaps, of hobbit and fairy blood on his mother's side, which led to "something a bit queer in his make-up ... that only waited for a chance to come out" (2006, 5). The fairy/human ancestry is itself a fairly common folktale motif (F305), perhaps best exemplified by Skuld, daughter of the *álfkona* and Helgi in *Hrólfs saga kraka* (Jónsson 1954, 27–9), who certainly inherits some unusual abilities from her mother. Bilbo is not at all strong; instead, Bilbo's primary feature, at least early in the saga, seems to be his luck, again a common motif, usually associated with heroes (N203).[36] Bilbo also has extraordinary sight (F642), is "a pretty fair shot with a stone" (183; F636.4), and has the traditional gifts of hobbits: "They can move very quietly, and hide easily, and recover wonderfully from falls and bruises, and they have a fund of wisdom and wise sayings that men have mostly never heard or have forgotten long ago" (83).

In the early stages of the adventure, Bilbo does what he can to help. The first "fight," the encounter with the trolls, has many different sources and analogues that are useful for understanding Tolkien's method and how *The Hobbit* merges traditional tales. The talking purse that gives Bilbo away is a magic purse (D1192), familiar enough in folktale, though not with an ability to speak. The dwarves are defeated, ready to be eaten: the motif of anthropophagy (G10; specifically, here, G11.2 "cannibal giant") is shared by all the monsters in the novel and is important in the analogues as well. Bilbo watches helplessly; only Gandalf's return saves them. The situation is precisely parallel to what will happen in Mirkwood, except Bilbo's development as a hero is demonstrated by the fact that he acts and acts successfully the second time. One influence in this scene is clearly *Alvíssmál* and Þórr keeping Alvíss talking until dawn, but Shippey (2003, 74–5) also notes that "ogres duped into fighting one another" is a common folktale motif (K1082; Grimm 20). The motif is part of *Örvar-Odds saga*, too, though there it is more specifically the "missile thrown among enemies causes them to fight one another" (K1082.1). Alvíss, of course, turns to stone, but the *trollkona* of *Grettis saga* is also suggested by some to have turned to stone in the first light of dawn, just as Grettir cut off her arm (F531.6.12.2: "sunlight turns giant or troll to stone"). Grendel and his ilk seem to have some dislike for daylight, and the goblins, too, are less than comfortable in sunshine (2006, 105). The defeat of the trolls leads the party to a cave where they find ancient swords and treasure, a common outcome in such a monster fight.

The turning point of the adventure comes when Bilbo finds the magic ring (D1076) in the monsters' lair, one of many folktale items granting invisibility (D1361.1), probably most closely associated in this context with the *Tarnkappe* that Siegfried wins from the dwarf, Alberich, in the *Nibelungenlied*. The parallels between Bilbo and Gollum are not fully realized in *The Hobbit*, but even here we see some similarities between the hero and the monster in their underground dwellings, and the ring changing hands must also be symbolic. Bilbo, uniquely, recognizes the suffering Gollum faces (2006, 102), pointing us further toward Tolkien's reorientation of heroism. The ring, his wits, and "pure luck" at the end of the riddle contest (92) allow Bilbo to escape Gollum and the goblins, and he emerges into the light to find himself on the verge of being left for dead. Escaping with the aid of an item discovered underground is, as we have seen, common in examples of AT 301. The rest and feast after the Misty Mountains comes at the hall of Beorn, the character to whom Tolkien transfers many of the traditional characteristics of the hero: Beorn is of uncertain origin (descended of bears or men), definitely a skin-changer (*eigi einhamr*), and possessed of great strength. Still, Gandalf's method of arriving at Beorn's hall is the same as, we suspect, the method he has advised the dwarves to employ for their arrival at Bilbo's, a few at a time, thus making Bilbo and Beorn "heroes" to be approached with a similar degree of caution.

Bilbo's luck is very much in evidence in the episode in Mirkwood. When he loses the dwarves, he guesses which way they went "by luck" for "he was born with a good share of it" (2006, 182). Using his stone-throwing abilities and some insulting verses, Bilbo this time rescues the dwarves from being eaten. Afterward, he is seen by the dwarves as possessing three things: "some wits, as well as luck and a magic ring" (192), though luck still seems to be the primary factor in their escape from the Elvenking and safe arrival in Laketown (207, 220). By the time the party arrives at the Lonely Mountain, the ring has been forgotten, and Bilbo is recognized as "a hobbit full of courage and resource ... [and] possessed of good luck far exceeding the usual allowance," luck that Bilbo is now beginning to trust (246). In the multiple encounters with Smaug and his eventual death, Tolkien's innovations are many. Bilbo's theft of the cup associates him with a very different role from that of hero, but the most important effect is that we see Thorin as the aged Beowulf to whom the stolen cup is brought. Bilbo's journeys reveal something of the character of Smaug (revealing him as *draco* more than *draconitas*), and the revelation of the missing spot of armor gives Bilbo a vital, yet non-active, role in the slaying of the dragon. Readers are attempted to associate Bard/Bilbo with Beowulf/Wiglaf, but the association is not parallel, for in a way it is Bilbo who "engages" Smaug so that Bard may slay him, and of course, neither Bard nor Bilbo dies. Bilbo's role, in fact, is more like Reginn's in *Völsunga saga*, giving advice to stab from below (though not leaving out a key detail as Reginn does).[37] The betrayal in this sequence is also transferred: Bilbo betrays his companions by delivering the Arkenstone to Bard and the Elvenking, although the theft is portrayed as a commendable act.

In the final sequences of *The Hobbit*, Tolkien seems specifically to be realigning the ending of *Beowulf*. Beowulf defeats the dragon with Wiglaf's help, though the rest of the Geatish warriors are proven faithless, and he is buried with the treasure, which is as useless to men as it ever was (3168). The final speeches of the poem seem to condemn Beowulf—"Oft sceall eorl monig anes willan/ wræc adreogan" (Often many men must suffer misery through the will of one man, 3077–78a)— and the Geats seem doomed to renewed feuding with the Franks and Frisians and Swedes (2910b–13a; 2922–27). Thorin's stubborn refusal to come to terms with Bard and the Elvenking—the bewilderment of the treasure—could have caused him to make many men suffer, but the goblins and bats and wolves arrive just as battle is set to begin. The Battle of the Five Armies, therefore, is the battle of "men" against monsters that forestalls the battle of men against men, which is the sure aftermath of *Beowulf*. Again, the temptation is to divide these conflicts in Augustinian terms, the kin of Cain (the monsters) at war with the kin of Abel (men), all while the kin of Cain (also, of course, earthly men) are at war with one another.[38] In any case, Tolkien resolves the feud among the non-monsters of the story by uniting them in a great battle against united monsters, and the fact that Beorn, the bear-hero, is the one figure responsible in the end for victory, is surely significant. Thorin, for his part, dies in the battle along with his nephews and is buried with significant items of value, the Arkenstone and Orcrist, the latter of which acts ever after as a warning against enemies, just as Beowulf's barrow is ever after seen from afar.

Bilbo is again thought dead after the battle, but Gandalf recognizes his luck in surviving (2006, 332). Thorin's parting words are vital to Tolkien's conception of Bilbo's heroism: "There is more in you of good than you know, child of the kindly West. Some courage and some wisdom, blended in measure" (333).[39] Bilbo's qualities are courage and wisdom, in balance, and the ring and luck are no longer reasons for his success. The formation is reminiscent of the *sapientia et fortitudo* that Robert E. Kaske finds to be central to *Beowulf*, with both positive and negative examples (1958). The most interesting pair in this context must be Hama and Hygelac as illustrations of wisdom and its lack, where

Hama takes the *Brosinga mene* away from the treachery of Eormenric, but Hygelac loses his treasure on his prideful venture against the Frisians (1197–1207a).[40] Tolkien is recasting strength as courage, but he leaves the last word to Gandalf. When Bilbo exclaims that the prophecies have in a way turned out to be true, Gandalf replies: "Surely you don't disbelieve the prophecies because you had a hand in bringing them about yourself? You don't really suppose, do you, that all your adventures and escapes were managed by mere luck, just for your sole benefit?" (351). Though Bilbo is recruited to be the fourteenth man, Mr. Lucky Number, as Smaug calls him, and though luck has a prominent role through most of the adventure, Gandalf hints that greater forces have shaped events. One might think of the *Beowulf*-poet's remark just before Grendel comes stalking toward the hall: "Soð is gecyþed/ þæt mihtig God manna cynnes/ weold [w]ideferhð" (Well known is the truth that mighty God always controlled the race of men; 700b–2a).

6.7   CONCLUSION

"At last then," Tolkien remarks in his lecture on *Beowulf,* "after inquiring so long whence this material came, and what its original or aboriginal nature was (questions that cannot ever be decisively answered), we might also now again inquire what the poet did with it" (1983, 9). In general, Bonniejean Christensen says that *The Hobbit* is "a retelling of *Beowulf,* but from a Christian rather than a pagan point of view, and as a fantasy rather than an elegy" (1989, 4), thus incorporating Tolkien's notion of eucatastrophe (1989, 9). Jonathan Glenn sees an "alternative to the heroic hierarchy of the Northern story": "Tolkien creates in Bilbo Baggins his answer to the defects of a Beowulf or a Beorh[t]noth or a Bóðvarr bjarki ... a person who ... in a way the Beowulfs of the world never can ... comes home again" (n.d.). Tom Shippey puts it more generally, and I believe best, when he says that "what chapter 16 ['A Thief in the Night'] and the scenes around it do most powerfully, perhaps, is to enforce a plea for tolerance across an enormous gap of times and attitudes and ethical styles" (2003, 85). In 1951, Tolkien himself offers an assessment of the work in an overview of his entire mythology: "[*The Hobbit* is] a study of simple ordinary man, neither artistic nor noble and heroic (but not without the undeveloped seeds of these things) against a high setting ... passing from fairy-tale to the noble and high and relapsing with the return" (Carpenter 1981, Letter 131, 159).

We have seen that Tolkien takes the two-fight structure of *Sellic Spell* or *Dat Erdmänneken* and expands it into a four-fight structure that incorporates new repetitions and motifs in each of its repeated movements. In the recounting of Bilbo's adventures, Tolkien incorporates patterns of repetition and structure that have much in common with oral traditional song and *Beowulf.* He uses allusions to other times and stories to add depth, and he imaginatively redeploys some traditional themes and motifs, though it has not been our purpose here to trace every borrowing, especially from *Beowulf.* At times, as critics have sensed in *Beowulf* and as we have seen in the stages of *Örvar-Odds saga*'s development, the tale also has compositional seams, for example, in the talking purse, the stone-giants throwing rocks, Beorn's serving animals, or the somewhat unsatisfying characterization of Bard. In creating his cast of characters, Tolkien takes the attributes of a hero like Beowulf, Grettir, or Örvar-Oddr, as Bonniejean Christensen has partially noted, and distributes them across several characters to achieve an effect that is utterly different from any other version of the tale (1989, 9). What is left to Bilbo is courage and wisdom: he has been characterized as a "mythological composite" (Hodge 1986, 219) linked particularly to the trickster figure, and assessed, at least according to traditional tales, as "though successful ... not a Hero" (Sullivan 2013, 72). However, we must also keep in mind that Tolkien offers a protagonist who develops and changes, slowly earning the role of leader as his adventures progress. By the end, Bilbo is a very different hobbit, bursting into spontaneous song, arriving home presumed dead, sufficiently changed never quite to fit in again.

In considering *The Hobbit,* we are in the remarkable position of being able to observe a teller of tales, whose goals and background we may guess with some authority, engaged in working through a creative process that is in many ways, and I would argue deliberately, the same process in which the *Beowulf*-poet and certain of the saga authors engaged. *Sellic Spell* looks back to the folktale that might have provided the plot of *Beowulf,* and *The Hobbit* is what a prose author, steeped in the tradition and with knowledge of later developments of the folktale, could yet do with that plot. *The Hobbit* participates in the same tradition as *Beowulf,* but it is not a retelling of the poem. Though Tolkien claims that "the analytic study of fairy-stories is as bad a preparation for the enjoying or the writing of them as would be the historical study of the drama of all lands and times for the enjoyment or writing of stage-plays" (2014a, 66), the success of his creative work would suggest otherwise.

NOTES

1. For an overview of Tolkien's published and unpublished work on *Beowulf*, see Drout (2015, 149–53).
2. He makes effectively the same remark—"to ask what is the origin of stories (however qualified) is to ask what is the origin of language and of the mind"—in "On Fairy-Stories" (2014a, 38).
3. See also Chapter 4, pp. 101–2.
4. Tolkien is responding in part to Chambers' comment that "the folk-tale is a good servant, but a bad master: it has been allowed in *Beowulf* to usurp the place of honour, and to drive into episodes and digressions the things which should be the main stuff of a well-conducted epic" (qtd. in Tolkien 1983, 12–13).
5. Tolkien also comments that "the comparison of skeleton 'plots' is simply not a critical literary process at all" (1983, 14).
6. See Acker (2016, 34–7) for extended and useful commentary on the story and *Beowulf* criticism.
7. Also cited in Acker (2016, 33).
8. Acker calls Lang's version of the story "condensed ... in the direction of a fairy tale" (2016, 33).
9. Tolkien comments on "spell" also in "On Fairy-Stories": "Small wonder that *spell* means both a story told, and a formula of power over living men" (2014a, 48).
10. I assume that the teller of stories throughout the passage is the Danish king, Hrothgar. See, however, Fulk et al. (2008, 233–4) for difficulties in translating and interpreting the passage.
11. For the full description of AT 301, see Chapter 1, pp. 31–2. AT 301A technically omits Movement VI, Recognition, as well, but *Dat Erdmänneken* has a partial recognition scene.
12. For a similar modern version of the tale, see Calvino (1980, 284–8).
13. See F696 in Boberg (1966, 128).
14. See also Tolkien's comments on *Sellic Spell*, p. 199, above.
15. See Anderson's detailed account of the genesis of the novel (2002, 7–15). The novel goes through three substantial editions (1937, 1951, and 1966–1967), with significant changes, particularly in Chapter 5, "Riddles in the Dark," to bring *The Hobbit* more in line with events of *The Lord of the Rings*. See Anderson (2002), for the latest edition with the text of previous editions in the margins. The differences make little difference to my analysis, but I cite from Tolkien (2006).
16. See Chapter 4, p. 109.

17. Among many studies treating Tolkien's sources, see in particular Shippey (2003, 55–73), Lee and Solopova (2005), Glenn (n.d.), Hodge (1986), Chance (2014), and Quigley (2015).
18. See also Hillman (2018, 33–58).
19. Day would further argue that "*The Hobbit* is a fairy-tale version of the epic reduced to its most elemental form" (2011, 124), but I believe *The Hobbit* is not at all a reduction, but rather an equal (though obviously different) product of the generative processes considered in the previous chapters, as I hope to show.
20. On the *Silmarillion* alone, see Rateliff (n.d., 2014).
21. Examples could be multiplied; for an especially complex paragraph, also inside an envelope, see "I should not have liked … to the days beyond" (83–4) or the envelope inside an envelope near the end of the riddle contest (the four mentions of Gollum's gleaming eyes) with parallel mentions of pockets and hissing (97–8). At times, Tolkien seems to lose control of his rhetoric, as in the repetitions of "grim" in various forms in descriptions of Bard (286–306, especially 286–88), which are then transferred to Thorin and the dwarves (308, 309, 313, and 321).
22. Tolkien (38, 55, 78, 81, 131, 180, 203, 256, 313/316, 340). The example that only partially fits is Bilbo's "Why, O why did I ever leave my hobbit-hole!" (78) as he bounces along on Bombur's back.
23. One might be tempted to connect Tolkien's "not for the last time" with the significant echoes of *ne wæs þæt forma sið* (that was not the first time): 716b (Grendel comes to the hall), 1463b and 1527b (Hrunting), and 2625b (Wiglaf) and the *forman siðe* in 740b (Grendel seizes a sleeping warrior) and 2286b (Beowulf looks on the pilfered cup). Taylor links *Beowulf* 716b to a sub-theme of death he calls "the fatal venture" and connects all these occurrences; see Taylor (1967, 255–61).
24. Glenn (n.d.) calls these "transitional formulas," noting that they help to "create order," but Glenn prefers to see an overall structure in which Bilbo acts five times, four of which become "focal points in the process of Bilbo's change."
25. The brothers of Böðvarr bjarki in *Hrólfs saga kraka* form another variation on trebling, being "animal" to different degrees because of Bera's graded reactions to be being fed the bear meat (Björn). As Böðvarr travels to Hrólfr's court, he meets each brother in turn.
26. Tolkien also uses gnomic wisdom to connect the world of *The Hobbit* and this world, as, for example, in his explanation of the origin of the saying "out of the frying pan into the fire" (115). A less satisfactory example of such a connection is the etymology of "golf" (22).
27. See also Chapter 1, pp. 17–19.
28. See Magoun (1955), Bonjour (1957), and Griffith (1993).

29. See Chapter 2, p. 62.
30. This point is made by Griffith (1993, 191). Griffith notes that the same thing happens in *Genesis A*, where the Elamites are called *herewulfa* (2015b) and *hildewulfas* (2051a).
31. See Chapter 4, pp. 129–34.
32. On the eagles as "eucatastrophe," see Neubauer (2015).
33. The key analysis of the flyting, though outside of an analysis of theme, is Clover (1980). For flyting as theme, see Anderson (1980) and Clark (1981). See also *Völsunga saga*, ch. 9; Lee and Solopova (2005, 136–77).
34. See Cross (1956) and Di Sciacca, (2008).
35. The letter is cited in Atherton (2012, 33).
36. See N203 in Boberg (1966, 200).
37. See Chapter 4, p. 109.
38. See Chapter 4, pp. 146–7n50.
39. See also Glenn (n.d.).
40. See Chapter 4, p. 141.

REFERENCES

Acker, Paul. 2016. Tolkien's *Sellic Spell*: A Beowulfian Fairy Tale. *Tolkien Studies* 13: 31–44.

Anderson, Douglas A. 2002. *The Annotated Hobbit*, revised and expanded ed. Boston: Houghton Mifflin.

Anderson, Earl R. 1980. Formulaic Typescene Survival: Finn, Ingeld, and the *Nibelungenlied*. *English Studies* 61: 293–301.

Atherton, Mark. 2012. *There and Back Again: J. R. R. Tolkien and the Origins of The Hobbit*. London: I.B. Tauris.

Bibire, Paul. 1993. By Stock or by Stone: Recurrent Imagery and Narrative Pattern in *The Hobbit*. In *Scholarship and Fantasy: Proceedings of The Tolkien Phenomenon, May 1992, Turku, Finland*, Anglicana Turkuensia 12, ed. K.J. Battarbee, 203–215. Turku, Finland: University of Turku.

Boberg, Inger M. 1966. *Motif-Index of Early Icelandic Literature*. Copenhagen: Munksgaard.

Bonjour, Adrien. 1957. *Beowulf* and the Beasts of Battle. *PMLA* 72: 563–573.

Calvino, Italo. 1980. The Golden Ball. In *Italian Folktales: Selected and Retold by Italo Calvino*, trans. George Martin, 284–288. San Diego: Harcourt.

Carpenter, Humphrey, with Christopher Tolkien (ed.). 1981. *Letters of J. R. R. Tolkien*. London: George Allen & Unwin.

Chance, Jane. 2001. *Tolkien's Art: A Mythology for England*, rev ed. Lexington: The University Press of Kentucky.

Chance, Jane. 2014. Tolkien's Hybrid Mythology: *The Hobbit* as Old Norse "Fairy-Story." In *The Hobbit and Tolkien's Mythology: Essays on Revisions and Influences*, ed. Eden, 78–96. Jefferson, NC: McFarland & Company.

Christensen, Bonniejean McGuire. 1969. *Beowulf* and *The Hobbit*: Elegy into Fantasy in J. R. R. Tolkien's Creative Technique. PhD dissertation, University of Southern California.

Christensen, Bonniejean McGuire. 1989. Tolkien's Creative Technique: *Beowulf* and *The Hobbit*. *Mythlore* 57: 4–10.

Clark, Francelia, 1981. Flyting in *Beowulf* and Rebuke in *The Song of Bagdad*: The Question of Theme. In *Oral Traditional Literature: A Festschrift for Albert Bates Lord*, ed. Foley, 164–193. Columbus, OH: Slavica.

Cleasby, Richard, and Gudbrand Vigfusson, with Sir William A. Craigie (eds.). 1957. *An Icelandic-English Dictionary*, 2nd ed. Oxford: Clarendon Press.

Clover, Carol. 1980. The Germanic Context of the Unferþ Episode. *Speculum* 55: 444–468.

Cross, James E. 1956. "Ubi Sunt" Passages in Old English—Sources and Relationships. *Vetenskaps-Societen i Lund Årsbok*, 25–44.

Day, David. 2011. The Genesis of *The Hobbit*. *Queen's Quarterly* 118 (1): 115–129.

De Lavan, Joanne. 1981. Feasts and Anti-Feasts in *Beowulf* and the *Odyssey*. In *Oral Traditional Literature: A Festschrift for Albert Bates Lord*, ed. Foley, 235–261. Columbus, OH: Slavica.

Diamond, Robert E. 1961. Theme as Ornament in Anglo-Saxon Poetry. *PMLA* 76: 461–468.

Di Sciacca, Claudia. 2008. *Finding the Right Words: Isidore's Synonyma in Anglo-SaxonEngland*, 77–148. Toronto: University of Toronto Press.

Drout, Michael D.C. 2015. Beowulf: A Translation and Commentary Together with Sellic Spell by J. R. R. Tolkien. *Tolkien Studies* 12: 149–173.

Eden, Bradford Lee (ed.). 2014. *The Hobbit and Tolkien's Mythology: Essays on Revisions and Influences*. Jefferson, NC: McFarland & Company.

Foley, John Miles (ed.). 1981. *Oral Traditional Literature: A Festschrift for Albert Bates Lord*. Columbus, OH: Slavica.

Foley, John Miles (ed.). 1987. *Comparative Research on Oral Traditions: A Memorial for Milman Parry*. Columbus, OH: Slavica.

Foley, John Miles. 1990. *Traditional Oral Epic: The Odyssey, Beowulf, and the Serbo-Croatian Return Song*. Berkeley: University of California Press.

Frank, Roberta. 1987. The *Beowulf*-Poet's Sense of History. In *Beowulf*, ed. Harold Bloom, 51–61. New York: Chelsea House.

Fry, Donald K. 1987. The Cliff of Death in Old English Poetry. In *Comparative Research on Oral Traditions: A Memorial for Milman Parry*, ed. Foley, 213–233. Columbus, OH: Slavica.

Fulk, R.D., Robert E. Bjork, and John D. Niles (eds.). 2008. *Klaeber's Beowulf*, 4th ed. Toronto: University of Toronto Press.

Glenn, Jonathan A. (n.d.). To Translate a Hero: *The Hobbit* as *Beowulf* Retold. Lightspill. Accessed October 12, 2019. https://lightspill.com/schola/nando/hobbit_beowulf.html.

Green, William Howard. 1969. *The Hobbit* and Other Fiction by J. R. R. Tolkien: Their Roots in Medieval Heroic Literature and Language. PhD dissertation, Louisiana State University.

Greenfield, Stanley B. 1955. The Formulaic Expression of the Theme of "Exile" in Anglo-Saxon Poetry. *Speculum* 30: 200–206.

Griffith, Mark S. 1993. Convention and Originality in the Old English Typescene. *Anglo-Saxon England* 22: 179–199.

Hillman, Thomas. 2018. These Are Not the Elves You're Looking For: *Sir Orfeo*, *The Hobbit*, and the Reimagining of the Elves. *Tolkien Studies* 15: 33–58.

Hodge, James L. 1986. The Heroic Profile of Bilbo Baggins. *Florilegium* 8: 212–221.

Hunt, Peter (ed.). 2013. *J. R. R. Tolkien: The Hobbit and The Lord of the Rings*. New York: Palgrave Macmillan.

Jónsson, Guðni (ed.). 1954. *Hrólfs saga kraka*. In *Fornaldar sögur Norðurlanda*, vol. 1, 1–105. Akureyri: Íslendingasagnaútgáfn.

Kaske, Robert E. 1958. *Sapientia et fortitudo* as the Controlling Theme of *Beowulf*. *Studies in Philology* 55: 423–456.

Keller, Thomas L. 1981. The Dragon in *Beowulf* Revisited. *Aevum* 55 (2): 218–228.

Lee, Stuart, and Elizabeth Solopova. 2005. *The Keys of Middle Earth: Discovering Medieval Literature Through the Fiction of J. R. R. Tolkien*. New York: Palgrave Macmillan.

Magoun, Francis P. Jr. 1955. The Theme of the Beasts of Battle in Anglo-Saxon Poetry. *Neuphilologische Mitteilungen* 56: 81–90.

Morris, Richard (ed.). (1874–1878) 1880. *The Blickling Homilies of the Tenth Century*. EETS os 58, 63, and 73. N. Trübner and Co.

Neubauer, Łukasz. 2015. "The Eagles are Coming!": Tolkien's Eucatastrophic Reinterpretation of the "Beasts of Battle" Motif in *The Hobbit* and in *The Lord of the Rings*. *Hither Shore* 12: 236–246.

Niles, John D. 1983. *Beowulf: The Poem and Its Tradition*. Cambridge: Harvard University Press.

Nist, John A. 1959. *The Structure and Texture of Beowulf*. São Paulo, Brazil: University of São Paulo.

Orchard, Andy. 2003. *A Critical Companion to Beowulf*. Cambridge: D. S. Brewer.

Pizarro, Joaquín Martínez. 1976–1977. Transformations of the Bear's Son Tale in the Sagas of the Hrafnistumenn. *Arv* 32–33: 263–281.

Pope, John C. (ed.). 2001. *Eight Old English Poems*, 3rd ed., revised by Robert D. Fulk. New York: Norton.

Propp, Vladimir. 1968. *The Morphology of the Folktale*, trans. Laurence Scott, 2nd ed. Austin: University of Texas Press.

Quigley, Logan. 2015. Middle-Earth and Midgard: the Viking Sagas in Tolkien's Legendarium. *Mallorn* 56: 11–15.

Rateliff, John D. n.d. A Fragment, Detached: *The Hobbit* and *The Silmarillion*. Tolkiendil. Accessed October 4, 2019. http://www.tolkiendil.com/essais/tolkien_1892–2012/john_d_rateliff.

Rateliff, John D. 2014. Anchoring the Myth: The Impact of *The Hobbit* on Tolkien's Legendarium. In *The Hobbit and Tolkien's Mythology: Essays on Revisions and Influences*, ed. Eden, 6–19. Jefferson, NC: McFarland & Company.

Shippey, Tom. 2000. *J. R. R. Tolkien: Author of the Century*. London: HarperCollins.

Shippey, Tom. 2003. *The Road to Middle-Earth: How J. R. R. Tolkien Created a New Mythology*, rev ed. Boston: Houghton Mifflin.

Sullivan, C.W., III. 2013. Tolkien and the Traditional Dragon Tale: An Examination of *The Hobbit*. In *J. R. R. Tolkien: The Hobbit and The Lord of the Rings*, ed. Peter Hunt, 62–73. New York: Palgrave Macmillan.

Taylor, Paul B. 1967. Themes of Death in *Beowulf*. In *Old English Poetry: Fifteen Essays*, ed. Robert P. Creed, 249–274. Providence, RI: Brown University Press.

Tolkien, J.R.R. 1940. Prefatory Remarks on Prose Translation of *Beowulf*. In *Beowulf and the Finnesburg Fragment*, trans. John R. Clark Hall, vii–xli. London: George Allen & Unwin.

Tolkien, J.R.R. 1953. The Homecoming of Beorhtnoth, Beorhthelm's Son. *Essays and Studies* 6: 1–18.

Tolkien, J.R.R. 1977. *The Silmarillion*, ed. Christopher Tolkien. Boston: Houghton Mifflin.

Tolkien, J.R.R. 1983. *Beowulf*: The Monsters and the Critics. In *The Monsters and the Critics and Other Essays*, ed. Christopher Tolkien, 5–48. London: George Allen & Unwin.

Tolkien, J.R.R. 1991. *The Two Towers*. London: Grafton.

Tolkien, J.R.R. 2006. *The Hobbit or There and Back Again*, 5th ed. London: HarperCollins.

Tolkien, J.R.R. 2014a. On Fairy-Stories. In *Tolkien: On Fairy-Stories*, ed. Verlyn Flieger and Douglas A. Anderson, 27–84. London: HarperCollins.

Tolkien, J.R.R. 2014b. Sellic Spell. In *Beowulf: A Translation and Commentary Together with Sellic Spell*, ed. Christopher Tolkien, 355–414. London: HarperCollins.

Tolkien, J.R.R. 2016. *A Secret Vice: Tolkien on Invented Languages*, ed. Dimitra Fimi and Andrew Higgins. London: HarperCollins.

CONCLUSION

Andreas Haarder observes succinctly that "formula analyses make boring reading" (1975, 199). His comment comes as he introduces what he sees as a shift in formulaic studies away from counting and deductions based on statistics toward "the working possibilities inherent in the formulas" and "a shift of emphasis from repetition to variation" (1975, 199). Almost thirty years later, Andy Orchard remarks that "it would be no exaggeration to say that the whole issue of the precise implications of *Beowulf*'s clearly formulaic style of composition has (rightly or wrongly) dominated recent literary appreciation of the text" (2003, 57). Neither Haarder nor Orchard, however, is taking formula in the sense I am finally using it here, as a compositional method that underlies everything from the half-line to the basic story-pattern, which, in the end, requires those half-lines to come to life. The notion of formula and formulaic system has been fully rehearsed—though their mechanisms might not yet be fully decided—but the notion that repetition at the level of structure, particularly in terms of envelope patterns and ring structure, might be part of that formula is less often considered. The link between theme as a cluster of motifs and formula is also well established, but digressions and episodes are also a part of the formula, from the way they are told, signaled, and set apart through structural repetition, to their impact on the way the story overall is told, with a lack of steady advance, with a sense of depth, with a collapsing of time. Finally, a story-pattern is the starting point, a skeleton from which to begin to think about what other parts of the formula to incorporate and precisely how to incorporate them. In all of this, of course, what must also be kept in mind is that variation is key: Jeff Opland has called it "the exploitation of tradition," that is, "the deliberate use of a traditional element in order to extend or deny its relevance in altered circumstances" (1984, 45; Olsen 1988, 149).

After recognizing these patterns of formula, it is possible to read the poem on that basis. Thinking about the half-line, its possible generative systems and its interlocking via different kinds of systems and via simple repetition of its constituent elements, can lead the reader, through a concatenation of associations, through most of the poem, to other poems, to other traditions, to observations that have not been made in the almost 200 years that the poem has been seriously studied. *Weox under wolcnum* (8a) is a particularly rich half-line, as it turns out, but the process could be undertaken with any half-line in the poem, where even an utterly negative result would also be a point worth making. Similarly, the perhaps artificial division that constitutes Fitt 1 of the poem still provides a fascinating glimpse into the poet's method, and the fact that fitt analyses have yielded results in different studies with different aims suggests that, as Yvette Kisor concludes in an observation that applies to every pattern we have seen and have yet to see in the poem, "the fact remains that the patterns are there" (2009, 76).

When, in the Sigemund-Heremod digression, the poet for the first time ventures into Germanic myth or legend, we catch a glimpse of another kind of depth, a third past that the poet coaxes into parallel with the historical past and the scriptural past. The passage is one of the most artful sequences in any verse in any tradition: a reader feels as if it is almost possible to step behind the words and see, though perhaps from a distance and through a slow-moving mist, the *uncupes fela* (876b) that time has stripped away. At the same time, the passage is a model of the poetic process, in a way both explicitly, as the horses ride and the scop sings, and implicitly, as we see just how, to use Tolkien's words, the "imagination might be kindled" when recent events recall events long ago.

Beowulf, Örvar-Odds saga, and *The Hobbit* are all products of the same formula. The *Beowulf*-poet takes a story-pattern, a tradition of formulaic composition in verse, an impulse and a method for digression and episode, a notion of structural patterns, an inventory of themes and motifs, and a poem is the result. The author of *Örvar-Odds saga* takes what I believe is ultimately the same story-pattern, but with a slightly different idea about what it might mean, a tradition of composition in prose, an inventory particularly of motifs, now clearly from some different traditions, and, over time, almost certainly with the participation of different authors, we see how a patterned narrative might emerge from the kernel of an idea. In the case of *Örvar-Odds saga*, the story-pattern we recognize seems to have been grafted to a prior tradition of a hero of enormous strength. In *The Hobbit*, we see an author with, as it were, inside information, imagining hundreds of years later what that generative formula might produce, complete with the influence of new traditions and new times, a hero for the modern world, where Mighty Warriors have no place.

Overall, I hope I have accomplished three things. The first is to show that *Beowulf* is so utterly the process of a compositional method or formula that to attempt to extract any one element of the poem is to find that the poem is bound so tightly in its formulas that every part resists extraction. The second is to model ways of reading the poem: these processes could be repeated with other half-lines, fitts, digressions, analogues, and even modern novels. The third follows from the second: if Tolkien's work demonstrates that the formula still works, I hope I have shown a contemporary relevance for *Beowulf* that transcends the difficulty of the language involved: at the level of story-pattern, certainly, the poem has much to offer a thoughtful student of literature and creative writing.

When Isaac D'Israeli began to publish his volumes titled *Amenities of Literature* in 1841, he had a rather harsh opinion of Old English poets and verse, and he used the word formula to explain the difficulty of understanding and appreciating an Anglo-Saxon poem:

> The torturous inversion of their composition often leaves an ambiguous sense: their perpetual periphrasis; their abrupt transitions; their pompous inflations, and their elliptical style; and not less their portentous metaphorical nomenclature where a single object must be recognised by twenty denominations, not always appropriate, and too often clouded by the most remote and dark analogies ... Such prescribed formulae, and such a mechanism of verse, must have tethered the imagination in a perpetual circle; it was art which violated the free course of nature ... An Anglo-Saxon poem has the appearance of a collection of short hints rather than poetical conceptions, curt and ejaculative; a paucity of objects yields but a paucity of emotions, too vague for detail, too abrupt for deep passion, too poor in

fancy to scatter the imagery of poesy. The Anglo-Saxon betrays its confined and monotonous genius: we are in the first age of art, when pictures
are but monochromes of a single colour. Hence, in the whole map of
Anglo-Saxon poetry, it is difficult to discriminate one writer from another.
(1841, 51, 55–6; Haarder 1975, 34)

D'Israeli's description of the mechanics of Old English verse is, in fact,
surprisingly accurate, and his further insights into Grendel, the scenes of
feasting in Heorot, and the overall exploits of Beowulf anticipate much
criticism to follow and place the poem appropriately in multiple traditions, including the classical, the folktale, and the mythic:

> This life-devourer, who comes veiled in a mist from the marshes, may be
> some mythic being; but though monstrous, it does little more than play
> the part of the Polyphemus of antiquity and the Ogre of modern fairy-
> ism ... The scene is truly Homeric ... The exploits of Beowulf are of a
> supernatural cast; and this circumstance has bewildered his translator amid
> mythic allusions, and thus the hero sinks into the incarnation of a Saxon
> idol,—a protector of the human race. It is difficult to decide whether the
> marvellous incidents be mythical, or merely exaggerations of the northern
> poetic faculty. We, however, learn by these, that corporeal energies and an
> indomitable spirit were the glories of the hero-life; and the outbreaks of
> their self-complacency resulted from their own convictions, after many a
> fierce trial. (1841, 85, 87)

Our understanding of Old English verse and *Beowulf* has, if not
advanced, expanded almost immeasurably since D'Israeli. His conception
of the formulas that informed the composition of Old English poetry
seems to have referred not to verbatim repetition, but to process, and
he was, therefore, perhaps the first to use the term as I have used it here.
D'Israeli's sense of the traditional story-pattern in which the poem shares
is also accurate, though our analysis of how that story-pattern evolves
and is evoked has demonstrated that the life-devourer does much more
than play the part of Polyphemos or the Ogre. As Tolkien would say,
the specific details as they are used now is what counts, not the recognition of what lies in their past. In the end, I find I cannot much disagree
with D'Israeli's conclusions, that "corporeal energies and an indomita-
ble spirit were the glories of the hero-life" and that sometimes, "after
many a fierce trial," one's "convictions" might lead to an "outbreak of
self-complacency."

REFERENCES

D'Israeli, Isaac. 1841. *Amenities of Literature*, vol. 1. London: Edward Moxon.

Haarder, Andreas. 1975. *Beowulf: The Appeal of a Poem*. Viborg: Akademisk Forlag.

Kisor, Yvette. 2009. Numerical Composition and *Beowulf*: A Reconsideration. *Anglo-Saxon England* 38: 41–76.

Olsen, Alexandra Hennessey. 1988. Oral-Formulaic Research in Old English Studies: II. *Oral Tradition* 3 (1–2): 138–190.

Opland, Jeff. 1984. Scop and Imbongi III: The Exploitation of Tradition. In *The Word-Singers*, ed. Norman Simms, 44–59. Hamilton, NZ: Outrigger.

Orchard, Andy. 2003. *A Critical Companion to Beowulf*. Cambridge: D. S. Brewer.

INDEX

© The Editor(s) (if applicable) and The Author(s),
under exclusive license to Springer Nature Switzerland AG 2020
M. Fox, *Following the Formula in Beowulf, Örvar-Odds saga, and Tolkien*, https://doi.org/10.1007/978-3-030-48134-6

239

Printed in the USA
CPSIA information can be obtained
at www.ICGtesting.com
LVHW082240211123
764609LV00005B/76